DATE DUE

HIGHSMITH 45-220

WESTERN WOMEN WORKING IN JAPAN

WESTERN WOMEN WORKING IN JAPAN

Breaking Corporate Barriers

Nancy K. Napier
Sully Taylor

Foreword by Mary Ann Von Glinow

Quorum Books
Westport, Connecticut • London

Library of Congress Cataloging-in-Publication Data

Napier, Nancy K.
   Western women working in Japan : breaking corporate barriers /
 Nancy K. Napier, Sully Taylor ; foreword by Mary Ann Von Glinow.
      p.   cm.
   Includes bibliographical references and index.
   ISBN 0–89930–901–1 (alk. paper)
      1. Women in the professions—Japan.   2. Americans—Employment—
 Japan.   3. Women—Employment—Japan.   I. Taylor, Sully.
 II. Title.
 HD6054.2.J3N37   1995
 331.4'81—dc20   95–9841

British Library Cataloguing in Publication Data is available.

Library of Congress Catalog Card Number: 95–9841
ISBN: 0–89930–901–1

First published in 1995

Quorum Books, 88 Post Road West, Westport, CT 06881
An imprint of Greenwood Publishing Group, Inc.

Printed in the United States of America

The paper used in this book complies with the
Permanent Paper Standard issued by the National
Information Standards Organization (Z39.48–1984).

10 9 8 7 6 5 4 3 2 1

For B.O.N., who was ahead of her time
N.K.N.

For my beloved family—Mother, Bill and Peggy.
And in memory of my treasured friend Anna,
whose life adventure sparkled with joy.
S.T.

Contents

Tables and Figures

FIGURES

TABLES

Foreword

The role of the *gaijin* has been explored in many contexts—negotiating with the Japanese, working in Japan, doing business in Japan—but rarely has it been explored in the way that *Western Women Working in Japan: Breaking Corporate Barriers* by Napier and Taylor does. In fact, I daresay that this is the first book of its kind to explore the life and experiences that professional business women working in Japan have. What makes this a special book is that it is about 111 female "lone fliers" or professional business women working in Japan either voluntarily or involuntarily sent on assignment, and about their adjustments. The conventional wisdom that women will find Japan a hostile environment for non-Japanese is no longer true, they assert, and they are the first to be able to document this claim. That's good news for many who have grown up with the myth that women are just not going to fare well in Japan, a country that is so vitally entertwined with the U.S. economy. What they reveal is that there are compelling reasons for women to live and work in Japan, and that in some cases, these women fare better than men do!

They begin by sculpting the terrain for us: globalization is widespread, and those that are capable of "global thinking," or firms that "have people able to act as chameleons," casually and comfortably adjusting to and thriving in multiple cultures and settings, will be more successful in the long haul. These globalists will be needed at many levels across most multinational enterprises (MNEs) and they offer us a new way of thinking about these people. The usual way to think about people who live and work abroad is to think about expatriates. But Napier and Taylor go much further in suggesting that these globalists really need to move beyond that single descriptive into new categories, and they offer us some: transferees, suitcase employees and armchair travelers. These are new words that will hit the international business ground running since it is high time that we became more descriptively adroit in referring to these people. Transferees are "employees working outside their countries of citizenship . . . including both people who move at the behest of the organization (often referred to as "expatriates") and people who independently relocate overseas because of their own decisions to pursue a job or career outside their 'home' country." Suitcase employees' "work requires them to travel abroad for unique projects, usually for less than a year at a time . . . employees and managers who oversee operations in one setting while being officially 'based' in another, making periodic visits to the locations for which they are responsible." And finally, the globalist couch potato who doesn't have to leave the armchair, so to speak. The armchair travelers are those whose "work requires them to interact with people from other countries, who need not travel," except via the fax, the internet and other electronic means. While the focus of this book is on the first category, the broader descriptive appeal of the latter categories is intriguing. Napier and Taylor reason that the demand for globalists is increasing, and that supply will not match demand, all things considered. For any number of good reasons, they point out that women are an important set of human assets that can more easily slide into the globalist role than has been acknowledged by global firms.

The bulk of the manuscript is targeted toward examining the adventurers that chose to live and work in Japan, and it is fascinating reading. While the sample size on the surface might look small, they were successful in getting almost 20% of the entire population of American businesswomen working in Japan in the early 1990s—an incredible feat! Their stories surprise and fascinate, but interestingly, very few of the women fall into the traditional transferee or "expatriate" category (5–10%), whereas "independent job seekers" moved voluntarily on their own initiative to Japan, and "involuntary transferees or trailers tended to move because of a spouse's or partner's career." Perhaps the thought of working in Japan is not for the faint-hearted and thus independent job seekers braved potential hurdles more successfully than can still be said of the MNEs who transfer their employees to Japan. They discuss poignant examples related to language capability, education, "tea-serving" jobs, and selection criteria that would be "unfamiliar to managers in a North American context." The selection criteria used seemed to be as important, or more so, than the more easily measured "technical criteria," which included "their cultural knowledge of Japan, and working with Japanese people." The ability to "switch" between both cultures was a key success factor. Additionally, the role of "luck," serendipity and other non-quantifiable aspects were discussed at length.

What is incredibly amazing to me is the complete lack of preparation the MNEs gave these female employees prior to their assignment in Japan. This is despite all that we have learned over the years on how important pre-departure training is for expatriates. They examine the expatriate transferees, as well as the existing "on site pool" of talent there in Japan that has received virtually no attention in the research literature. In summary they note that foreign women professionals in Japan seem to feel that "gaining professional acceptance is not an automatic process and is somewhat tougher than it would be for foreign men," but they felt it was feasible. This study explicated some of the fears about foreign women working in Japan, in that Japanese clients and customers will not work with them, thus detracting from a firm's ability to secure business. While confirming some of these difficulties that women face, they also discuss means for overcoming these challenges. Their recommendations to firms and to women seeking jobs in Japan are thoughtful, and right on target. For MNEs wise enough to heed this advice (in particular, let the women decide if they want an international transfer), they will systematically advantage themselves; for those that don't, they will once again miss the boat. This is more than an enjoyable book to read, it is a *must read* for managers in MNEs that have a female pool of talent anxious for a Japanese assignment, or for those MNEs with an on-site presence in Japan, who can now avail themselves of involuntary transferees or trailers who are already there and probably networked! This study is one-of-a-kind, and will set the new standard in international research on globalists.

Mary Ann Von Glinow
President, Academy of Management

Preface

"A foreign woman working in Japan? How intriguing—too bad it would never work." Such a comment seems outlandish, even quaint, in the 1990s. Not so long ago, however, such sentiment was common regarding American women professionals working in Japan. We wrote *Western Women Working in Japan* in part to ensure that such thinking remains squelched, to give strength to the women who have made it work or want to make it work in Japan and to firms considering sending foreign women to professional posts in Japan.

Western Women Working in Japan is a book that demanded to be written, for several reasons. First, with a focus on Japan, we examine life for foreign women professionals in a country that has become one of America's—and many of the world's countries'—largest and often most frustrating and baffling economic partners. From 1975 to 1992, for example, trade between Japan and the United States grew over 500 percent in dollar volume. In 1988, Japan surpassed the Netherlands as the second largest investor in the United States, trailing only the United Kingdom. Even with the bumps and potholes of trade policy and political changes, it is likely that Japan will remain a strong trader with many of the world's countries, making it all the more important to understand how to operate successfully in that climate.

Aside from its position as a major trading partner, Japan has long had the image of being a particularly difficult working environment for "Westerners" (i.e., North Americans and Europeans). Its people, culture and business systems have seemed impenetrable to many non-Japanese.

Indeed, numerous scholars and managerial writers have tried to "make sense" of the Japan that business people encounter (e.g., Reed, 1993).

Nevertheless, many American and European firms have in fact successfully conducted business in Japan. IBM has operated there for over 30 years; indeed, one of our Japanese colleagues many years ago commented that, while he was growing up, he assumed IBM was a Japanese company, like Sony or Matsushita. BMW and other luxury car manufacturers have made headway into Japan in the last decade. Hewlett-Packard's joint venture with Canon remains strong and growing. Thus, dispelling some of the myths about the difficulty of doing business in Japan was a second reason for writing the book.

Japan has long been perceived not only as a somewhat hostile environment for non-Japanese in general, but as even more so for women. Thus, a third purpose for this book relates to the previous one but extends the questions to women. Interestingly, the bulk of the research on foreigners who work or have worked in Japan focuses primarily on men (and usually American men) who have been transferred by their firms. Thus, while information does exist on how well (male) "expatriates" adjust to working in a tough Japanese business environment (e.g., Black, 1988), little exists on women in similar situations.

A conventional aphorism for many years was that Japanese would never "accept" women as business partners or counterparts. Indeed, the environment for Japanese women in the workplace has long been quite inhospitable, as we discuss in Chapter 4. Many businesspeople have likewise assumed over the years that the environment for foreign women would be similarly frosty. This premise has only recently been challenged, as more foreign women professionals have begun to work in Japan.

Indeed, despite the growing number of women professionals working overseas, little research exists—in the academic or business press—on particular issues facing them, the firms they work in or their colleagues. The initial and still most comprehensive research on women expatriates, conducted in the early 1980s by Nancy Adler, Professor at McGill University (Montreal, Canada), has only recently been updated (Adler and Izraeli, 1994). Other work on businesswomen working in Japan (e.g., *Doing Business with Japanese Men: A Woman's Handbook*) offers "how to" tips for women, ranging from etiquette to hotels catering to businesswomen, as well as general suggestions on doing business. On the basis of the two consultants' experiences and interviews with several hundred women, it is a useful handbook, especially for women making their first visits to Japan. Other than these works, however, there has been remarkably little recent research or information on whether Japan is indeed as "hostile" to foreign women as conventional wisdom argues. Thus, we wanted to examine this assumption and test its validity.

In addition to Japan's importance as a trading partner and perceptions about its impenetrableness to foreigners and women, we wanted to write this book because of our own circumstances, as professors and as professional women working overseas. Each of us has extensive experience in various parts of the world—living or working in Western Europe, Latin America, Southeast Asia, and Japan. Indeed, over the last nearly 20 years, we have spent significant chunks of time living and working overseas; a good portion of that time was in Japan and working with the Japanese. One of us worked for a blue chip Japanese steel firm, teaching English to managers and employees; this experience was followed by living in Japan to do research for a doctoral dissertation. The other has conducted numerous academic and business research projects for Japanese firms (e.g., Hitachi Steel, Nippon Mining, and Mitsubishi Research Institute) interested in the U.S. market, as well as for American firms interested in learning about Japan. Last, in our research on Japanese human resource management practices over the years, we have encountered and worked with numerous Japanese managers, employees, and scholars, becoming friends with many of those people.

Our experiences in Japan and with Japanese ranged from being stimulating to frustrating and, in some cases, downright hilarious. We have been treated as oddities and near royalty and "part of the team." Always, the experiences prompted us to ask why things happened as they did and how we could (the next time) handle situations "even better."

Given the abhorrent lack of information about women professionals working overseas, however, we had no sense of whether our experiences were typical. Further, during our early careers, we had little guidance on how to handle some of the more difficult situations we faced. Often, we were the first American women professionals our Japanese hosts had encountered. During the late 1970s, when one of us was scheduled to visit Japan to work with a large firm, the U.S. office received several telexes asking questions that had never arisen for the men who traveled to Japan: (1) is she married, (2) what does she eat, (3) how tall is she, and others. We never learned just what purpose such questions had, other than to give the Japanese counterparts some assurance that this "new being" was predictable.

Because we were frequently lone fliers in Japan, we had no road map on how to act as women professionals. We found our own paths, dealt with challenges as they arose—often with humor—and moved forward. Only later, as we compared stories with other women and finally discovered some research, did we realize our experiences were in no way unique. Thus emerged the idea for a project examining more systematically the challenges and advantages of American women professionals working in Japan.

Finally, we wrote this book for our students. Over the years, many women—undergraduate and graduate students alike—have approached us to ask how they can get jobs in "international business." They have the drive, the ambition, the guts, and the willingness to take on the challenges of living overseas, yet they feel thwarted. Often their professors (usually male) comment that working overseas in certain countries or regions (e.g., Japan, the Middle East, Italy, South America) is impossible for women. Finding models of women who do what our students want to do has been difficult. The "models" are often already overseas, in their words "just doing it." Thus, our students often have few people to talk with who are encouraging about their prospects. We hope this book heartens them and other young women seeking international business careers and assures them they are following a track that is feasible and open to them.

Western Women Working in Japan is based upon an ongoing international research project (described in more detail in Appendix A) that examines the experiences of women professionals who work outside their home countries. The full project will explore women's experiences in many countries, including several in Western Europe, Southeast Asia, and South and Latin America. In this book, however, we focus on foreign women professionals' experiences in Japan, for the reasons stated.

In the project, we collected information from over 100 women, through written surveys and in-depth interviews. We jointly conducted comprehensive interviews in Japan with over 20 women, spending 2–3 hours with each. Their time, candor, and insights greatly enhanced our understanding of issues facing women today. We also surveyed over 90 women through two organizations—Foreign Executive Women and the American Chamber of Commerce in Japan.

Our focus for this project is on women who work in professional capacities other than teaching English in Japan. Typically, the teachers of English far outnumber the professional population and, further, usually belong to well established organizations with clear procedures and structures. We were more interested in women whose jobs involved managing others or providing some technical or professional expertise in environments that are often less structured. Such positions can bring the job holders into contact with Japanese clients, suppliers, subordinates, peers or superiors. Women professionals holding such positions in foreign or Japanese firms in Japan have only in the last decade become a large enough group for more systematic study.

We estimate the total number of American women working in Japan to be nearly 2000. The much smaller group of professional and managerial women (non-clerical/secretarial or English teachers) is probably about 500–700. It is these women, likely to manage or work as peers with Japanese counterparts in professional capacities, who were of interest to us. These are the women we teach as students in business administration programs; they are the ones who have fought their way up corporate ranks and now find themselves transferred overseas in challenging settings; they are also women who independently move to Japan seeking work and whom firms hire on-site.

We have clustered the book's chapters into three parts. Part I, "Wanted: Adventurers for the Next Century," focuses on the general trend of globalization and its implications for women working outside their home countries. In Chapter 1, "The Environment of Globalization," we argue the need for employing more global managers, and in particular, for viewing women professionals as a good pool.

In Part II, "Foreign Women Professionals in Japan: The Realities," we examine the findings of our research on women working in Japan. Chapter 2, "The Adventurers: Who Were They?" describes the women we studied—who they were, what types of jobs they held, and their initial perceptions about their jobs. The focus of Chapter 3, "Getting Jobs," examines the challenge of securing a job and the various ways the women we studied did so. Indeed, among our first surprises during the project were the resourcefulness and range of ways that these women used to find work in Japan.

Chapter 4, "The Working Environment," examines the setting in which the women worked. As we mentioned, Japan is often perceived as a particularly hostile environment for Westerners, and especially for women. In this chapter, we explore that environment to understand in more depth the scene in which our group of women operated.

Part II closes with two chapters (Chapter 5, "How Do Women Fare?: Adjustment on the Job," and Chapter 6, "Women's Lives Outside Work") that examine how well the working women did—on and off their jobs. Specifically, we examine the advantages and disadvantages those women faced working in Japan and how they dealt with them.

Part III, "Piercing the Bamboo Wall," focuses on what firms and women can do to improve the use of and effectiveness of American women professionals working in Japan. Chapter 7 and Chapter 8 examine and offer, respectively, "Recommendations for Firms" and "Recommendations for Women" on the issue of foreign women professionals working in Japan. We close the book with Chapter 9, "What Next for Foreign Women Professionals?" in which we briefly review findings and suggest future research directions.

Acknowledgments

We are delighted to offer this book to colleagues, students, and current, future or would-be foreign women professionals working in Japan. It developed out of a desire to understand our own experiences, and those of other women who have worked in Japan. It ends with a hope that the path will be smoother for foreign women professionals who work in Japan in the future.

Our scholarly debts are to several researchers who have contributed tremendously to our understanding of expatriates in general and of women expatriates in particular. Among the many, several deserve note. Stewart Black, Mark Mendenhall, Hal Gregersen, and Gary Oddou have crafted new and useful ways of thinking about the expatriate experience. We are truly grateful for their guidance—direct and indirect—in structuring and carrying out our work. Before we knew each other, we had each been touched by Nancy Adler's early research. Having worked extensively overseas, we felt alone, and wondered whether we were unique in what we had encountered. Through her work, we realized that many women had faced similar experiences. Separately, we concluded she was describing us in the 1970s and 1980s; as we began sharing our experiences, we wanted to know more about what women were experiencing in the 1990s.

Many people and organizations contributed ideas, energy, or resources to this effort. We wish to thank several and hope we have neglected none of the key contributors. The project had its beginning when Patti Salvagio and Catherine Moss, present and former Presidents respectively of the Foreign Executive Women (FEW) group in Tokyo, encouraged us to pursue our questions and use the organization as a focal point for finding an appropriate group of women to study. Patti also led us to our collaborator, Iris Harvey, who truly made the project fly. Based in Tokyo in her own consulting business, Iris arranged for us to meet with the many women we interviewed and surveyed. With a background in marketing research herself, she forced us to recognize the limits and advantages of doing such work in Japan. In addition to FEW, we used the American Chamber of Commerce in Japan as a major resource for our sample of women. Of course, the women we interviewed in Japan deserve special thanks. We have changed their names, to protect their privacy, but deeply appreciate their time and willingness to describe the experiences, frustrations and exhilaration of working in Japan. We wish them well.

The funding for the project came from three key sources. The East-West Seminar, headed by Mr. M. Shibusawa in Tokyo, provided a grant to conduct interviews in Japan and encouragement to pursue the project. Our universities also subsidized the effort. The Portland State University Foundation and the Boise State University Office of Research each contributed needed funding to support our visit to Japan and an extensive mail survey.

In addition to those directly involved in supporting the project, we thank others who listened, argued and urged us on. Schon Beechler heard us play with the early ideas, as we debated in hotel rooms during Academy of Management meetings. Mike Tharp, of *U.S. News & World Report*, offered ideas, encouragement, and contacts. Without the encouragement and support of numerous colleagues at both Portland State and Boise State, it would have been difficult to carry out this research. Students in our classes—and classes of other professors kind enough to let us visit—provided valuable feedback and insights. Masami Nishishiba gave us helpful comments on Chapter 4. Our administrative assistant and secretarial help were wonderful. Many thanks to Joy Brady, Gloria Wilson, Laura Farrington, and Leslie Brown for "production help." Our graduate assistants were amazingly resourceful in finding important data, creating graphs and charts, and teaching us much as we went through the process. In particular, Archana Rai and Manrique Vega at Boise State and Kathie Lennertz and John Weisensee at Portland State were marvelous assistants and colleagues throughout the process.

We also spoke to several groups during the course of the project—academic and professional groups alike. The chance to test the ideas in front of "live audiences" was extremely helpful in deciding what to focus on in the book.

Our personal supporters, of course, deserve highest honors. Donna Philbrick, Bob Hazen, Joanne Mulcahy, and Pam Tierney not only encouraged Sully's efforts but made it possible for her to travel to Japan. Chase Olbrich and Quinn Olbrich have greeted their mother's travels and projects with bewilderment at times, but as a result are becoming wonderful globalists themselves. Tony Olbrich contributed many weeks of single parenting and managing a household for this effort—the price one pays for marrying a person with traveling genes. He also spelled us both for a needed concentrated effort in the mountains of McCall, Idaho, to hammer out final decisions and directions. Thanks much for all the help.

Part I

Wanted: Adventurers for the Next Century

Part I argues for the need to expand the pools for potential "globalists" or people comfortable working "across borders." As the world's economy becomes more fluid, with goods, capital, services, and people crossing boundaries more easily, firms will increasingly need human resources able to comprehend and succeed in such a "global environment."

In Chapter 1, we examine the idea of globalization and some of its implications, especially as they affect foreign women professionals who work in Japan (or want to). A concept that has swept the business world in the last decade, "globalization" urges managers and employees to think of doing business in a "borderless world," in which capital, goods, services and people move relatively unimpeded by regulation, barriers, or thinking (Bartlett and Ghoshal, 1989). We discuss globalization in a broad context, and follow it with a discussion of the increasing economic links between the United States and Japan. Next, we move on to an argument for the need for more "globalists," or managers and professionals who can function successfully in the changing global environment. Finally, we close with a call for considering women as a viable pool for the globalists that firms will need.

Chapter 1

The Environment of Globalization

GLOBALIZATION—NO ESCAPING IT

As I write this chapter on my 3 pound (1.4 kilo) notebook computer (made in South Dakota, USA), I sit in Hanoi, Vietnam. The house in which I live and write was built by the French in the 1930s, was renovated in 1993 by funds from the Swedish government, and is now rented from the Vietnamese Communist party, which has a propaganda printing office in its basement. Down the street, nestled between the Department of Defense and an officers' compound, the Korean giant Daewoo has renovated its local office. Another kilometer farther, the Japanese trading firm Mitsubishi's sales office building in resplendent white, is even more impressive.

After a lunch of local vegetables, soup, and "Coca" (Coke) or *bia* (beer) from Singapore, I spend my afternoons teaching instructors of the country's first M.B.A. program, at National Economics University. These 30 ambitious core faculty members are also preparing executive development and training courses to offer to managers in Vietnamese and foreign firms.

As part of a multinational team of professors from Canada, the United Kingdom, Denmark, Hong Kong, and New Zealand, I came prepared to teach with overhead transparencies and handout packets (in case there was no overhead projector or electricity). I expected to overwhelm the participants with my Powerpoint generated overhead transparencies. Upon arrival, I was chagrined (and yet relieved) to learn that the 20 computers assigned to the M.B.A. instructors have newer versions of Powerpoint, Harvard Graphics, and Word for Windows than I have in the United States.

I ride to work in a 1993 Toyota Landcruiser, print my faxes on a Hewlett-Packard LaserJet made in my hometown (Boise, Idaho), and nightly eat dinner with a Canadian woman coordinating the M.B.A. program and her two colleagues (one from Scotland, the other from Singapore) who are consultants with a firm based in Hong Kong. On my first evening in Hanoi, we were joined by an Australian attorney setting up his law firm's first Vietnamese office, an optimistic Filipino marketing manager who was moving to Ho Chi Minh City (Saigon) to open a sales office for BMW, and a husband (Singaporean) and wife (Malaysian) team starting a textile operation in the country.

Such experiences, somewhat jolting in the juxtaposition of the diversity of products, markets and people in Vietnam, are becoming more commonplace, even in developing countries. Borders increasingly mean less and less. The world economy is indeed becoming more global.

Components of Globalization

"Globalization," as suggested earlier, is generally defined as viewing the world economy as an open and yet integrated system, in which capital, people, goods and services flow easily across borders. Rather than focusing on single countries or regions for marketing, production or staffing (Hill, 1994), global managers sell, produce, and hire on a worldwide basis, adapting and modifying for local tastes only where necessary. Global production, likewise, means locating the "creation" of products or services where it makes most sense economically, politically or socially. For example, in early 1994, Hewlett-Packard's storage division transferred its production facilities from the United States to Penang, Malaysia, in part to take advantage of lower wage rates and proximity to growing markets. West German firms, since reunification, have faced pressure to locate in the former East Germany, for somewhat political reasons—shoring and building up the newly merged former East German unit with the existing, much stronger West. Moreover, firms sometimes shift sourcing or production because of social concerns, as Levi Strauss claimed in 1993 when it began pulling production contracts out of the People's Republic of China, in protest of "pervasive violations of human rights."

Finally, globalization ties into the management of human resources by identifying and effectively using "globalists"—people who think "across borders," in their tasks of marketing, producing, or managing resources. Such "global thinking" demands that firms have people able to act as "chameleons," casually and comfortably adjusting to and thriving in

Figure 1.1
United States–Japan Exports and Imports, 1975–1992

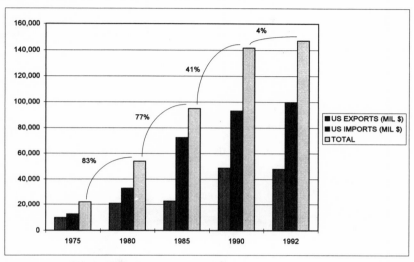

Sources - Direction of Trade Statistics Yearbook 1982. Page 380.
Direction of Trade Statistics Yearbook 1988. Page 406.
Direction of Trade Statistics Yearbook 1993. Page 403.

multiple cultures and settings. These people may actually live outside their countries of citizenship or simply conduct business globally from a "home" setting.

Increases in International Activity Worldwide

Globalization means that countries and firms are increasingly active in and dependent upon other parts of the world. Evidence for such globalization trends is widespread. The U.S. trade picture has changed dramatically since 1975, for instance. The dollar volume of trade between 1975 and 1992 increased 572 percent (Figure 1.1), for example, with marked increases in each 5 year time period.

When assessed other ways, the situation further reveals increasing globalization. In direct foreign investment (DFI), for example, multinational firms based in the United States accounted for more than 60 percent of all foreign direct investment (FDI) worldwide in the 1960s. This proportion has given way to several other countries, resulting in a more even spread of foreign investment outflow. Nevertheless, in the 1990s, seven countries account for 90 percent of all investment, dominating the world scene: the United States, United Kingdom, Japan, Germany, France, Holland, Canada (Hill, 1994: 15). Also significant in the investment shifts is the rapid growth of Japanese foreign direct investment,

Figure 1.2
1991 Value of Trade (Exports and Imports) from World Regions (Percentage of World Trade)

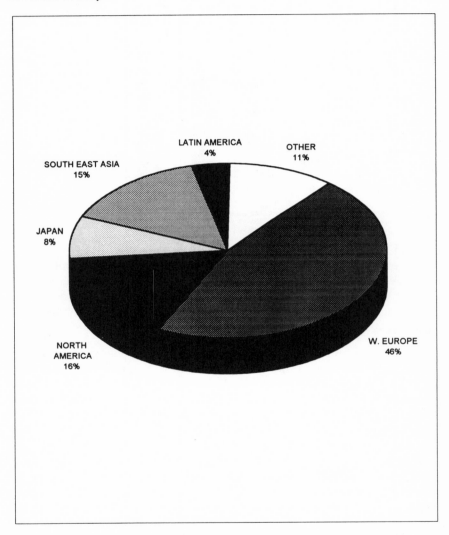

Source - Adapted from Handbook of International Trade and Development Statistics 1992. United Nations. 1993. Page 2-11.

Table 1.1
Gross Domestic Product, 1980–1992 (Average Annual Percentage of Growth)

	1980	1981	1982	1983	1984	1985	1986	1987	1988	1989	1990	1991	1992
China	7.8	4.5	8.7	10.2	14.4	12.3	8.2	11.0	10.7	4.3	5.4	6.4	12.8
S. Korea	-3.3	6.9	7.4	12.1	9.2	6.9	12.3	11.8	11.4	6.1	9.0	8.4	6.5
Thailand	4.7	6.3	4.0	7.2	7.2	3.4	5.1	9.6	13.4	12.2	10.3	8.0	7.5
India	6.7	6.5	3.8	7.4	3.7	5.4	4.8	4.7	10.3	5.4	5.6	1.2	3.5

Source - World Table 1993, The World Bank, 22-25.

much of it to Southeast Asia. Indeed, the Japanese ambassador to Thailand in 1991 estimated that a new Japanese factory would open in Thailand every 3 days throughout the mid-1990s (Pyle, 1991).

Despite changes in world trade and investment patterns, the three largest industrialized areas of the world—Japan, North America, and West Europe—dominate world trade. In dollar volume, total imports and exports among the three areas was $2.366 billion in 1990, 70 percent of all world trade (Figure 1.2), nearly double that in 1980. Clearly, the "triad" (Ohmae, 1985) regions (Japan, North America, and Western Europe) will continue to play a major role in trade patterns for the next several years.

In addition to the triad, other regions are gaining in importance in terms of their economic growth and increasing role in trade. During the 1980s and early 1990s, the annual economic growth rates of several Asian countries (Table 1.1) outpaced those of developed countries (Figure 1.4). Average annual rates of South Korea and China (10 percent), Thailand (7.5 percent), and India (5.5 percent) regularly surpassed that of Japan (4 percent), the United States (3.2 percent) or Germany (2 percent) (Hill, 1994: 47; taken from World Development Report, 1992, Table 2). Furthermore, while the region has long pointed to the "four little tigers" (South Korea, Taiwan, Hong Kong, and Singapore) as the fast growth sites for multinational expansion, these countries are in turn becoming major investors themselves. Hong Kong and South Korea, for example, invest more than the United States in places like China.

Moreover, as the traditional "little tigers" become more developed, other countries will replace them as low cost alternatives. Thailand, for example, enjoyed annual double digit growth in the late 1980s, in large part because of its attractiveness to multinationals seeking low cost production sites that were close to growing Asian markets. Indeed, Japan's "three plants per day" (Pyle, 1991) pattern helped spur Thailand's dramatic growth. Joined by the other three "new" little tigers (Malaysia, Indonesia, and the Philippines), Thailand may itself in the coming years face an onslaught of newer low wage havens, such as Vietnam.

Thus, increasing trade and global independence among countries is likely to continue into the 21st century. The world's two largest economies—the United States and Japan—will doubtless become even more intertwined. One result, clearly, will be more foreigners (including professional women) working in Japan in the future. Before discussing those women and their opportunities, we review briefly the links between these two countries.

UNITED STATES–JAPAN LINKS

Given the focus on Japan in this book, we turn now to review briefly the positions of the United States and Japan and their economic ties. After Canada, Japan is the United States's largest single trading partner, in both exports and imports. In 1992, the United States shipped 11 percent of its exports (about $50 billion) to Japan; in turn, it received about 18 percent ($96 billion) of its imported goods from Japan (Figure 1.3).

The links in foreign direct investment are also increasing, more from the perspective of Japanese investment in the United States than the reverse. Indeed, in absolute dollars, U.S. firms have in the last decade invested far more in Europe than Japan, although their involvement in Japan has more than doubled since 1980 (Figure 1.4). In contrast, Japanese investment in the United States grew tenfold, from less than $10 million in 1980 to close to $1 billion by the early 1990s. During the Japanese economic boom of the late 1980s alone, the pace of investment in the United States increased five times, clearly fusing the economic links between the two countries. As countries such as the United States and Japan further cement their economic bonds, their firms will doubtless expand those connections through interactions by employees in each country. In the next section, we discuss the growing need for human resources who can successfully interact across borders.

THE NEED FOR "GLOBALISTS"

The dramatic changes in the global economy in the last 30 years foreshadow similar developments for the coming decade. For firms to succeed in the next century, their managers will need to think of the world as their production, marketing, and staffing backyards. Furthermore, as firms and industries continue to operate across borders, they will increasingly clamor for "globalist" managers and professionals who can work in environments that demand an understanding of the global economy, the marketplace, and a variety of cultures.

The first step is understanding what it means to be a "globalist" and the challenges firms will face in finding such people. In the balance of this chapter, we address these issues in three subsections. First, we offer

Figure 1.3
Direction of U.S. Merchandise Trade with the World, 1992

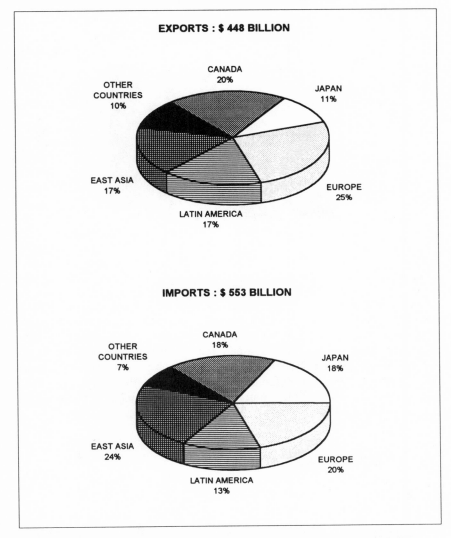

EXPORTS : $ 448 BILLION

CANADA
20%

OTHER
COUNTRIES
10%

JAPAN
11%

EAST ASIA
17%

EUROPE
25%

LATIN AMERICA
17%

IMPORTS : $ 553 BILLION

CANADA
18%

OTHER
COUNTRIES
7%

JAPAN
18%

EAST ASIA
24%

EUROPE
20%

LATIN AMERICA
13%

Source - Adapted from Direction of Trade Statistics Yearbook 1993. Pages 403-405

a way to define "globalists," drawing from ideas of various scholars and managers as well as our own research and experience. Following these definitions and for the balance of the book, we will focus on a particular subset of globalists—those who live outside their "home countries."

Figure 1.4
Foreign Direct Investment Between the United States and Japan, 1980–1991

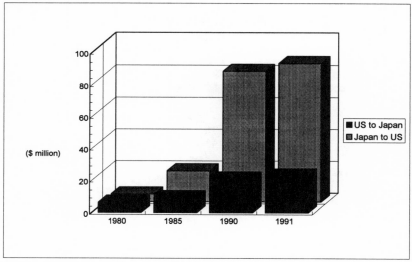

Source - Statistical Abstract of The United States. 1993: 798, 801

Next, we discuss the likely future demand for and supply of such globalists. While we have no crystal ball, we sought to estimate roughly the general "demand" that may occur in coming years. Following this, we discuss the "supply" of globalists, particularly in terms of the forces that are driving down traditional sources of employees (usually men) whom firms typically transfer overseas. We close the chapter by suggesting that professional and managerial women may be an increasingly important and viable pool of "globalists."

What Is a "Globalist"?

In the 1980s and early 1990s, numerous scholars (Bartlett and Ghoshal, 1992; Trompenaars, 1993) and managers, such as Percy Barnevik, CEO of Asea Brown Boveri (Taylor, 1991), offered definitions of the global manager and employee. In the main, they concur that a globalist's perspective is one in which the world is viewed as a potential market and resource base.

To meet customer needs, then, firms increasingly assign managers and professionals to positions that demand global perspectives, in which citizenship means less than competence and skills. Examples of such approaches were myriad during the early 1990s: Volkswagen's CEO came from the Czech Republic; the top manager of the powerhouse consulting firm McKinsey came originally from India; since 1989, Sony has added three non-Japanese to its corporate board of directors; when Whirlpool established a joint venture with the Dutch firm Philips, it was initially managed by a Swede out of its headquarters in Italy (Reich, 1991).

If globalists are employees who view their jobs and their firms from a global perspective, they will no doubt be needed at multiple levels of an organization. As such, we define globalists as people who work in an environment where national borders have little relevance with regard to marketing, production or provision of services, transfer of capital, or building of a career.

Types of Globalists

Given such a definition, we see at least three types of globalists within firms: transferees, suitcase employees, and armchair travelers (Napier, Tibau, Janssens, and Pilenzo, in press). They differ as a function primarily based upon their main "home base" and the amount of time they spend overseas in their jobs. We briefly discuss each.

Expatriate transferees. Transferees are those employees working outside their countries of citizenship. This group includes both people who move at the behest of their organization (often referred to as "expatriates") and people who independently relocate overseas because of their own decisions to pursue a job or career outside their "home" country.

Typically, transferees live abroad at least a year. The means and method by which such employees find themselves overseas may vary, but the premise that they live outside what would be considered their "home countries" remains. In effect, then, this includes a broader range of employees than the expatriates who have traditionally been examined in scholarly or managerial work.

Suitcase employees. For a variety of reasons, some global firms are more cautious about transferring employees overseas than they were even 10 years ago. Pressure from local markets to hire and develop local managers and professionals, concerns about costs of transfers, and terrorist attacks against foreigners are among the forces driving firms to consider alternatives to traditional expatriate assignments.

One solution is short term assignments, particularly when employees have some specific expertise required at another location. Suitcase employees' work requires them to travel abroad for unique projects, usually for less than a year at a time. This category of globalists includes employees and managers who oversee operations in one setting while being officially "based" in another, making periodic visits to the locations for which they are responsible. A typical example of a manager based in one place but managing other sites is P. J. Martin, president and general manager of Xerox's Americas operation. In 1992, Martin managed the firm's operations in Latin America, Canada and the Pacific Rim from his office in Connecticut (Piturro, 1992). Spending over 50 percent of his time on the road, Martin visited Xerox's Western Hemisphere operations (Mexico, Canada, Brazil) on a monthly basis and Asia three or four times yearly.

Suitcase employees also comprise those employees who travel for business meetings or negotiations, as well as those who remain at a given site for several months, assigned to a specific project. The last group of suitcase travelers often includes people who have technical expertise that must be transferred to local operations or who act as trouble shooters. Mercedes Benz, for example, sends German service technicians for several months at a time to its new operations to train and monitor on-site programs.

Armchair travelers. A final group of globalists remain physically in one country but nonetheless do their jobs in a global environment. Such "armchair travelers" include employees whose work requires them to interact with people from other countries, who need not travel. They interact instead through technology and other means: telephone, fax, electronic mail or the postal mail. Procurement managers at Hewlett-Packard's Idaho facilities have for years, for example, communicated daily with counterparts in Mexico, Singapore or Malaysia, without meeting them face to face. Nevertheless, the ability to understand a person who has another "first" language (and thus may speak English with an accent), or who may have different customs and holidays (and thus require better planning and coordination), demands more global thinking, even from one who never leaves "home."

Need for Transferee Globalists

Given the trends toward more emphasis on global thinking, firms will doubtless need all types of globalists—transferees, suitcase employees and armchair travelers. While the suitcase and armchair travelers are critical, our focus is on transferees, those employees who live and work for extended periods outside their country of citizenship. These globalists often face the greatest challenges as they adjust (or do not) to a variety of cultures and business practices, often with little preparation. They must balance work and non-work aspects of living in diverse settings, ranging from managing subordinates who think and act differently from them to ensuring successful child care and educational arrangements for family members. They frequently face multicultural relationships within and across units of their organizations and must deal with external stakeholders like customers and suppliers.

Finding successful "globalists" is daunting for any firm. Doing so in an increasingly competitive environment, where many organizations are chasing the same people and where certain pressures thwart finding and developing such people, will be even more difficult.

Demand for transferees. To understand more fully the challenge facing managers seeking globalists in the coming decade, we examine the possible demand for and supply of transferees in particular. While it is difficult to specify the total numbers of transferee globalists that firms may need, we have tried to estimate existing numbers of traditional expatriates and, from that, gauge possible future needs for such overseas employees. We estimated these expatriates in part because it is possible to identify them (through their firms), whereas it is more difficult to do so with other types of transferees.

As mentioned previously, "traditional expatriates" include managers and professionals working for global firms who are transferred overseas by those firms. We estimate roughly the number of such traditional expatriates in the largest firms in the world to be about 100,000 annually. This estimate is based upon (1) research that examined a sample of the world's largest 150 firms (as reported in *Fortune* magazine, 1992) (Peterson, Sargent, Napier, and Shim, 1993), (2) through a written survey of the world's largest manufacturing firms and (3) in-depth interviews with human resource managers of 27 of those firms based in Japan, the United States, the United Kingdom, and Germany. While the firms range widely in their actual numbers of expatriates (e.g., from 200 to over 4000 in the 27 interviewed firms), our estimate rests on the assumption that each firm has an average of 500–800 expatriates overseas in a given year. Thus, we estimate that the largest 150 firms have a total of 75,000–120,000 expatriates working abroad each year. The estimate itself will likely change markedly in the coming years. Many of these large firms have reduced their absolute numbers of expatriates over the last decade and anticipate some reduction over the next 10 years. Nevertheless, they are still likely to have 50,000–100,000 traditional transferees yearly. Further, if expatriates rotate every 2–4 years, the largest firms will need an estimated 30,000 new expatriate transferees annually.

Source of expatriates. Firms seeking a ready source for future globalists have often looked to undergraduate and, more specifically, graduate programs of business. In some regions such programs appear to be a promising source. For instance, the number and quality of M.B.A. programs, particularly in Europe, have increased in the last decade. An estimated 4000 students graduate annually from the 20 top M.B.A. programs in Europe. Of these, if 30–40 percent are willing to take on expatriate career tracks, firms can anticipate 1200–1600 people who could eventually move into expatriate assignments.

Unlike their European counterparts, however, most American students have been more reluctant to pursue international careers. Instead of traditional M.B.A. programs, many North American firms have had to recruit at specialized international business programs. At the master's level, traditional sources have included such schools as the American Graduate School of International Management ("Thunderbird") (about 1000 students annually), the University of South Carolina (about 150 students), the University of Southern California's International Business Education and Research program (about 40 students), or Wharton's Lauder program (about 100 students). The total number of students from such specialized programs in the United States is thus estimated roughly to be about 2000–3000 yearly. Yet, not even all of these students will pursue "globalist" careers. Indeed, Thunderbird, the oldest and largest of the specialized programs, has graduated over 30,000 people since the 1940s, but many have remained in their home countries.

Other sources will include the numerous M.B.A. programs with specialties in international business (New York University, Columbia University) or several electives in international business (University of Washington). Even if an estimated 10 percent (7000) of the annual 70,000 M.B.A. graduates in North America pursue careers that allow them to become traditional transferees or expatriates, this may not fully serve global firms' future needs.

Perhaps firms will venture into undergraduate business or related international studies programs to find a future supply for globalists. At the undergraduate level, in 1990, just under one million people received bachelor's degrees (Schwartz, 1992: 137–138). An estimated 194,000 received business degrees; of those, approximately 46 percent were women, or about 90,000 students. If some of those business students pursue international careers *and* if students from other, related degree programs (e.g., languages, international relations) pursue global careers, firms may have another 10,000–15,000 or so students annually to draw upon in coming years.

Will Supply Match Demand?

Although such numbers look potentially promising, recent trends in the number of students pursuing business degrees (at both the graduate and undergraduate levels) are less encouraging. In the last 2–3 years, the proportion of students receiving business degrees has begun to decline in the United States, possibly inhibiting the availability of students from universities.

Other factors may influence the number of available globalists who come from the traditional expatriate ranks. In the next section, we discuss several broad issues: growing numbers of dual career couples, and job and career related fears in the form of restructuring, financial uncertainties, and apprehensions of repatriated (i.e., returning) expatriates. Each of these factors can limit the pool from which expatriate transferees have typically emerged.

Dual careers. Increasingly, the traditional group of expatriates—long term male employees of global firms—are less likely to be part of a pool for overseas assignments. Increasingly, men in countries such as the United States and Germany have spouses and partners who are likewise engaged in demanding careers. As the numbers of women managers and professionals increase, the corresponding numbers of men available for posts abroad will likely decrease.

The issue of dual careers applies most pointedly to the seasoned managers who would be likely candidates for development positions abroad. As mid-career managers and professionals, they are more likely to face the challenges of dual career pressures, maintaining financial security, and balancing other family demands (such as caring for older parents, meeting teenage children's expectations). As a result, it becomes more difficult for firms to find seasoned male managers prepared to take overseas assignments.

Restructuring gloom. In addition to personal factors such as dual career pressures, the fervor of "restructuring" continues to make many managers and professionals skittish about their future in their organizations. As firms continue to "restructure," many employees—especially middle managers, whose jobs are often targeted for "downsizing"—may be reluctant to move away from the center of the corporate action. Moving out of the country becomes more treacherous than ever. The "out of sight, out of mind" adage takes on new meaning in times of restructuring. In leaner economic times, being plugged into a network and understanding coming changes outside as well as inside firms become critical for managers anxious to hold their positions. The perception that taking an international post will endanger one's career may well cool interest and willingness to transfer.

Financial security—a thing of the past? Furthermore, because of fears of restructuring and involuntary layoffs, managers may increasingly be anxious to create as much financial security as early in their career as possible. International moves have traditionally been a way to achieve such financial security, given the extra compensation and expatriate perquisites common in many firms. In the present environment, however, international assignments are becoming less attractive financially for individual transferees. In certain regions, such as Europe, some firms are, for example, reducing the perquisites for overseas assignments to be more in line with local compensation conditions.

Moreover, transfers of expatriates are increasingly less attractive—for financial reasons—for global firms as well. The costs of transferring executives can be 1.5 to 2 times their salary, with huge portions going for living, education, and related allowances. In countries such as Japan, where apartments alone can cost upwards of $100,000 annually, costs of transfers become exorbitant.

As a result, many firms are seeking ways to cut the costs associated with transferring people. One approach has been to develop new compensation schemes and packages. An example is the emerging "Euro-contract," which pegs newly hired Europeans within some firms to a common compensation package that is transferable across Europe. While more appealing to individual employees than local contracts, these "Eurocontracts" are less attractive (and as a result, much less expensive) than the more traditional expatriate packages that were customized by country.

Jobs upon reentry: Few guarantees. A final pressure dampening the pool of existing male expatriates is that many firms transferring managers and professionals overseas can (or will) guarantee neither a promotion nor—in some cases—a particular job upon the expatriate's return. Indeed, coupled with restructuring, stepping out of an existing job and risking not having one to return to make transfers even less attractive (Peterson, Sargent, Napier and Shim, 1993). Given such trends, global firms may have difficulty finding managers and professionals from their traditional potential expatriate ranks. Such challenges force new ways of solving the problem of finding and developing future globalists.

SEEKING TRANSFEREES—A NEW WAY OF THINKING

In this final section of Chapter 1, we present two ideas that may help firms fill the globalist positions they will have in the future. First, we argue for a broader definition of "transferee." Rather than considering only the traditional source of transferees (i.e., long term careerists from the firm's home base country who become expatriates), we urge managers of global firms to broaden their definitions of and searches for globalists, particularly for transferees.

In addition, we recommend that within a broader category of transferees, managers consider women as a key potential pool. Women have typically represented 3–5 percent of the traditional expatriate pool in global firms (Adler, 1994). While many women face some of the same pressures that male expatriates do, there are some pressures that prod firms to more aggressively embrace women in their potential pool of globalists.

A Broader Definition of Transferees

Given the pressures facing firms seeking to transfer expatriates, we suggest that the sources of transferees reach beyond traditional expatriates. In this section, we discuss four types of transferees: (1) expatriates,

(2) inpatriates, (3) independent transferees, and (4) involuntary transferees.

Expatriates. As we have discussed, transferees have traditionally been defined as "expatriates," employees identified by their firms for transfer and assignments abroad. "Expatriates" work outside ("ex") their home countries (from the French word for country, *patrie*). Present day expatriates have a long line of ancestors, ranging from early colonialists—whether Portuguese, Belgian or British—who established "subsidiary" operations to exploit countries ranging from Indonesia to the Congo. British managers of the Atlantic & Pacific Tea Company, American engineers of the Arabian-American Oil Company (ARAMCO), and Japanese Honda motor scooter salesmen trying to build U.S. markets all represent the traditional expatriates. In each case, the organizations initiated a transfer of employees. This group of traditional expatriates has been chronicled, examined, praised and damned during the many years people have moved and worked overseas. As we have suggested, however, firms need to consider other sources of overseas employees, discussed later.

Inpatriates. While expatriates have been the most visible—and perhaps best understood—of transferees, they represent only one of at least four types. In addition to the expatriates who move from their "home countries" to others, firms are beginning to use "inpatriates" to increase the firm's "globalization." These transferees move from outpost locations to firms' home bases. Such "inpatriates" typically move to headquarters or other operations from their own home countries, usually for training or development reasons. The German pharmaceutical giant Hoechst, for example, brings Americans, and more recently, Southeast Asians (e.g., Thais) to work in and learn from the headquarters operations in Germany. The intention is primarily to train and then return such transferees to their home bases, although some of them move to other countries, becoming "third country nationals."

Independent transferees. A third category of transferees includes those adventurous souls who choose to move to a location outside their home countries and seek work locally, upon arrival. The lure of working in another environment, the challenge of operating in another culture, or the lack of opportunities in the home countries may propel certain transferees to move abroad.

Such "independents" or "voluntary expatriates" (Parker, 1991) have likely existed as long as the more traditional expatriates, yet there is little information about them. Part of the reason is that, unlike their counterparts in multinational firms, they are often difficult to identify. They often work for local firms, not multinational firms; further, if they work for global firms, they are often considered "local staff." Also, they frequently establish their own businesses, as opposed to working for foreign companies. Finally, many voluntary transferees work as free-lance or contract workers, outside organizational boundaries. Thus, the total number of such voluntary transfers is difficult to estimate.

Trailers or involuntary transferees. Finally, a last group of transferees arrive abroad sometimes involuntarily, usually for reasons other than their own career goals. Trailing spouses or partners of traditional expatriates make up the largest portion of "involuntary transferees." While their moves typically stem from personal reasons (i.e., to keep a family together), they often make a move expecting or wanting to seek work on site. Those who find it thus become another group of "transferees," living and working outside their home countries. Those unable to find work (but who want to) nonetheless represent a possible pool of globalists, again very difficult to identify.

One reason to rethink the way we describe globalists is because of the major role that women can and will play as a source of globalists. In the next section, we discuss factors that encourage women to become, and organizations to draw upon them as, a potential source of future globalists.

WOMEN AS A POTENTIAL POOL

If the trends mentioned—the increasingly global nature of business, the demand for globalists, a declining pool of traditional expatriates— were not enough reason for firms to look to women as a potential pool for future transferees, other forces push in that direction as well.

This section points out that several influences should lead firms to factor women into their search for transferees in the future. We examine three such forces: (1) availability of trained women; (2) government regulation pushing firms toward finding and promoting women into upper level positions, including overseas assignments; and (3) likelihood that capable women will already be overseas, whether as voluntary or involuntary transferees.

Availability of Trained Women

As we mentioned earlier, growing numbers of business graduates in general are positioning themselves to become globalists in the future. In this section, we argue more specifically that women are playing a major role in that shift.

Increasingly women are pursuing preparation and careers that place them in a position to take up jobs outside their home countries (Figure 1.5). In the United States, for example, the proportion of undergraduate business degree recipients who were women grew from 8.0 percent in 1965 to 46.7 percent in 1990. The story is similarly dramatic among grad-

Figure 1.5
Women as a Proportion of Business Students

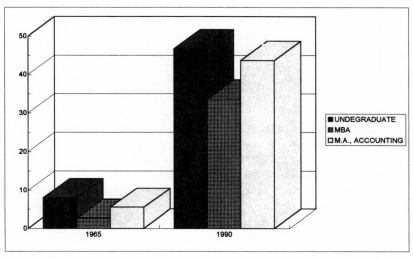

Source - Schwartz, 1992 : 65

uate programs of business: the percentage of women M.B.A. graduates went from 2.6 in 1965 to 8.3 in 1980, to 33.6 percent in 1990 (Schwartz, 1992: 65, 137–138). Such trends suggest that, like men, women increasingly have the basic business preparation for international careers.

Indeed, once women receive the appropriate preparation, they also show interest in pursuing such international careers. In past surveys, about 10 percent of American business students claimed they wanted to pursue internationally oriented careers. Further, the percentages of women and men desiring overseas assignments are fairly similar, despite a myth (Adler, 1984b) that women are uninterested in global careers. Indeed, in the early 1980s, when Adler conducted her initial research on women in international business, she found that the proportion of women M.B.A.'s wishing to get into international business was similar to that of men.

Government Regulation

A second force encouraging firms to consider women for overseas posts is legislation requiring equal treatment in selection and promotion of women and minorities in the United States. Briefly, the 1991 Civil Rights Act requires multinational firms to follow the same Equal Employment Opportunity guidelines for international staffing as they must for domestic (i.e., in the United States) staffing. An implication of the

Act, therefore, is that global firms are reexamining their selection practices for overseas positions. In particular, Taylor and Eder (1994) suggest four ramifications for firms, which will each have varying effects on the future numbers of expatriate transferees. One implication that may mean fewer expatriates is the push to seek more local (i.e., "host" country) staff members or to transfer temporarily those "host country" managers and professionals to the headquarters or "home country" operation (i.e., inpatriates). A second result of the Civil Rights Act of 1991 could well be more aggressive pursuit of women and minorities for overseas posts. This supports our contention that women professionals should and will be considered for traditional transferee assignments. Moreover, in such a scenario, the training and development programs for transferees will necessarily change, adapting to address issues that may be of particular concern for women and minority employees.

Finally, the selection process itself, according to Taylor and Eder (1994), will become more open, with assignments being posted throughout a firm, rather than decided upon by an "old boys' network," one of the more traditional approaches to international staffing. Thus, law in the United States will encourage more use of U.S. firms' existing talent pools, which include women candidates for upper level positions.

Already at the Site: Voluntary and Involuntary Transferees

A final catalyst that should lead firms to consider women more frequently for overseas posts is that they are often already at the locations where firms may need talent. If firms build on the idea of considering "transferees" as a broad category of current or potential employees, it becomes clear that firms need not always do the "transferring." Indeed, we were surprised early in our research to learn how few women were traditional expatriates in Japan, and rather how many were voluntary transferees. Indeed, of the 500–700 foreign women professionals estimated to be working in Japan in the early 1990s, a former president of the Foreign Executive Women organization estimated that only 5–10 percent of the women were traditional transferees or expatriates. The balance were mostly voluntary expatriates—independent job seekers—who looked for work on-site.

Finally, many professional women find themselves becoming involuntary transferees. When their spouses or partners accept overseas assignments, many women must leave (or transfer if possible) their professional or managerial careers to "follow" the expatriate. Thus, many talented, ready-to-work professional and managerial women are already overseas, many of them looking for a match with a local or foreign firm. Such a pool, while more challenging to access, may again offer another solution to firms' future needs for globalists.

SUMMARY AND CONCLUSIONS

Globalization—the open flow of goods, people and services across borders—is increasingly commonplace in developed and developing countries alike. One result of this trend will likely be a greater need for globalists, or people with a perspective that is worldwide, rather than focusing on their own "home country" issues or markets.

Firms will likely need several types of globalists—those who transfer long term (1–4 years) overseas ("traditional transferees"), those who travel on short term assignments ("suitcase travelers") and those who remain in their home countries but have jobs with international components ("armchair travelers").

Globalization will increasingly affect businesses and individuals alike. Savvy employees—or potential employees—of global firms will recognize the need for gaining experience in international transactions and in working with people from cultures other than their own. Likewise, shrewd managers in firms operating globally will seek such "globalists" to launch their firms into the next century. Unfortunately, however, finding people with the skills and attributes for such work is challenging, given the many pressures that limit the pools of candidates and the difficulty for many such candidates to adjust to ways jobs are changing in a global environment.

Global economic forces push firms to seek new pools of candidates for global positions, especially ones where employees work outside their home countries. Moreover, firms, especially in the United States, increasingly face government regulations, reluctance to live overseas from traditional expatriate pools (i.e., white males), as well as a growing pool of talented women, prepared and adventurous enough for complex global assignments. All of these forces point to foreign women professionals as a possible source for staffing positions abroad.

Clearly the need exists for more foreign women professionals who can help fill the gaps for staffing in overseas assignments. Indeed, contrary to the reactions so common even a decade ago about sending women to overseas posts, the evidence mounts daily that many professional women perform beautifully in countries outside their own. The balance of the book shows this in one particularly challenging setting, Japan.

Part II

Foreign Women Professionals in Japan: The Realities

The forces moving firms toward needing and seeking more globalists and the factors that lead women to become part of the potential pool of such globalists have already begun to surface in Japan. In Part II, we illustrate how those factors operate. Specifically, we report the findings of our research on foreign women professionals working in Japan—who they are, what type of work they do, and how they have reacted to their situations on and off the job.

The next five chapters discuss the lives and learning of the women we studied. In Chapter 2 we describe these "Adventurers"—their backgrounds and what brought them to Japan. As we suggested in Chapter 1, one of the initial (and more surprising) findings in the project was the range of ways that women came to and found jobs in Japan. Rather than following the traditional expatriate route (i.e., being transferred from the home country by one's firm), many of the women we studied moved independently to Japan. While other researchers have focused most heavily on the traditional expatriate, ignoring other routes to overseas posts, we sought to understand as well the other tactics that women used to arrive on the scene.

Following a discussion of the sample of women, we move to issues related to job seeking in Chapter 3. First, we review how these adventuring women identified the opportunities they pursued, and the selection criteria and processes that they used. Next we address the preparation the women received (or did not) prior to and just after taking their jobs. In addition, we discuss their perceptions of the barriers and advantages to being women going through the selection process. Finally, we examine the types of compensation and benefits packages these women received.

Chapter 4 on "The Working Environment" examines the setting in which the foreign professional women worked. As we mentioned, Japan is often perceived as a particularly hostile environment for Westerners, and especially for women. In Chapter 4, we explore that environment to understand in more depth the scene in which our group of women operated.

Part II closes with two chapters on how women adjusted to living and working in Japan. Additionally, we examine the advantages and disadvantages those women faced and how they dealt with them.

Chapter 2

The Adventurers: Who Were They?

In Chapter 2, we introduce the women in the study. To comprehend better the issues facing these foreign women professionals working overseas generally and in Japan specifically, we used several sources for insights and information. In addition to our own experiences, we drew upon earlier research (e.g., Adler, 1984a; Adler and Izraeli, 1994; Black, Gregersen and Mendenhall, 1992).

While these sources were useful for creating a theoretical understanding of the challenges and advantages that foreign women face working in Japan, we depended most heavily on two traditional research methods for gathering information: a written survey sent to a sample of foreign professional women working in Japan and in-depth interviews, in Japan, with several women professionals. In the following two sections, we describe those sources generally; Appendix A reports in more depth on the research method and these two key data sources.

INFORMATION SOURCES ON THE WOMEN IN THE STUDY

We used two primary sources of information to learn about foreign women professionals working in Japan. A written survey and series of interviews with a smaller group formed the main sources. We discuss each in turn.

Survey

Building upon previous research done on male (Black, 1988) and female expatriates (Adler, 1984a, 1984b, 1984c, 1994), we adapted and further developed a written survey for this study (Appendix B). It asked a wide range of questions about the lives and reactions of foreign professional women working in Japan. The questions explored, for example, the extent to which the women were satisfied with their jobs, the degree to which they had received preparation before taking those jobs, the compensation package they received, the extent to which they and their families (i.e., partners and children) had adjusted to life in Japan, and the extent to which they saw their situations as similar to or different from those of men in comparable posts.

We sent the survey to members of two key organizations for foreign women who work in Japan. The Foreign Executive Women (FEW) group, founded by a group of foreign women seeking a support and networking group, now boasts some 200 members, most of whom are located near Tokyo. Most of the members hold jobs but, increasingly, women join FEW to use its network in seeking jobs. We sent the survey to all FEW members, and received 55 usable responses.

The second group receiving surveys were the female members of the American Chamber of Commerce in Japan. Screening out overlaps, there were 93 women in the Chamber to whom we sent surveys. Of those 36 returned usable responses. Coupled with response from the FEW group, this number made a total of 91 completed surveys.

Interviews

In addition to the survey findings, we interviewed several women to gain more insight into the situation of foreign women professionals working in Japan. In the following chapters, we draw heavily upon comments and perspectives gained from in-depth interviews with 20 women professionals. Through the Foreign Executive Women group, we worked with a local contact in Japan who identified and scheduled a variety of women for us to interview. We spent from one to three hours with each of the interviewees, using an interview protocol described in Appendix C.

The purpose of the interviews was to gain more insight from women who had experienced a diversity of job situations, who had spent varying lengths of time in Japan, who had different personal circumstances, and who had experienced (what they perceived to be) various levels of success. Furthermore, we wanted to—and did—speak to women who were from dissimilar backgrounds: three of the women were African-American, two were Japanese-Americans; nine were married (one to a

Japanese and one to a Korean); their estimated ages ranged from late-20s to mid-40s; three had children. They had been in Japan from 2 months to over 16 years and held jobs in banks, consumer products firms, consulting firms, or relocation companies or had started their own businesses.

One issue that could influence the project findings is the period during which we investigated the experiences of these women. We collected interview and survey information between December 1992 and June 1993. At that time, Japan had just moved out of a long term growth cycle, a so-called economic bubble. By mid-1992, the "bubble had burst." Thus, the experiences of the women we studied were, for the most part, based upon the late 1980s and early 1990s, before the economy in Japan became much tougher. Although some of the findings we uncovered may result from the women's working in "good" economic times, many of the insights nonetheless seem widely applicable. Indeed, the findings confirm those from research done by Nancy Adler a decade earlier, persuading us that much of what we learned will be of value to women in a variety of settings and time periods.

CATEGORIES OF FOREIGN WOMEN PROFESSIONALS WORKING IN JAPAN

When we first started our project, our intent was to replicate much of the earlier research that had been done on expatriates (Adler, 1994; Black, Stephens and Rosener, 1992), or those people who are transferred overseas by their firms. Since most of the work used male samples, we wanted to see whether the issues facing that group were similar for women.

One of the first surprises during the research, as mentioned, was that *very* few women fall into that traditional transferee or "expatriate" category. Indeed, when we first contacted FEW about our wish to study women expatriates, the response was quite startling—only an estimated 5–10 percent of the members had been transferred by their firms! Thus, it quickly became clear that we needed to learn about these *and* other groups of women working in Japan. We uncovered at least three groups or categories of women, based upon how they ended up in Japan.

Three groups of foreign women professionals emerged. First, as we suggested in Chapter 1, the "traditional transferees" (or "expatriates") were typically transferred by their organizations. "Independent job seekers" moved "voluntarily" or on their own initiative to Japan. Finally, a group of "involuntary transferees" or "trailers" tended to move because of a spouse's or partner's career.

Before defining each of these groups in more detail, we note that a unique aspect of our research was the chance to learn more about the latter two of these categories, women who arrived in Japan through means *other* than being transferred by the firms they worked for in their home countries. To date, each of these groups has been largely neglected in the research and managerial writing; instead, as we have mentioned, most focus has been on the first group—traditional transferees or expatriates. Very little research (Parker, 1991) has addressed the situation of other types of overseas employees, such as "seekers"—women who independently find jobs in Japan—and "trailers"—those who follow a spouse or partner whose job takes him to Japan. Particularly through our interviews, we were able to learn more about their situations.

Traditional Expatriates

As have men over the years, women *have* come to Japan as "traditional" transferees or "expatriates." To date, however, their numbers are overwhelmed by those of their male counterparts. Nevertheless, given the pressures firms will likely face in coming years, as we discussed in Chapter 1, we expect that women *will* more often come to Japan as traditional transferees. Thus, we wanted to learn from some of the current expatriates just what experiences they have had.

The women expatriates we interviewed had been transferred to Japan in large part because of their expertise and, in some cases, for management or career development. While most went readily, some were extremely reluctant to transfer. Thus, while their individual stories ranged in the degree to which they sought such transfers, the women were nonetheless similar in that they had moved to Japan under the auspices of their organizations. As such they tended to have very different compensation packages (typically much more attractive) than other groups of women.

Of the eight women who had been transferred by their firms in the United States, seven held jobs in American firms and one worked for an international service organization headquartered in the United States with offices worldwide. They worked in banking, law, consulting, and consumer products. Most tended to hold mid to upper management positions. In only one case was the "title" a misrepresentation of such a high level position; in that case, the woman felt the title did not reflect her true job.

Independent Job Seekers

A second group of women moved to Japan voluntarily. In this category, there were two "types" of voluntary expatriates. First, some women moved independently to Japan—without jobs—and sought work once they were on-site. A second type were hired in their home country for jobs in Japan; they became "local staff" once they were in Japan. The first subgroup of "seekers" often referred to themselves as "local hires," since they found work once they were living in Japan, were hired "on-site" by firms and were treated as local (i.e., Japanese) staff in terms of compensation and personnel practices. The second group were more "hybrid," in that they were hired outside Japan but became similar (in terms of compensation) to independent job seekers once on-site.

Such "voluntary expatriates" (Parker, 1991), like their traditional transferee counterparts, had different personal reasons for being in Japan, but essentially they all had made a decision to *go* to Japan and work there. They included women working for Japanese firms, working for foreign firms, or working independently as consultants or entrepreneurs. In some cases, although the women worked for foreign firms, they were the only non-Japanese employees in the office.

During the project, we interviewed eight such "local hire" seekers. They varied widely in how they "became" seekers. For example, one was initially transferred from the United States but, to be able to remain in Japan, later moved to another firm, losing her "expatriate" status. Another initially arrived in Japan as a "trailer" (wife of a military officer) and returned much later to become an independent business owner. Finally, a third married a Japanese man while she was studying in Japan and decided to remain after finishing her degree.

The second type of independent job seekers—so-called hybrid seekers—was the group of women who were neither transferred by firms as expatriates nor hired *in* Japan as "locals." Instead, these women were hired in the United States (usually directly out of graduate programs) by Japanese or American firms and then were sent to Japan. While each had previous experience and interest in Japan, the offer to work in Japan was typically one of several that the women considered. Thus, they did not necessarily initially seek out the Japanese opportunity, although most were quite interested in moving to Japan. Two of the three we interviewed, for instance, were Japanese-Americans, reared in bilingual households and with exposure to extended family members in Japan. The third had spent a year studying in Japan during college.

Once employed, however, these hybrid seekers were typically treated as local hires in terms of their compensation packages and personnel status. Thus, in many cases, the issues and challenges faced by both of these groups of "seekers" were similar once they got into their jobs.

"Trailers"

A final group of women went to Japan because they wished to remain with their partners or spouses who were offered a transfer, usually a traditional (expatriate) transfer. Such women become "trailers" or "involuntary expatriates" (Parker, 1991) and moved *with* or *after* the partner or spouse who transferred. If they came later, they typically followed their partners within a year.

The decision of when and how to leave jobs and careers in the home base was often difficult. Some women left (i.e., quit) their jobs outright; some were able to rearrange their jobs in such a way that they could continue working. Many went to Japan intending to seek work on-site; once they were there, they joined the ranks of "seekers" and were typically treated as "local hires" if they were able to find work.

Similar to those of the other groups of women, individual stories varied markedly. One woman, with an educational background comparable to her husband's, reluctantly left a management level post in a nonprofit firm to accompany her banker husband. Another had followed her military husband to several bases in Asia, including one in Japan, nearly two decades before. A third was an independent consultant in the United States and chose to continue her consulting for several months, by commuting from Japan to the United States. Ultimately, however, she phased out her American projects and began building a consulting practice in Japan.

Thus, the study comprised a variety of women, in terms of the ways in which they landed in Japan. We now move into a more detailed description of those women.

THE ADVENTURERS

In the following several sections, we describe in more depth the women we studied. First, we review selected demographic information—their age ranges, educational backgrounds, nationality, marital status and the like. Next, we examine their work backgrounds and current job situations and organizations. We conclude with general observations about these foreign women professionals working in Japan.

Who Are These Adventurers?

As mentioned earlier, we estimate that there were about 500–700 foreign women professionals (non–English teachers) working in Japan in the early 1990s. Through our questionnaire and interviews, we sought a sample of women who represented a wide range of those foreign women professionals working in Japan. In the succeeding section, we describe the women we studied in terms of their personal backgrounds—age, education, language capabilities, nationality, family and marital situations, and, lastly, their prior experience with living or working overseas.

Age range. The foreign women professionals we studied tended to range in age from their mid- to late-20s through early-40s. Most of the

Figure 2.1
Age Ranges of Women in Sample, by Type (Expatriates, Independents, and Trailers)

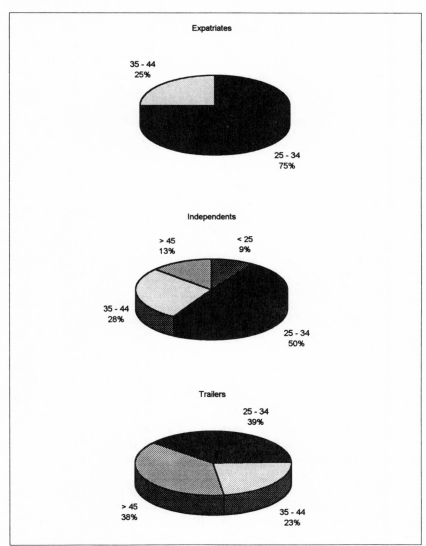

women were relatively young: over 50 percent of those responding to the survey and half of our interviewees were between 25 and 34 years old. This held true especially for expatriates and independents (Figure 2.1). Typically, these younger women had completed college, and in some cases graduate study. Many had worked in their home countries (usually the United States) before moving to Japan. Thus, they often took with them technical or business related skill or interest.

Typical of this group was Linda, a young woman who had been an exchange student in Japan during high school, had studied business during college and was interested in learning about international business and international marketing in particular. She sought work in Japan after completing her bachelor's degree and worked for a Japanese firm for 6 months before seeking another employer. When we interviewed her, she had recently attained what she considered to be a good position selling advertisements at an international public relations firm. She was the only foreigner in the subsidiary office of about 20 employees. She was enthusiastic about living and working in Japan and intended to remain in Japan for up to another five years before returning to the United States.

The next most common age group was women who were 35–44 years old (26.4 percent of survey respondents and 35 percent of interviewees). Many of these women arrived in Japan as traditional transferees, moving with their firms, or as trailers following their spouses or partners. Like their younger compatriots, they had technical skills, usually much more extensive, and often had extensive management experience. Deborah, who transferred to Japan to assume leadership of a research and development team, had a master's degree in engineering and some 10 years of work experience in technical and management capacities in U.S. electronics and computer firms before moving to Japan.

Fully 15 percent of the women we studied were 45 years old or older and were usually trailers or independents. Many of them had chosen to remain indefinitely in Japan. In one case, a woman had moved to Japan 10 years earlier, to "follow" her fiancé. When the relationship fizzled, she chose to remain in Japan and raise her son there. Another woman moved initially as a military wife, returned later with her (by then retired) husband, and eventually established a business in Japan.

Thus women of all ages work in Japan. We will examine later the differences among age groups, particularly in terms of such factors as language skills and job levels.

Educational backgrounds. On the whole, the foreign women professionals working in Japan in this project appeared to be highly educated. Almost all of the women in our study had graduated from college— most often receiving a bachelor's degree. Many had graduate education as well. All except 4 of the 91 women who responded to the written questionnaire had attended colleges or universities. Most had liberal arts degrees; others had bachelor's of science degrees; some had studied in business or related administrative programs as undergraduates.

Over 50 percent (Figure 2.2) of the survey respondents had graduate degrees. Their degrees were master of arts (e.g., in Asian History) or,

Figure 2.2
Educational Background of Women in Sample, by Type (Expatriates, Independents, and Trailers)

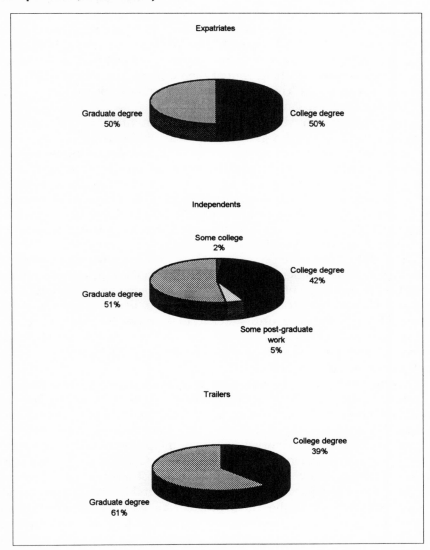

more commonly, administration or management oriented degrees, including master of business administration, master of public administration, or master of international management. Many women studied Japanese history or language at some point during their educational career. A typical example was Donna, who had studied music and Japanese language during a year overseas while obtaining an Asian History undergraduate degree; she continued her Japanese language training while she sought a master's degree in international management.

Language capabilities. Any foreigner (particularly from North America or Europe) who has wrestled with learning Japanese knows how challenging it can be. On the other hand, knowing the language of the country where one lives can help temper the normal uncertainties that come with such experiences. Thus, we wanted to learn how capable the women felt in their Japanese language abilities.

One of the areas in which our sample women differed most was their language abilities. Of the group of women we interviewed, the independent job seekers were by far the most accomplished, many having studied Japanese or lived previously in Japan. Furthermore, since they were hired as "local status employees," they were typically thrust into an all-Japanese-speaking environment. Thus, skills of speaking, writing, and reading Japanese were a requirement. Indeed, as we discuss in Chapter 3, these women were often interviewed by potential employers in Japanese as one test of their competence.

The traditional transferees or expatriates, on the other hand, usually held higher level positions and spoke English in their jobs. Furthermore, the attitude that some of them held verged on being "anti–Japanese language." One woman commented, for example, that since she was the "boss," her (Japanese) subordinates had to learn English, not the reverse. Most who came with such an attitude, however, eventually decided that learning basic speaking skills was useful to making life more manageable both in and out of the office.

Despite—and perhaps even because of—the range of expectations about the extent to which Japanese was a requirement on the job, we were surprised by the number of women, especially independents, who claimed that their Japanese speaking skills were quite good (Figure 2.3). Figure 2.3 illustrates the survey results of the proportion of women, by type (i.e., expatriates, independents and trailers) and their level of Japanese speaking ability. Most women had at least basic Japanese ability: 25 percent of the expatriates (only two people in this case, however) and 45 percent (N = 67) of the independents claimed fluency. Such figures make sense for the independents, in particular, given their backgrounds, which often included time spent as exchange students in Japan. Trailers (N = 13) reported much lower overall ability levels in speaking Japanese. The pattern was similar among interviewees as well: independents tended to have much better ability to speak Japanese, particularly since several of them were the only non-Japanese employees in their offices.

A second figure (Figure 2.4) compares self-reported fluency in Japanese in speaking, reading, and writing for the three groups. The women

Figure 2.3
Speaking Ability—Percentage of Women with No, Basic, Intermediate, or Fluent Knowledge of Japanese, by Type (Expatriates, Independents, and Trailers)

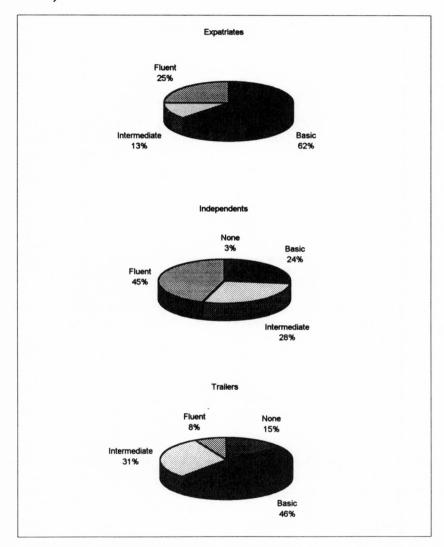

rated the extent to which their Japanese was fluent in each area. Again, the small number of expatriates (N=8) skews the results somewhat: two expatriate women reported they were fluent in all three areas. The proportion of independents, on the other hand, reported better skills in speaking and reading than the other two groups.

Figure 2.4
Fluent Knowledge—Percentage of Women with Fluent Knowledge of Japanese (Speaking, Reading, and Writing), by Type (Expatriates, Independents, and Trailers)

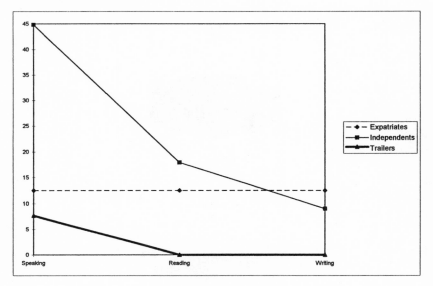

The reports of skill in reading and writing Japanese were more modest, perhaps in part because foreigners so often find those skills much more difficult to learn. Indeed, of the surveyed women, an average of only 16.5 percent of the women surveyed claimed fluency in reading, and 7.7 percent in writing.

Nationality. The majority of the women in the study were from the United States. Among the women we interviewed, all were American; two came from Asian-American families with close ties to Japan. Of the women who responded to the survey, all the expatriates, 87 percent of the independents and 85 percent of the trailers were from the United States. The balance were from Canada, the United Kingdom and Hong Kong (Figure 2.5).

While we had hoped to have more representation of women from other countries, the organizations we worked with (particularly the American Chamber of Commerce in Japan [ACC]) primarily had Americans as members. Throughout this study and other research we have done, however, we heard about (limited numbers of) women expatriates from countries such as Germany, the Philippines, or Australia. Unfortunately, in our current study, we had too few for detailed assessment of their particular experiences.

Family backgrounds and marital status. The women we interviewed came

Figure 2.5
Nationalities of the Women in the Survey Sample (Percentages), by Type (Expatriates, Independents, and Trailers)

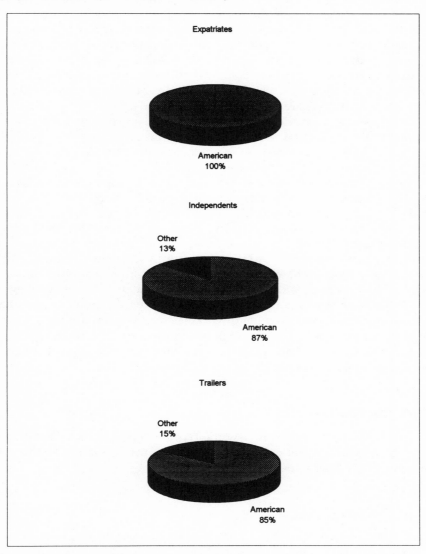

from a variety of family and demographic backgrounds. As mentioned, two had been reared in Japanese-American families; three were African-American. Several commented that they came from a very conservative background. One of the young job independent seekers said her parents were baffled by her desire to live and work in Japan. She commented that she was already bracing for her return (in the coming 1–2 years), planning how to prepare her family for the next career step she hoped to take—graduate school and more international business.

Just under half of the women we studied were married. Of the survey respondents, 44 percent were married, compared to 40 percent of the interviewees. Of interviewees, one had children living at home, while four had grown children or stepchildren living in another part of the world. Of the survey respondents, 18.7 percent had children. None of the traditional transferees had children living with her.

Overseas experience. Many of the sample women were unfamiliar with overseas living. Indeed, over 60 percent—in all groups—of those responding to the survey had never worked or lived abroad prior to going to Japan (Figure 2.6).

The interviewees likewise had a range of overseas experience. Three had worked abroad in various capacities: two had worked previously in Japan, one in Australia immediately before taking a job in Japan. Six of the other interviewees had lived in Japan as exchange students in either high school or college. The two Japanese-American women had lived in and traveled extensively in Japan because their extended families still lived there. One woman, during her university exchange program, had met a Japanese man and returned to marry him after finishing college.

Of the women with some overseas experience, the length of time that the women had spent living and working overseas varied widely. Of all the surveyed women, nearly 30 percent had spent 1–2 years overseas; another 17.6 percent had spent 3–5 years and just over 13 percent had 5 or more years of experience overseas (Figure 2.7).

THE JOBS AND FIRMS

In this final section, we review the types of jobs and organizations in which the women worked in Japan. As was true of other aspects, the experiences varied widely.

Jobs and Organizations

The types of jobs that the women held also ranged widely (Figure 2.8). By far, most were related to marketing: 33 percent of the total surveyed respondents and 40 percent of the interviewees held jobs that involved marketing. Following that, human resources (23.1 percent and 20 percent, respectively) was the next most common job function area for survey respondents and interviewees. Other areas in which several women worked were positions in finance/accounting, information management

Figure 2.6
Overseas Experience (Before Japan) of Sample Women (Percentages), by Type (Expatriates, Independents, and Trailers)

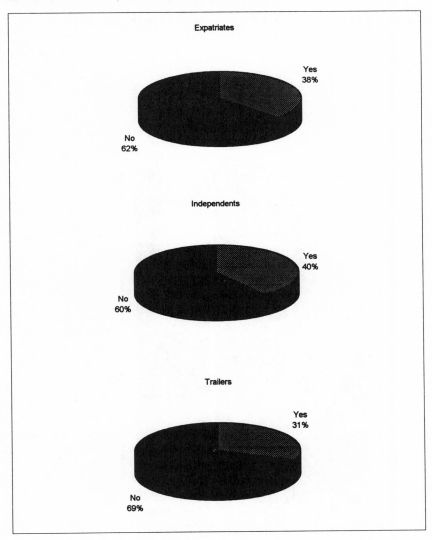

or technology, and general management. Some, albeit very few, worked in the law or production area.

When divided out by type (i.e., expatriates, independents, trailers) the jobs that the groups of women held varied mostly in terms of the variety of categories. The expatriates' jobs fell primarily into four main

Figure 2.7
Number of Years of Overseas Experience, by Type (Expatriates, Independents, and Trailers)

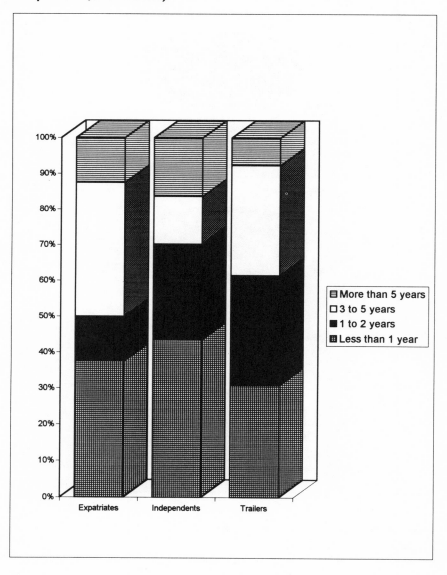

Figure 2.8
Job Functions of Sample Women (Percentages), by Type (Expatriates, Independents, and Trailers)

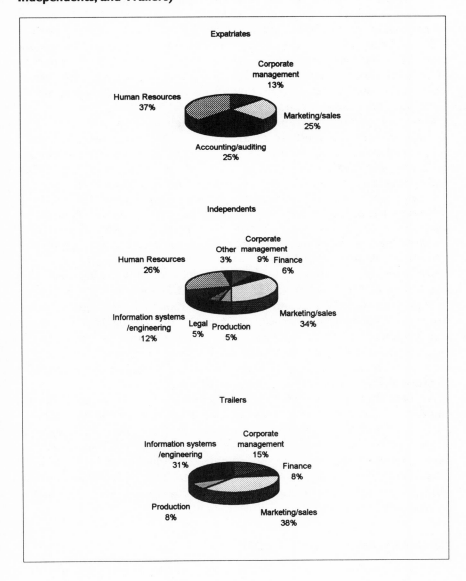

41

groups: corporate management, human resources, marketing/sales and accounting/auditing. The other two groups reflected a wider range of job types. Independents, for example, included most of the same categories as expatriates, but also worked in information systems and engineering, in production, and in legal advising.

The women worked for either fairly small (i.e., fewer than 500 employees) or very large (more than 1000 employees) firms. Nearly a quarter of the surveyed women, in fact, worked for firms that had fewer than 100 employees, while over 50 percent worked for companies having more than 1000 employees. The main business of their firms tended to be general services (e.g., consulting, marketing, public relations, trade, printing, research), followed by financial services, manufacturing, transportation and communications.

Many of the women among the interviewee group, for example, worked in subsidiary offices of global firms. These offices were often very small (fewer than 30 employees), and, in many cases, the women were the only foreigners working in the offices. As a result, they often played the role of "liaison" with the headquarters offices.

Other women worked in much larger subsidiary offices, which tended to be regional offices of major consumer products companies or financial institutions. In such cases, the subsidiary employment was often several hundred people, with up to 20 traditional transferees, and sometimes several offices throughout Japan.

The women's bosses were fairly evenly divided between Japanese and non-Japanese. Of the total group of surveyed women and interviewees, 38.5 percent and 35 percent, respectively, reported their bosses were American (Figure 2.9). Likewise, another 41.8 percent of those surveyed and 35 percent of those interviewed worked for Japanese supervisors. Other nationalities, such as British or Canadian, accounted for the balance; in some cases, the women worked as independent consultants or business owners, and thus had no formal supervisors.

Women who were managers overwhelmingly had Japanese subordinates. Over 70 of all the surveyed women were responsible for overseeing other people. Of those, most supervised Japanese subordinates (Figure 2.10). The expatriates and independents reported that 75 and 80 percent, respectively, of their subordinates were Japanese. Just over half (54 percent) of the trailers supervised Japanese. The nationalities of other subordinates tended to be mostly American but several women had subordinates from other countries in Asia (e.g., India).

SUMMARY AND CONCLUSIONS

Foreign women professionals already appear to be a labor source for some global firms. Interestingly, however, the largest group is those in-

Figure 2.9
Nationalities of Supervisors of Sample Women (Percentages), by Type (Expatriates, Independents, and Trailers)

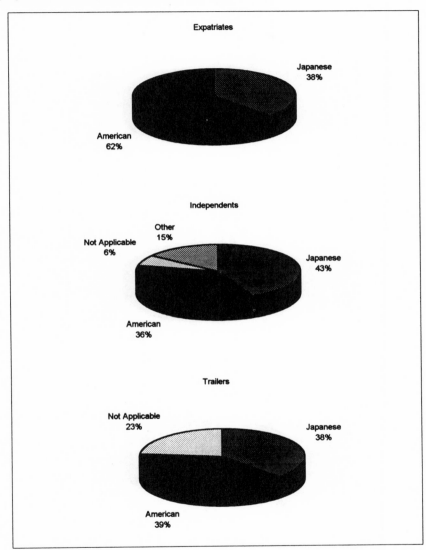

dependent women who arrive in Japan (or are hired in their home countries but for specific positions in Japan) on their own. This on-site pool has received almost no attention in the research literature but could well become a substantial portion of foreigners (women *and* men) hired by global firms.

Figure 2.10
**Nationalities of Subordinates of Sample Women (Percentages), by Type
(Expatriates, Independents, and Trailers)**

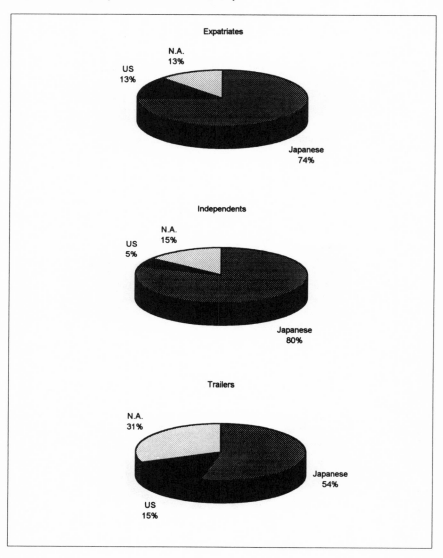

The foreign women professionals we studied had wide-ranging backgrounds, with some common elements. Highly educated, many had
graduate degrees as well as undergraduate degrees; a number had prior
experience in Japan, primarily as students in high school or college. As

expected, many of the independents had strong language skills, no doubt enhanced by the daily use in their jobs. Even so, the bulk of the women—even expatriates and trailers—claimed to have basic or intermediate ability.

While these women have strong technical and academic backgrounds, basic language skills and talents that would enhance their ability to operate globally, many of them nevertheless found the Japanese environment particularly challenging. As we discuss in Chapters 3 and 4, the process of finding and settling into jobs in Japan drew upon their resourcefulness and imagination.

Chapter 3

Getting Jobs

Dreaming of working in Japan (or having an opportunity arise to do so) was the first step for many of the women we studied. The reality of getting or moving into a job brought the dream into focus. As we discussed in the previous chapter, women found their jobs through myriad approaches. Common to all were some of the fears, expectations, preparation (or lack of it), and general reactions upon beginning to work in a new country. In Chapter 3, we explore those similarities as well as the many differences we discovered among the various groups of women.

To learn more about the women's experiences and accomplishments during the "getting a job" phase, we probe five topics in particular: (1) how women found job opportunities in Japan; (2) what selection criteria and processes firms used in hiring women for professional positions in Japan; (3) what type of preparation women had before assuming their posts in Japan; (4) what expectations, advantages or barriers they expected and found as they moved into jobs in Japan, in terms of both professional and personal issues; and (5) what types of compensation packages were common for our 111 foreign women professionals working in Japan.

Where possible, we report on the findings from both the survey of 91 women and the interviews with 20. Some knowledge came more from one source than another (e.g., most of the detailed insights about job sources, selection criteria and processes, and expectations about barriers were gleaned from interviews rather than the survey). We will discuss each of the five topics in turn, presenting similarities and differences across the categories of women.

FINDING A JOB: HOW DO WOMEN FIND THEIR OPPORTUNITIES?

If our sample group of women is representative, on the whole, successful foreign women professionals working in Japan appear to be energetic and entrepreneurial in the ways that they find and conduct their jobs. As we have noted, one of our earliest surprises—and cause of the greatest differences—was the range of approaches that women used in arriving and becoming employed in Japan. Rather than finding large numbers of expatriates, which other researchers found when they studied men, we discovered that most women came independently. Less common were traditional transferees and trailers. Thus, we discuss in turn how women in each of the groups—expatriate transferees, seekers, and trailers—found jobs.

Traditional Expatriates

The traditional expatriates arrived from their home countries under the auspices of their firms, avoiding much of the mundane hassle of finding work and setting up living quarters in Japan. While they were similar in that fundamental aspect, they nevertheless differed in the specifics of how they became interested in or "tapped for" an overseas post.

Our research suggests that these women followed at least three routes in securing their jobs in Japan. Essentially, they varied in terms of the source or initiative for finding or receiving their jobs. The initiative for a given person's job tended to come primarily from the company management (most common), from the individual woman herself (least common), or from a joint decision by the woman and management.

"What an opportunity for you!" In some cases, a woman's boss or upper management initiated the idea that she take a job in Japan. When the woman was uninterested, the boss had to encourage, offer inducements and in some cases cajole her into taking the position in Japan. In one case, a New York law firm seeking to replace a returning lawyer and to increase its Japanese business approached a junior level associate to work with an established senior partner in the Tokyo office. The firm had key Japanese corporate clients in the United States and wanted its Japanese office to be able to provide more timely and personal service to those clients in Japan.

The law associate had no interest whatsoever in going to Japan. Amanda was on track to make partner status, wanted to remain in New York City to advance her career, and had no previous exposure to living or working abroad. Nevertheless, the company had approached her because she had done some work for Japanese clients in the United States and she had corporate experience. Because the firm needed someone in Tokyo very much and because the associate was so reluctant to go, the firm did have to provide major incentives for her, including benefits for her fiancé (whom she later married). Thus, in such cases, the firms must convince reluctant transferees that Japan posting is desirable.

In another case, a young consultant who began life as a potential "trailer" negotiated her way into becoming a "traditional expatriate." In this situation, the firm approached the husband initially, requesting that he move to Japan because of particular technical expertise he could provide for clients. The husband and the wife were neither committed to pursuing international careers, nor strongly opposed to working in Japan. But they were only willing to go if the wife could be transferred as well. Thus, they negotiated with the firm for a joint transfer, in which each would receive benefits accorded "traditional transferees."

"What an opportunity for me!" In other cases, much less common within the group of traditional transferees, some women approached their firms about making a transfer to Japan. In one case, for instance, a woman working with an international service organization had reached a point in her career where she wanted to "try something new." Connie had been quite successful in the United States, frequently becoming the "first woman" to hold certain technical and management positions. Yet she sought a change and put it in altruistic terms: she wanted to feel she had a broader impact on making the world a better place for people. In addition, she sought the chance to live and work overseas as part of her own personal development and learning.

She approached the international division of her organization to ask for a job overseas; working together, but mainly on her initiative, they identified the Japan office as a place that might be interested in hosting an American. She then worked to "create" a job in the Japan office that, as she described it, would help develop program offerings and manuals for the Japanese branches to use.

Unfortunately, idealism gave way to realism. While not all self-initiated transfers fail, this one did, miserably, which we discuss in Chapter 7. The vagueness of the job design, the lack of enthusiasm of the Japanese office, and the gap in cross-cultural understanding between Connie and her Japanese counterparts led to an irreconcilable state.

Among all of our interviewees, this woman was the most disillusioned and the least successful (by her own admission), indeed; she was leaving the organization the day after our interview. She had lost confidence in her abilities and felt betrayed by her home base organization.

While we cannot generalize on the basis of this single case, several factors signaled its probable failure. Connie initiated the transfer for rather unspecific, idealistic motives: she wanted to "do some good somewhere" and experience living overseas. Her organization, while receptive to the idea of a move, was unable to secure a job with substantive content; indeed, the Japanese office allowed a new job to be created that (perhaps) was unneeded.

"What an opportunity for you and us!" In the best situations, the traditional transferees reached a conclusion jointly with their firms that a transfer was good for both the woman *and* the firm. In several cases, women acknowledged that they were ambitious, looking for new challenges, and that the Japan opportunity met their own and their firm's needs at a given time. In some cases the women considered several options; the Japan opportunity tended to be the one that fit their desire for more responsibility at a particular career stage.

An American banker who had been working in Australia for several years had reached a point where she was ready to move, preferably back to the United States. Simultaneously, however, Helen's previous (New York) boss was leaving his Japan assignment to return to headquarters. He suggested (to his management and to her) that she replace him in Japan, giving her more responsibility for a region of major importance to the firm, and simultaneously filling his post. Her experience in Australia had been a good one, albeit very "similar to the United States," so she was willing to try a new international assignment.

In another case, the match between what the firm and the woman wanted at a given time fit superbly. Carol, in the customer service area of a large telecommunications firm, had been tapped for inclusion in a select group of potential top leaders for the firm. These people, sponsored by mentors throughout the firm, were expected to be able to move into positions at least two levels higher than their present ones. According to Carol, management (and others) apparently saw in her the ambition and ability to take on broader responsibility, including an international assignment.

Anticipating her future career path, Carol had reached a similar conclusion: given the emphasis on globalization within her firm and industry, she had decided that she needed an overseas post. By her own admission, she "was not a good networker," but had found a compatible mentor who encouraged and sponsored her career move. In her favor, however, was experience with one of the firm's major Japanese customers.

A final example of a "win-win" situation was a woman who transferred with a large American computer firm to establish and manage a team that was to design a VLSI chip in Japan. Deborah's firm initiated the discussions about a transfer, but it fit beautifully with her own interests, one of which was studying aikido, Japanese martial arts. She readily agreed to a 2 year transfer.

In such cases, the firms sought these particular women for certain positions and the women were at stages in their careers (and personal lives) where such a move made practical sense.

Independent Job Seekers

While the traditional expatriates are the most pampered of the women working in Japan, in many ways, the true adventurers of our study were those women who independently found ways to work in Japan. For these women, the lure was Japan and the chance to work and live there. In some cases, the women had been exchange students in the country, during either high school or college, and thus spoke Japanese and were familiar with the customs and culture. In other cases, the women came initially through other routes (e.g., as traditional transferees, as trailers) but decided to remain long term in the country.

"Local hires." By far the largest group of seeker were younger (25–34 years old) women who moved to Japan without jobs and sought them on-site. These women often had studied in Japan at some point during their academic careers. Their main motives for seeking work in Japan were to learn how to conduct business there and to improve their Japanese language skills. In some cases they wrote to companies before arriving, but most often they conducted their job campaigns once they were in Japan.

In their searches, they used a variety of methods; the most common were "networking" and "cold calls." The main networking body they used was Foreign Executive Women. A number of seekers mentioned that they had made helpful initial contacts through the FEW group; in some cases, women were hired by FEW members to work with or for them.

The primary way that women sought jobs through "cold calling" was by contacting firms that were members of the American Chamber of Commerce in Japan (ACCJ). The ACCJ directory lists several hundred individual members, their positions and firms. Most of the women used the directory to select and contact firms that were in their fields of interest. Typical was Kiri, who married a Japanese man while she was studying in Japan. After deciding to remain in Japan, she sought consulting positions through the Chamber, eventually becoming the only foreigner in a 21 person subsidiary office of a worldwide compensation consulting firm.

In other cases, the seekers contacted Japanese firms or Japanese subsidiaries of foreign firms. Indeed, in several instances, the women we interviewed commented that they took their initial jobs "just to get into the system in Japan," changing into new jobs within months.

In two typical examples, young women joined Japanese firms and, before completing a year with those firms, left them. Sandy, a former exchange student, joined a firm that specialized in planning events for Japanese and American firms in Japan. She left two months later, claiming that her Japanese managers had given her little "real" work, and that she was more of a "token foreigner" than a real contributor. Further, she felt that being female relegated her to more "female tasks," such as tea serving. For her next position, she consciously sought a firm that hired (and fully used) women professionals. She found a job at a moving and transfer firm that worked with expatriates being transferred to or from Japan. A majority of the employees were women, including the second in command, and the owner/manager made a point of explaining that he hired and promoted women.

In a second case, the oft mentioned trait of "being persistent" paid off well, as it did for many of these seekers. Linda, who arrived in Japan almost immediately after completing her undergraduate degree, claimed, like many of the others we talked to, that she "had no contacts" and was not "good at networking." Nonetheless, she said she was (initially and remained so during her stay in Japan) aggressive about talking to anyone she met (on subways, in restaurants, even in job interviews) about a range of potential opportunities.

Such persistence paid off for her, as it had for others. Linda, whose interests were in international marketing and advertising, initially joined a Japanese telecommunications firm. She took a position in "sales and advertising," and found herself also serving tea. Frustrated, she sought a job at a European consumer products firm within the first 6 months of joining the Japanese firm. Figuring that her lack of direct international marketing experience would work against her, she decided to take a more novel approach to seeking the consumer products marketing job: she sent her resume in a large package resembling one of the candy bar boxes sold by the firm. Although her creative job seeking tactic did not land that job, the European interviewer was so impressed with her approach that he recommended her for another job, in the Japanese office of an international public relations firm. There, Linda was the only non-Japanese professional in the office, providing her the chance to do a wide range of tasks and be the key liaison with the New York headquarters office.

Other "seekers" were themselves "sought." The woman mentioned earlier who was transferred by a computer firm to manage a VLSI design team found herself pursued by a headhunter firm after she had been in Japan for nearly two years. By that time, she had decided she wanted to remain in Japan longer term and was beginning to consider her options. Also, her company would have had to send her back to the United States for tax reasons. Her chance came in the form of overseeing a large data center operation for a major financial institution, allowing her to stay in Japan, learn Japanese and aikido, and continue in a satisfying career.

A final group of "seekers" are very rare—women entrepreneurs who start businesses in Japan. Their reasons for going this very difficult route are, again, as varied as the women. Lorna initially went to Japan as a "trailer," nearly 20 years ago, with her military husband. Returning on and off, she eventually decided to stay in Japan, in part because of her disillusionment with the United States—few good job prospects for her, declining American values—and because of her increasing interest in Japan and fluency in the language. She saw a great need for the Japanese to have a well run school teaching English as a second language and thus started the difficult process of building a business.

Most of the other entrepreneurs we encountered operate as individual consultants, having decided to leave firms or their consulting practices for a fresh start in Japan. Irene, reaching a mid-point in her career with a well regarded international financial institution, decided she needed a change that was unlike anything she could find in the United States. Having no prior knowledge or experience with Japan or the Japanese, she nonetheless decided to move overseas for 1–3 years. Her approach was to move to Japan and begin consulting on organizational development and human resource issues. Drawing upon contacts gained through the FEW organization and through other African-Americans she met in Japan, she developed enough work to have a comfortable life-style and interesting career.

Hybrids. A subset of the independents was one we called "hybrids." As mentioned earlier, several women came to Japan because of offers they received in the United States after graduate school. These women were recruited by American or Japanese firms that were seeking to fill positions in Japan. Once they were in Japan, hybrids typically were treated as Japanese local staff in terms of conditions of employment (e.g., pay, benefits).

Trailers. Finally, four of our interviewees initially came to Japan as a result of following their husbands or partners. Some came reluctantly, giving up careers and jobs that they perceived as quite significant and meaningful. Once they arrived, however, their job searching approaches often mirrored those of the other "seekers" who had come independently. Like the other seekers, the trailers commented on the importance of the FEW group to their search. One advantage that some of the trailers had that differed from the qualifications of the more typical seekers is that they were able to draw upon contacts within their spouse's or partner's firms. Such assistance, however, tended to be informal and not always as helpful as the women anticipated before moving to Japan.

Interestingly, some of the trailers noted that when they sought jobs, potential employers looked favorably upon them if their partners were expatriates. The potential employers assumed that the expatriate partners have access to certain networking groups and clubs (e.g., the American Club of Tokyo) and thus the trailers would be able to capitalize upon that access. Indeed, one woman who followed her husband commented that her first boss in Japan, a Japanese banker, "actively looked for trailing spouses." His rationale was threefold. First, he reasoned that the spouses could open doors at key American expatriate locales that were inaccessible to him; they could thus more easily generate business for the bank. Further, she remarked that this (unusually enlightened) manager felt that having foreign females on his staff would be "mind expanding" for Japanese men working in the unit. Finally, not having to pay (high) expatriate wages was another likely attraction.

The overall theme from the women regarding finding a job in Japan was the importance of ingenuity, flexibility, and to some extent serendipity. Even among the traditional transferees, the process of finding a job depended in large part on all the "pieces coming together at the right time." Stage of career and personal life as well as availability of a position that offered growth and responsibility were critical.

Particularly among the independent seekers, furthermore, the women agreed that chance and persistence were key. Unwilling to remain in situations where serving tea became a key job component, these women had clear ideas of the types of jobs they wanted. As a result, they had few misgivings about moving among jobs to find ones that satisfied their goals, which usually revolved around learning how to do business in Japan and improving their language skills.

SELECTION: HOW DO FIRMS CHOOSE WOMEN FOR JOBS?

In this next section, we discuss the criteria and selection process that firms appear to use in selecting the women professionals. While much was similar to what women encountered during domestic selection processes, there were some differences, in both the criteria and the process itself.

In the selection process in Japan, the women reported that "soft" criteria (i.e., interpersonal skills) seemed to be more important, particularly for the independent job seekers. Furthermore, differences emerged in the requirements for women in the various job categories. For example, among the independent job seekers, knowledge of the Japanese language—speaking as well as reading and writing—was typically a requirement for employment. Among the traditional expatriate transferees, Japanese language expertise was rarely expected, although most tried to learn some basic Japanese.

Selection Criteria

The criteria that the women in our sample identified comprise two broad categories: technical qualifications and non-technical, more interpersonal relations oriented criteria. While the technical criteria often matched those that would be required for domestic jobs, the less technical were more elusive and connected to doing business outside the home country.

Technical criteria. The technical criteria mentioned by women during their interviews were ones that are typical for most selection processes in North America: educational background, experience, and, in some cases, specific expertise/qualifications relating to working in Japan. The three hybrid seeker women, for instance, all had master's degrees. Two of them had focused on international management and marketing; both had interest and expertise in the Pacific Rim region. The third woman's graduate degree was in technical writing. The firms that hired them all sought out those expertise areas from the women. The New York lawyer had an extensive educational background, with degrees from Ivy League colleges in the eastern United States. Such degrees, her knowledge and competence, and the support of the senior partner in the office helped establish her credibility with—initially skeptical—Japanese clients. Indeed, the firm's senior partner in Tokyo made a point of introducing her to clients by reciting her imposing pedigree. Likewise, the engineer transferred to manage a VSLI design project had an impressive education background, with bachelor's and master's degrees from a well-known university that was highly respected by her Japanese counterparts.

In addition, business or related working experience was important for all groups of women. Again, the reluctant lawyer was tapped in part because of her extensive corporate experience with American and some Japanese clients in her firm's New York office. The senior bank auditor was offered a transfer in large part because a former boss (who was leaving Japan) knew of her experience in a similar post in Australia and in New York. Likewise, when the engineer made a job change within Japan, her experience as a project manager with the firm that had initially transferred her was the primary basis for her subsequent selection. A woman who worked with expatriate managers seeking to find and establish new offices in the Tokyo area was hired in part because of her entrepreneurial background: she had started and managed her own travel agency in a U.S. city before coming to Japan.

The requirements for language expertise differed widely. For the younger independent job seekers, language skills seemed to be a key selection criterion. Those who found work in Japan as well as the three "hybrids" who were hired in the United States and then posted to Japan each spoke, wrote and read Japanese, which they needed in their work.

Indeed, one of the women commented that, in her telecommunications firms, all employees *except* the expatriates were required to be bilingual.

Language ability was much less important for expatriates. All but one (the former expatriate engineer who chose to remain in Japan) of the traditionally transferred expatriates had limited expertise in the Japanese language. The engineer learned Japanese partly to improve her aikido understanding and skills. Interestingly enough, however, she felt her Japanese skills helped immensely on the job as well, because she was able to gather critical technical information from lower level Japanese employees directly, rather than depending upon mid-level managers who would normally translate (as well as interpret) information for her.

Non-technical criteria. The other types of criteria that were important in selection decisions were less technical. Indeed, some would be unfamiliar to managers in a North American context. Further, these criteria seemed, in some cases, to be as important as (or more so than) the more easily measured "technical criteria."

First, the independent job seekers often mentioned that their cultural knowledge of Japan and working with Japanese people was frequently a critical component in their selection. For instance, the women who were the only foreigners in an office viewed themselves as acting as a bridge between the Japanese and American counterparts or offices. As a result, their understanding of both cultures and ability to "switch" between them was, in their view, crucial in their being selected for their positions.

Furthermore, as foreigners, they were asked (and indeed expected) to take on some tasks that the Japanese office members would not. For instance, Linda, who worked in the all-Japanese subsidiary of a large advertising and public relations firm, was in charge of developing new business for the firm, particularly through "cold calls" on potential clients. Uncomfortable calling people (by phone or in person) whom they did not know, the Japanese were only too happy to have her take on such a job; her outgoing entrepreneurial personality was "made" for such a job and she relished it.

For the traditional transferees, who tended to be in senior positions, knowledge of their firm and the "politics" of the firm were sometimes mentioned as criteria that the women believed influenced their selection. Others discussed such criteria in terms of being good at "networking" and knowing with whom to deal within their firms to accomplish goals. In addition, one woman commented that having "good negotiation skills" to work within the firm as well as with customers was a key factor in her transfer decision.

As it did in finding a job, "luck" appeared to play a role for several women in the selection process as well. Several women mentioned that when they sought their posts, they were the sole true contenders: either no other candidates emerged or, if they did, they were much less qualified for the particular position. For instance, the lawyer commented that the firm had approached two of her male counterpart associates about transferring to Japan. Neither pursued the idea because of dual career complications, making them unwilling to move. The lawyer (at the time of her transfer) was single, making her the "obvious" choice. In the case of the young seeker who wanted to work for the public relations firm, the other candidate (also an American woman) had no Japanese expertise, thus eliminating her from serious competition.

Some women noted that chance played a role in timing: particular jobs opened at the times when they were looking for a change. In the case of the senior manager in a telecommunications firm, she was "ready" for a global position just at the time one was available: her personal life was such that she was "free" (i.e., she had no children at home), her professional life was at a point where she wanted a new challenge, and thus she was prepared and searching for an opportunity. The firm was simultaneously building a program to encourage women and minorities to move into global positions and saw her as a key future senior manager. Thus, the timing from both perspectives was right.

Other women talked of more "intuitive" or "hard to define" criteria as being important in the selection process. One commented that she was "smart enough" but not "brilliant" in her job; rather her strengths included good customer relations skills, common sense and an ability to identify quickly key issues in a problem and know (through her knowledge of the firm and how it operated) how to address them. In her case, the woman felt she was not the "typical" employee who would be picked for promotion or transfer but acknowledged that her different approach may nevertheless *have* been an important selection factor.

Intriguingly, many women mentioned that the simple fact they were female played a role in their selection. Their gender came into play in different ways, however. For instance, in several cases, the women commented that they were hired because their jobs would put them into contact with people who were going through major life or professional changes and their employers believed that women would be more "empathetic" for those clients. Sandy, who worked for the moving and transfer firm, spent much of her time with wives of expatriate men from Europe and North America who were being transferred to or from Japan. During such a stressful time in a family's life, reasoned the owner of the firm, the wives would prefer to deal with another woman rather than a man.

In a similar situation, Donna worked typically with expatriates who were seeking space and then establishing offices in Japan. Again, her being female was assumed (by her British boss) to be an advantage in that the men with whom she dealt would be more comfortable with a woman.

A technical writer, working for a large Japanese firm, commented that her (female) Japanese boss believed that women make better writers and teachers of technical writing (more empathy again). Further, the female boss did not want to have to supervise a male, figuring that there would be some resistance from him in working for a woman.

Sometimes various attributes worked together. A last example is the woman engineer who managed several men in both the VLSI project and then in a job establishing an international bank's data center. In her view, being female and older (in her late-30s) worked in her favor because she was "in the middle" (some people were older, others younger than she), making her less threatening for some people. Further, as a foreign woman, she was also perceived as less threatening than a foreign man would be in a comparable position. Finally, her management style, which she described as unabrasive and more acceptable to Japanese, allowed her, in her estimation, to get more done than a foreign man in the same post would have been able to. Clearly, the theme running through these women's experiences is that *they* perceived being female as an advantage in the selection process.

Furthermore, the reason why gender was seen as being an advantage was that the women were (again, in their view) seen as being "less threatening" than a foreign man in a comparable position would be. Such findings support what Adler (1984b) found in the early 1980s. In addition, as Adler discovered and we heard repeatedly, these women saw themselves as "already" being quite different, just by being *gaijin* (i.e., foreigners) in Japan. As women, they were that much more unusual; rather than considering differentness a handicap, however, they "used" it to their advantage when they sought new jobs.

The women made comments and exhibited behaviors that suggested they attributed their successes to their own efforts, their failures to factors beyond their control. When the women felt the job matches to be good, they commented on the strengths that clearly the firms had identified and seized upon in hiring them. When the situation was less successful, the women "blamed" their firms for not recognizing their strengths or desires for the job. The woman who transferred with the international service organization, for instance, commented that her Japanese host firm managers "should have realized" that she was a "creative program designer." That, according to her, should have helped them understand and anticipate her expectations for the job. That her Japanese employers did not recognize and use those talents was a major reason for the venture's failure, she concluded.

Other women, even the "seekers" who typically understood more about Japanese culture than others, sometimes commented that in their first jobs, they were expected to serve tea. They would then make the remark that their Japanese firm managers should have realized that they were looking for "real" work, not serving tea. Such attributions placed more blame on the Japanese employers for the women's dissatisfaction with those initial jobs.

Selection Process

By definition, the selection process for traditional transferees was conducted within the home country, by the transferring firm managers. The women we interviewed described the processes as fairly informal, depending heavily upon networking within the organization or upon the advice and recommendation of their bosses or upper management.

The selection process for independent job seekers and trailer women, conducted in Japan, tended to be quite different from typical American processes. The selection process for the hybrid seekers, for example, involved people based in the United States as well as Japan. The women commented that they were typically interviewed by American or Japanese managers who visited their (U.S.) university campus for interviews. In all cases, the managers went to specific universities to recruit. In the case of the editorial/technical writer, her university was known as having an excellent writing program; the Japanese manager for whom she would work was the main interviewer. For the other two hybrid seekers, the employers went to their universities because of their reputations in international business and marketing.

Because, in some cases, the women who were selected played key roles in the "globalization" process for their firms, the competition was fierce. Terri, who worked in sports marketing for a major American consumer products firm, was one of only six new hires chosen from 650 applicants from American college campuses in the year that she was hired. She reasoned that the young graduate students were employed for their Japanese language and business skills, but also as liaisons to help bridge the gap between senior management in the Japanese subsidiary (who were all Americans) and their Japanese middle managers and other subordinates.

Other women described the selection process as less rigorous. Eileen, who worked for a large telecommunications firm, said the "hybrids" were the "third tier new hires." First tier hires for the firm were top university graduates from Japanese universities; these people were hard to attract, however, because few Japanese students knew of (and thus sought out or responded to) the American firm. The second tier hires were Japanese students studying in the United States. The firm's managers sought these students because they were likely to know of the American firm, having lived in the United States, and could be hired for positions in Japan. A final source, the so-called third tier hires, included

Eileen's group: Americans studying in the United States who were bilingual and had an interest in working in Japan.

Interestingly, Eileen was interviewed by two managers—one was Japanese and one was American—about potential jobs at the firm's subsidiary in Japan. The Japanese manager said that, during her first year in his division, Eileen would do typing and "learn the business aspects by doing them"; after she had spent one year learning the business in Japan, then she would be able (allowed) to meet customers. The American manager focused only on being sure she understood his performance expectations and not about how she would "learn" the business or do her job; he wanted her to meet and work with customers as soon as possible. She chose to work with the American manager.

For the local hire job seekers, the selection process often consisted of at least two interviews, often with the general manager or president of the subsidiary or firm. In most of these cases, the women worked in offices that were all or primarily Japanese employees and for a Japanese boss. In many cases, the interview questions seemed to have less to do with the job than with "non-technical" criteria discussed earlier. Frequently, the women commented that they wished they had had the chance to discuss the job *content* in more depth but acknowledged that in Japan, "job descriptions" are a foreign concept.

Others chuckled at (but understood) the wide ranging nature of the interview questions, particularly since they so often had little to do with the job or working at the firm per se. For example, when Kiri interviewed for a consulting position in the all Japanese office of an international compensation and consulting company based in the United States, one of the key questions was what salary she wanted. When she gave an answer, the follow up question was whether that salary would cause problems "at home," since she would (likely) make more money than her student husband.

Because the independent job seekers so often joined firms where they operated in an all Japanese setting, the interviews were typically conducted in Japanese (since that was a criterion for the jobs). The women usually met and interviewed with senior managers, and rarely with potential co-employees or counterparts.

In sum, our findings support other work that suggests the "soft" criteria are important in jobs overseas; the Japanese managers or offices, in particular, seemed to be concerned about whether the women would "fit" into the office. Further, the Japanese bosses focused more on giving the women time to "learn the job" through tasks that were "job related" as well as many tasks the women considered unrelated (i.e., tea serving).

PREPARATION FOR WORKING IN JAPAN

Much of the literature about international management and traditional transferees and expatriates laments the deplorable lack of preparation that firms offer their people before they transfer (Adler, 1991). Our survey data confirmed that many women had little or no formal preparation by their firms before going to Japan or taking jobs in Japan.

General Approaches

Since so many of the women were not traditional expatriate transferees, we were interested in the range of preparation (or lack of it) they encountered or pursued. We discovered at least four approaches to the issue, each of which we will discuss in turn. First, we discuss an unusual situation: in one case, a woman commented that she pointed *avoided* preparing for her move to Japan. Although we report just this case, such an attitude may not be completely novel. Next, we examine cases of several women, particularly traditional expatriates, who reported that their firms offered little formal preparation.

Third, we consider situations where the women did have some preparation, offered by their firms either before they transferred (in the case of expatriates) or by their firms on-site in Japan. Some of the women expatriates reported that their firms offered preparation or orientation, which ranged in its nature and duration. Finally, and by far the most frequent situation we encountered, many women themselves took the initiative to prepare for their assignments and for working in Japan.

Avoiding preparation. As we mentioned, in one unusual case a woman admitted that she "avoided" preparing for her move. She was reluctant to relocate to Japan in the first place and felt the idea of "formal training" would be difficult to sit through. Her view was that she needed no language training, since she would not speak Japanese in her job. Further, she commented that to "sit in a room [and be told] about Japan would have been torture."

While she went to Japan with that attitude, after living there for a year, she decided to learn the language and more about the culture. She acknowledged later that her lack of preparation made adjustment extremely demanding; indeed, she admitted that living and working in Japan were much more difficult than she had anticipated. This supports the notion that preparation is a useful though not the only contributor to successful adjustment.

No or little formal preparation by firms. Remarkably, despite the two decades of research calling for preparation of expatriates before transfer, several expatriate women reported that their firms offered no formal language training or preparation prior to their taking on the Japanese

Figure 3.1
**Preparation Before Taking Job in Japan (Percentage of Women), by Type
(Expatriates, Independents, and Trailers)**

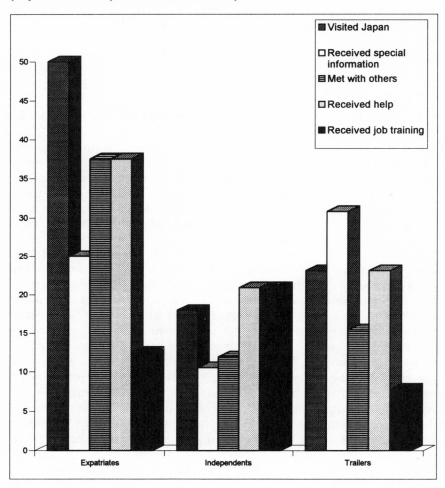

posts. Of all the surveyed women, for example, only 2.2 percent reported working with a trained professional prior to taking the job in Japan. Only 14.3 percent of the full group of 91 reported that they received any specific information about Japan or the job, or that they were encouraged or assisted in meeting other returned expatriates. Finally, some women, mostly expatriates, visited Japan before taking a particular job or moving with a spouse or partner (Figure 3.1). Indeed, the expatriates, as expected, received the most "thorough" preparation, including visits (50 percent), information (25 percent), meeting with others who had worked in Japan and help from the firm on settling into the job (37 percent on both aspects). Despite such efforts, however, most women reported that preparation for living and working in Japan was insufficient for the challenges they faced.

Our interviews confirmed such dismal reports. The telecommunications manager, the senior manager bank auditor, the husband-wife consultant transferees—none of these people who worked for large, well established global firms reported that they had received substantive formal preparation in understanding Japanese history, culture or business practices. The only training they received was "survival Japanese," yet none of them used Japanese extensively in their jobs.

Likewise, reports were discouraging regarding on-site assistance or ongoing company support during the initial period after taking a job. Only 23.1 percent of the surveyed women reported any form of assistance once they arrived in Japan; even fewer (7.7 percent) had access to ongoing support from their organizations once they started their jobs.

One of the hybrid seeker women who was hired in the United States and then moved to Japan commented that, although she received no training from her Japanese employer, the firm has since begun an orientation program for foreigners. The initiative for the program came from one of the firm's foreign managers. From his own and compatriots' experiences, that manager recognized the importance of giving new foreign employees some exposure to doing business in Japan and working with Japanese. Even so, claimed the woman, the program (put on by the Japanese) was quite superficial.

The one woman who did report more extensive preparation was a "trailer," whose husband's firm offered training to both of them. They received one day of training with a cross-cultural consulting firm. The training included an overview of Japan's history and customs and was in addition to 40 hours of language training. The cross-cultural training was conducted by a woman who had worked in Japan, and who was quite bleak about the trailing spouse's likely opportunities to find work. In fact, the trailer woman we talked to came away with the impression that she would be unable to find a line job or to work with Japanese clients.

When we asked women why they received so little preparation, their reasons often included "lack of time": the new job arose so unexpectedly or quickly that they had little time to prepare formally, even if the training had been available. In addition, some women had a sense that managers in the firms felt these were intelligent women who could pick up what they needed to know on-site, rather than needing training beforehand. Nevertheless, each of the women commented that having some preparation would have smoothed her transition and made her more productive sooner.

Even so, the one woman who did receive training (as a trailing spouse) was dissatisfied with it. In particular, she commented that the extent of language training (40 one hour lessons) was minimal; her impression was that the firm assumed that once spouses could visit the grocery store successfully, "that would be enough" to satisfy them. As she said, that may be true for 25–30 percent of the trailing spouses but for many who wanted to seek work, that was hardly "enough." Furthermore, she felt the one day overview glossed over the difficulties of living in Japan. Perhaps it was too brief or perhaps it simply gave a more positive perspective but she felt she was not fully prepared for the shock and challenge of being in Japan.

Company Training Related to the Job or Work

Some women received training to prepare them for their work, rather than for living and working in Japan (Figure 3.1). The independent job seekers, in particular, tended to report more company sponsored training than did traditional transferees. The approaches included training prior to beginning the job (less common), on the job training (most common), or special off-site programs once the woman had been in the job for several months or a year.

Pre-job training often focused on technical aspects of the job. For instance, Eileen, the woman who worked for the U.S. manager (based in Japan) of the telecommunications firm, spent two months on the company's "Japan desk" in the United States before moving to Japan. The key areas of the training were sales and technical training so she could move into customer relations more quickly. Subsequent to her move to Japan, she attended annual technical and sales training programs sponsored by the firm.

While pre-job training included technical aspects, it sometimes included "social components" as well. One woman who worked for a global advertising agency was sent to a large Japanese firm for an "etiquette seminar." Topics included, for example, "Japanese manners," polite ways to answer the phone, and tips on how to remain courteous on the job, especially in stressful situations.

Several women reported that they had received on the job training (OJT), either through working with their predecessors or creating/developing the job themselves. For instance, the woman who worked for the moving and transfer firm overlapped 4.5 months with the former job holder, giving her ample time to learn the job before doing it alone. Many women used a combination of OJT and training programs once on the job. Another frequently cited approach was rotation through functions with various departments.

Finally, several women developed the specific jobs themselves and then attended various training programs through the firm once they had been working for a while. Kiri developed her job as survey analyst at the compensation consulting firm and also attended a training program in Brussels for new employees. In addition, she continued her training through attending sessions held twice yearly in Singapore. Linda, at the public relations firm, spent two months with her predecessor, learning the job, before she was on her own. Subsequently, she attended the firm's "world college" training program and others to improve her interpersonal and customer relations skills.

Self-Initiated Preparation

By far, the most often cited means of preparation was learning about Japan on one's own. The self-initiated preparation typically took one of two forms: (1) background experiences that the women had that prepared them generally for life in Japan or overseas and (2) specific activities that the women undertook prior to moving to Japan or on-site once they arrived.

Personal background. Women frequently cited their educational or personal background as preparation for living and working in Japan. Their backgrounds often included experience as exchange students in high school or college. Indeed, most of the independent job seekers had lived previously in Japan and studied Japanese; those two factors were typically the driving forces for wanting to return. Others had lived in or made extensive visits to Japan because of their family situations. We have cited before the two women from Japanese-American households who have extended family members in Japan. While their parents may have spent much of their lives in the United States, the women often had family members still in Japan. As a result, these women often visited those relatives, spoke Japanese and were comfortable living in Japan.

Coupled with the experience of living in or visiting Japan, many of the women had also formally studied international management, and Asian or Japanese cultures in particular. Indeed, as we mentioned earlier, several women had master's degrees in international management, in addition to undergraduate degrees in Asian or Japanese history or language.

Finally, some women had exposure to Japanese firms prior to living and working in Japan. One had worked for a Japanese company in the United States; another's mother was an executive at a Japanese subsidiary in the United States. Thus, through personal experience or hearing family and friends talk about working for Japanese firms, the women had some background in what types of situations they might experience.

Personal preparation for the current situation. Women used a variety of approaches to prepare for the jobs they held in Japan when we met them.

Some did formal "research," in terms of reading about the country and culture. Others focused on the language and began lessons before arrival and then continued afterward.

Still others prepared and sent very specific questions to their potential bosses about the job, living conditions and the like. In one case, a woman interviewed in the United States sent a list of 25 questions to her potential employer before agreeing to take the job. Her questions ranged from what her office would be like (e.g., private? size?) to the nature of her living conditions (e.g., how much would the firm subsidize an apartment?). Another woman—one of the senior manager traditional transferees—asked only what type of reaction she should expect from Japanese subordinates and counterparts.

Several of the women reported that they used informal networking approaches to learn about their specific jobs and about working in Japan in general. They were quite creative in their approaches. One woman spoke to expatriate women in her firm but focused most of her questions on what those (older) women had experienced as employees of the company 20 years earlier, figuring that their experiences as women in the United States during the early 1970s would have relevance for what she might experience in Japan in the 1990s! The woman whose mother is an executive with a Japanese subsidiary in the United States continued to use her mother as a mentor and sounding board even after taking her job in Japan. When she faced specific work related problems, she sought her mother's advice on how to handle them.

Others sought mentors or colleagues in Japan, to whom they could turn with questions or concerns during their stay. The types of on-site mentors ranged widely. Sometimes those mentors were predecessors in the job—male and female. The senior bank officer drew upon her male predecessor (and former boss) to clue into potential general challenges she would face. Another expatriate drew upon insights of two female predecessors (in other units) who were leaving Japan. The woman engineer joined the Foreign Executive Women group and began networking there. Eileen, one of the hybrid seekers hired in the United States who moved to Japan, became close to a woman in her firm's human resource department. The human resource person was instrumental in giving her key advice, such as "when to rock the boat and when not." One of the most interesting approaches to preparation came from an African-American woman. She commented that hers came mostly from having spent her life being black in an all white business environment. Having always been in a "white world," she had learned how to play by others' rules. Further, she was able to move easily into and out of that world and her "black world." Since she felt she had never been truly "accepted" in that white business world, she had no expectations of being accepted in Japan. So, in a sense, her previous experiences were excellent preparation for Japan.

Moreover, she noted that white male expatriates seemed to have a much more difficult time adjusting to working and living in Japan than she had. Since they had never experienced being outnumbered or unaccepted, they were ill prepared for the discrimination (overt and subtle) that they felt. They were, in her words, having a hard time "learning to be the minority."

BARRIERS AND ADVANTAGES IN JOB SEEKING

During the phases of job seeking and early establishment of credibility in jobs, women faced several occasions where they experienced barriers and sometimes advantages. In this section, we discuss such issues both with regard to work-related as well as personal aspects. For simplicity, when we examined barriers, we reviewed them in terms of whether they were expected or unexpected.

Barriers the Women Expected

The women we studied rarely went to Japan without anticipating challenges in doing their jobs. The principal expectations were that, because they were female, they would experience discrimination or problems from their Japanese work colleagues (i.e., superiors, subordinates or peers) or from Japanese clients or others outside the firm.

At times these barriers were overt and stated by members of the organization. Typical was the experience of the lawyer transferred from New York City. Prior to her arrival in Japan, two other American women had worked in the law office in Japan, with limited degrees of success; as a result, there was an expectation that she would likewise have difficulty with Japanese clients. Similarly, the consultant who transferred with her husband was told by home office people that she would likely have trouble with Japanese clients.

More frequently, the women anticipated challenges but those concerns were not explicitly discussed or raised by representatives of their firms. The bank executive transferring from Australia said she had expected (and experienced) "machismo" and discrimination from men in Australia. She had little knowledge about what to expect in Japan and thus asked her predecessor and others in the Japan office what she should anticipate.

Several women acknowledged that the expectations they had were based upon their own concerns or fears. For instance, one of the African-American women said she expected (likely negative) reactions from the Japanese because of her race. She also commented that this was more "her" issue than a problem for the Japanese or for her firm. In fact, once she established credibility within her firm in Japan, she experienced few overt problems. What she did encounter (and greatly bothered her), however, was curiosity from the Japanese on the street.

For other women, although they anticipated being female would be a challenge, they encountered fewer problems than they expected. On the other hand, they saw evidence of problems for "other women." For example, the "hybrid job seeker" working for a telecommunications firm said she felt no problems and, in fact, had become "proof" for the firm that Japanese-American women could be effective in business. Indeed, she had been asked to "mentor" a young Japanese woman to become "less girlish" in her interactions with Americans.

Other barriers that the women expected to encounter related to problems with age. By their very nature, the independent job seekers tended to be women in their late-20s or early-30s. Particularly when they were in professions that put them in advising positions (i.e., consulting) or in situations where they interacted with (typically older) Japanese clients, several of the women said they felt that their age worked against them, at least initially.

Unexpected Barriers

Some women encountered unexpected barriers or surprises as they took on new jobs. Those surprises ranged from general perceptions (but not serious obstacles) to insurmountable hurdles. For example, one woman, during her selection interview, was told by the Japanese man interviewing her that she could "expect problems, being a young single woman working in Japan." Indeed, he continued, he would worry about her as he would his own daughter. The woman ended up *not* working for this man but felt his attitude was not uncommon.

Other times, women were surprised that the nature of the job itself seemed to work against them. When coupled with other barriers (some of them expected, some not), the obstacles seemed formidable. For example, the transferred lawyer perceived barriers because of the way the Japanese saw the role of the two American attorneys in the Tokyo office. The Japanese viewed the American lawyers more as "technicians," expected to follow instructions of the Japanese lawyers working for the client firms, rather than actively advising clients. In addition to this, the lawyer lamented that she "looked young," that her voice "sounded young," that she was female and that she was not a partner of the firm. All this, she felt, created a major challenge to her establishing credibility with Japanese clients, at least initially. Indeed, she relayed stories of clients who called the office, learned that the senior partner was unavailable and preferred to have their question or problem unattended to, rather than having to deal with her, even though she could have readily solved their problems. She was able to overcome such reluctance and skepticism of the clients in large part because of the senior American partner in the office. He worked hard to build her credibility in initial client meetings, by giving her a lengthy—and glowing—introduction to the clients. Once her credibility was so established, she was able to work successfully with Japanese clients.

One of the more common surprises the women reported was the difference between what they had expected in their jobs and the reality. In several cases, they learned that "serving tea" was part of the job; in other cases, they had expected to initiate or oversee the introduction of some new program (e.g., quality management in a bank, development of training manuals) but discovered that they were expected to do more clerical tasks.

The experience of the woman who worked for the service organization was among the most dramatic in terms of mismatch between her expectation and the realities of the job. Connie was completely unprepared for the extent to which her gender would influence expectations about her job and behavior. As mentioned, she had seen herself as a "doer" in the United States and went to Japan anticipating that she would help the Japan office advance the volunteer program. Instead, she came to view herself as an "ornament," an American with a big title and no responsibility. She was expected to serve tea, clean up, run the postal and copy machines, and be available and charming to foreign visitors.

Furthermore, she felt isolated once she took the Japanese position. According to her, the U.S. home office ignored her pleas for support as well as her complaints about dissatisfaction with the position. Her assessment was that, because the Japanese office represented such an important subsidiary politically, the home office could not allow her problems to influence relationships at the higher levels. Her experience (news of which spread through the organization) and the perception that international experience offered no career benefits meant that no American men were willing to take her job when she left.

Advantages

In addition to barriers in their work situations, many women reported unexpected benefits or advantages that they encountered seeking jobs or establishing careers in Japan. Sandy, the seeker working for a moving and transfer firm, was pleasantly surprised to discover that over half of the employees in her firm were female, including several of the senior managers; further, the owner, a Canadian man who had spent many years in Japan, fully supported and indeed sought women employees because of the nature of the business. Thus, she had strong backing in her job.

Lorna, the entrepreneur who started a language school, found that being female was neither an advantage nor a barrier but rather that being persistent was the key, especially in starting her business. As she showed continuing commitment (i.e., through being successful in her business and seeking to open a branch office) to remaining in Japan, the government became increasingly more supportive. Indeed, she was pleasantly surprised when a government inspector offered assistance in helping her prepare for an interview with bankers when she sought a loan. Further, the local government has allowed her and her husband to be the only foreigners to live in a highly regarded subsidized housing area.

Personal Challenges

Women who work in Japan face many challenges as they try to balance their work with demands of life off the job. Many of them commented that seeking, taking or remaining in jobs in Japan presented challenges and hurdles that were often difficult to manage. We discuss these trials in terms of what women faced in seeking a job and what they experienced subsequently in deciding whether to remain in it.

To seek or not? Several women, particularly the expatriates, had personal situations that influenced their decisions regarding whether to take an overseas assignment. Carol, a senior level expatriate, was a single mother whose only daughter had just finished high school. The timing for her to take on a new assignment outside the country was "right" and matched her career stage. For Donna, the "trailer" who followed her fiancé and then found work in Japan, the timing was also appropriate, given her personal situation. She had sold her United States–based business and her 4-year-old son was able to begin school at an international school in Japan, rather than switch once he had started in the United States.

Often, however, the timing and personal constraints were quite complex. A senior manager at a global financial institution was married to a man who was a foreman in a trade profession. The bank's human resource department wrote letters to his employer requesting leaves of absence (when she was in two different overseas locations) for him to be able to join her. While they lived in Japan, he was able to work intermittently in construction and other trade positions. The nature of his job allowed them, as a couple, the flexibility to pursue her overseas opportunities. Nonetheless, after 2 years, his employer requested that he return or lose his job; furthermore, he was becoming more discouraged with living and working in Japan. He was unable to work as often as he wished, disliked driving in Japan and found the commitment to doing things by "rote" frustrating. Thus, he returned to the United States, leaving her in Japan. Disliking having to live apart, she decided to seek a post back in the United States.

In the lawyer's case, when she moved to Japan she was unmarried but very committed to a man who was a computer consultant. He agreed to go to Japan since his profession allowed him tremendous flexibility. Thus, he became a "trailer," and was hired within 3 months of arriving. Had he been unwilling to move or unable to find work in Japan, she would no doubt have been even more reluctant to transfer.

Reasons for remaining in Japan also vary widely. One woman married a Japanese man who "shares the load" at home, making it much easier for her to work at a job that demands long hours (because of time differences) since she is the liaison with U.S. contacts. Although they have discussed moving to the United States eventually, for the time being they will remain in Japan. Although her husband is an engineer in a field that would allow him to find work in the United States, his written language skills are not strong; thus, he feels some reluctance to leave Japan. On the other hand, they have discussed that when they have children, they wish to be in the United States when the children reach middle school years, feeling that the education they would receive there surpasses what they see in Japan.

The woman with the four-year-old son decided to remain in Japan after her relationship with her fiancé fell apart. A main reason for remaining was that she felt her son would be safer living in Tokyo than in any American city. Making such a decision as a single mother, however, raised extreme challenges. She spent several years finding a suitable live-in child care giver. Subsequently, she had ongoing arguments with the local government about gaining a visa for the Filipino sitter. She encountered overt discrimination and comments from the immigration officers who told her that her "title was not high enough to sponsor a maid for 3 years," that she would have to return annually to renew the visa, and furthermore, that she should "be home" with her son rather than hire a care giver.

COMPENSATION PACKAGES

A final area of concern to women working in Japan is the type of compensation package they receive. While we did not go into extensive detail with the women, we wanted to get a sense of the range of foreign women professionals' benefits and pay. Moreover, in our investigation of the various compensation "packages," we wanted to understand the range of issues that the women viewed as important: (1) the major components of the package, (2) the areas in which they felt slighted, and (3) the ways in which they addressed their dissatisfaction.

Major Components

Most of the women we studied, particularly the traditional transferees, reported that, to their knowledge, their compensation packages are comparable to those of men in similar posts. There were some areas of dissatisfaction and inequity (discussed later), but for the most part, the women believed their packages to be comparable.

Typical components for expatriate women included, for example, overseas allowance, housing allowance, cost of living allowance and home leave. In addition, memberships and "extra" pay were common. Women who were hired as independent job seekers (both those hired on-site in Japan as well as the hybrid women hired in the United States but placed in Japan) generally had much less attractive or lucrative packages than their expatriate compatriots (Figure 3.2). Trailers received the least attractive packages; the trailers we interviewed commented that this happened largely because firms assumed they had "expatriate packages" of their husbands or partners.

Nevertheless, even within the ranks of independents, the range of benefits varied widely. Sandy, working for the moving and transfer firm, had perhaps one of the more appealing packages, including a company car, housing, paid home leave every 2 years and language training. Kiri, in the Japanese office of a consulting firm, had the same package as comparable Japanese (men), including pay and a bonus based upon performance. Donna, working for the corporate relocation firm, had perquisites such as club memberships, but no pension benefits. Further, since she was working for a conservative British firm, she anticipated no long term career path options, unless she was willing to leave Japan.

Most of the independents, especially when they had been hired locally, noted that their packages were not particularly lucrative and often meant the women had to economize in various ways, particularly if they were single. Linda, for example, working for a public relations firm, paid for her own health benefits, received no overtime for the long hours she worked, and had to share an apartment with three other women because her pay was relatively low (although she boasted that it was double the salary of teachers of English!). Catherine, a "trailer" who found work in an American firm, received a straight salary and health benefits, but no housing support or bonus. She did, on the other hand, receive subsidized language training.

The women also noted that they were able to negotiate individual components that were particularly important to them; this was most common in traditional transferee situations, and usually where the women were hesitant movers. For example, the lawyer who moved reluctantly to Japan convinced her firm to move her "friend" (whom she later married) from California to Japan. Subsequently, after they married,

Figure 3.2
Overseas Compensation Package (Percentage of Women), by Type
(Expatriates, Independents, and Trailers)

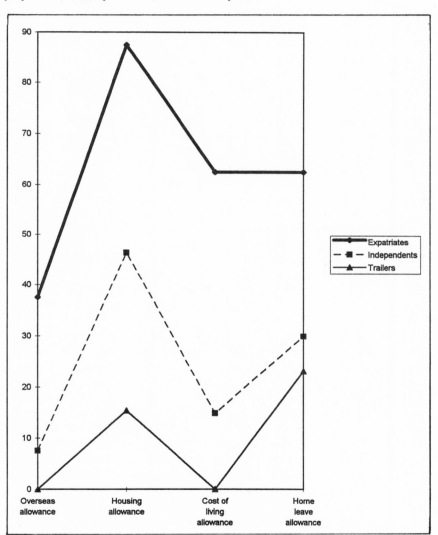

the firm treated his three children as her dependents as well, providing travel allowances for the children to visit Japan. Likewise, the consultant woman whose husband was initially offered a transfer and who then became a transferee herself received a promotion (earlier than she would normally have received it) *before* she was transferred as an incentive to move.

Areas of Dissatisfaction

Several of the women noted particular areas of dissatisfaction with their treatment. The dissatisfaction was mainly felt by the independent job seeker women who were hired on a local status; additionally, some of the women who were traditional transferees or trailers voiced criticism. The complaints ranged from feelings that the firms misrepresented what they promised, did not compensate the women as they did men in comparable positions, or treated them differently because they were not Japanese.

Misrepresentation. Sometimes, women felt misled because they were "foreigners," who might not be expected to understand or know what to expect in a contract. One of the "hybrid seeker" women, hired out of graduate school in the United States, believed that her firm had lied to her about the extent to which it would support her housing expenses. She had expected a certain percentage of coverage by the firm and leased an apartment based upon that expectation. The company ultimately backed out of the promise, leaving her stranded with an expensive apartment, which absorbed more of her take home salary than she had planned. She speculated that the firm figured, as a foreigner, she would not have "fully understood" what they had agreed to or "would never know" that the firm had backed out of an agreement. She was, however, quite sure of her understanding of the Japanese contract and felt that the firm had cheated her.

Another woman who felt discriminated against as a foreigner worked initially for the Japanese office of a global advertising firm. Although she was "treated as a Japanese" in pay (and in lack of housing allowance and lack of home leave), she received no indefinite (i.e., long term) contract. The impression she had was that the firm managers "expected" her to leave, on the basis of their own stereotypes of Americans, and thus guaranteed no job security. As a result of such a stingy package, she claimed other foreigners were unwilling to work for the firm.

Other women felt they were mistreated because they were women. Trailers and independents most often commented on this concern. The consultant who moved with her husband commented, for instance, that the firm did not want to offer her an "expatriate package" because her husband had "already received such benefits." She argued that she too was a traditional transferee employee and, while there could be some areas of synergy (e.g., housing allowances), she was nonetheless deserving of a comparable package.

Another of the hybrid seeker women found, upon arrival in Japan, that she (and the other women from the United States hired by the firm) had been hired through the "Japanese human resource department," in a "secretary status." Eileen's male compatriots moving from the United

States were hired in through the "international human resource department," gaining them compensation that was one third higher than her own for the comparable job. When she realized what had happened, she went to a senior expatriate in the firm and was advised to "be patient." She was greatly disappointed but agreed to wait; ultimately, she moved into a higher pay scale but fumed for two years before it happened.

Finally, one "trailer" pointed to areas of dissatisfaction from her perspective. She noted that most firms, when they offer "support" to traditional transferees in a move, think in terms of tangibles such as a housing allowance, cost of living allowances, or schooling for children. One of the greatest needs, from her perspective, is support to the accompanying spouse or partner in finding work. Networking with other companies and more extensive and longer term subsidized language lessons are such types of support that are typically neglected.

Ways and Timing Used to Address Dissatisfactions

Given their dissatisfactions as well as the general nature of these women to be assertive, many sought remedies for the areas that they felt were unfair. The key tactic seemed to be persistent but gentle pushing until they got what they desired. Typically, the process was long and wearying. The woman working for a British relocation firm finally received a housing allowance after one year on the job—and a year of haggling with the firm. Terri, a hybrid seeker hired to work in marketing, renegotiated her pay after two years in her job, receiving a 20 percent increase.

The independent who discovered she was making one third less than her male compatriots who had also been hired as "hybrids" took the advice of her friend in human resources to "be patient." Difficult as it was, she complied: she waited. After one year, she was promoted one salary level but remained below that of comparable men. After two years and two job evaluations, she was finally promoted and her pay elevated to a level comparable to that of the men (her Japanese female counterpart in a similar position was *not* promoted, however). She commented that she *could* have "blown the whistle" and made an issue of the inequities. That she did not raise a commotion gained her some respect throughout the firm. Nonetheless, she lost two years' worth of pay she felt she was due her and had, at the time we spoke with her, requested back pay for overtime.

SUMMARY AND CONCLUSIONS

Foreign women professionals working in Japan appeared to be remarkably resourceful in finding and settling into jobs. The expatriates pursued or were pursued by their firms and seemed to negotiate good arrangements for their time in Japan. The independents and trailers showed the most imagination in "packaging" their skills, in networking to find positions, and in finding ways to leverage their positions into good learning experiences.

On the whole, however, the preparation—particularly formal—that women received prior to their move and on-site in Japan was lamentably poor. Again, the more resourceful women found ways to prepare themselves or learn from others once they were in Japan. In Chapters 7 and 8, we will discuss recommendations for both organizations and women to enhance the preparation and likelihood of on the job success, rather than depending primarily upon women's willingness to train themselves.

Chapter 4

The Working Environment

A key reason why many U.S. firms rarely send women abroad stems from a perception that most foreign countries are inhospitable to women in the workplace. The expectation is that a negative business climate will severely hamper a woman expatriate's ability to perform her job and, ultimately, to enhance the firm's business. Such a perception of inhospitability and likely probability of failure has led some decision makers to avoid selecting women for overseas positions. Indeed, although fewer than 15 percent of U.S. human resources directors publicly acknowledge that they intentionally favor men over women in international selection decisions, the fact remains that 95 percent of the expatriates in American firms are male (Black, Gregersen, and Mendenhall, 1992).

Japan is frequently viewed as a particularly difficult environment for women, in part because of a prevailing image of female subservience in Japanese society. A perception exists that Japan is "culturally tough" for Westerners and has great differences in social values from North American and European countries. Consequently, senior managers often conclude that sending foreign women to Japan for business is sheer madness.

To fathom whether such perceptions are justified, in this chapter we examine the Japanese work environment. First, we will discuss the work climate for and roles of Japanese women professionals in Japan. Second, we explore how the women in our study felt the Japanese working environment affected their ability to carry out their jobs, particularly with regard to work relationships. We will look at how their relationships with bosses, colleagues, clients and subordinates appear to be shaped by the Japanese working environment for women, and whether they believe these relationships would be easier or more difficult for foreign men holding the same job.

WORKING ENVIRONMENT IN JAPAN: HOW DO JAPANESE WOMEN FARE?

The workplace environment for Japanese women exhibits some paradoxes. On the one hand, Japan's economy has long depended heavily upon women's involvement in the work force; on the other hand, their participation is often perceived as peripheral when it comes to strategic decision making and management of firms. Thus, in the following four sections, we discuss components of this issue: (1) what types of women participate in the work force, (2) what kinds of jobs they hold, (3) what environment they work in, and (4) what trends affect the workplace climate in Japan.

Japanese Working Women: Who Are They?

Japanese women form an important part of the work force in Japan. Of the total work force in 1994, women represent approximately 40 percent. Holding positions ranging from salesperson to secretary, factory worker to manager, they are highly visible in most workplaces. In fact, women have played critical roles throughout the industrialization process in Japan. In the early 1900s, when Japan's economy developed rapidly through growth in its textile industry, it was women who were the primary mill workers in the industry (Reischauer, 1974). In a sense, then, Japan built its modern economy as a result of the efforts of working women.

During the 1990s, women have continued to participate actively in the working environment. Indeed, some 58 percent of all married women in Japan work (Lam, 1992). Their involvement, however, often fluctuates over the course of their lives. The general pattern has been for young women to join the work force after graduating from high school, junior college or a 4-year university. Typically, they work until they marry or have their first child. As a result, most women leave the work force by their mid- to late-20s (after marrying and having a child) and remain at home until their children are in school. They often then return to work. In general, women with higher educational levels rejoin the work force at a lower rate than others. While 43 percent of primary and middle school graduates return to work, only 25 percent of graduates of vocational, 2-year, and 4-year colleges and post-graduate schools do so.

Some scholars (Lam, 1992) describe this pattern of joining, leaving and rejoining the work force as the "M curve" of labor force participation. The middle of the letter *M* represents a nearly complete withdrawal from the labor force of women in their mid-20s to mid-30s when they are bearing and then raising young children (Lam, 1992:14). Labor force participation typically resumes for women in their late-30s, and continues until they reach their early-60s. Although the "M curve" continues, in recent yearly the pattern has begun to show some changes. Three trends are causing young women to remain in the work environment in larger percentages. As women pursue and achieve higher education levels (and subsequently seek to apply that knowledge), marry later and have fewer children, the decline in labor force participation among women in the 25–34 age group is less steep (Lam, 1992).

Japanese Women's Jobs

Although Japanese women hold a range of jobs, by far the largest percentage occupy lower level positions, especially clerical and sales jobs, or work only part-time. In addition to meaning low pay, such positions tend to offer few opportunities for advancement. Several researchers have commented on the structure of the workplace and positions that women and men hold. As Lam summarizes:

> The sexual imbalance [in the work force] is striking. Over one-third of women work as clerical workers, and another quarter work as production process workers or laborers, [while] only one percent of them work as managers and administrators. The concentration of women in some occupations is obvious if we look at women's share relative to that of men: women constitute 51.3 percent of service workers, 58 percent of clerical workers and 41.6 percent of unskilled laborers. They are severely under-represented in administrative and managerial jobs, constituting a mere 7.7 percent of the total. (Lam, 1992: 50)

Unfortunately, the picture is even more disheartening in reality. Although women statistically hold 7.7 percent of administrative and managerial jobs, the figure is somewhat misleading. Most of those positions are with small Japanese firms, rather than the larger "blue chip" Japanese companies. Indeed, others estimate that women occupy only 1 percent of the managerial decision-making positions in large Japanese firms, where the best paid and most challenging jobs are (Steinhoff and Tanaka, 1994).

Women's exclusion from higher level (i.e., higher paid and more responsible) positions in business has numerous causes, including laws, cultural beliefs, and enduring business practices that limit women from gaining ground. First, Japanese business firms continue to heed the Labor Standards Law, amended in 1986 (Japan Economic Report 33A, 1991). In essence, the law prohibits companies from requiring late evening work for women, thus "protecting" them from overtime and keeping them out of other higher wage or salaried positions. Second, embedded cultural beliefs in Japan that children are best raised by a mother at home force the "M curve" pattern of labor force participation. This limits predictable career advancement for women with children. Finally, the much-discussed Japanese practice of "lifetime" employment (which actually applies to only about 20 percent of the Japanese work force) encourages a firm to train and invest in employees likely to remain long term with the firm. Such skills would be lost with women who quit to raise children. Thus, businesses are reluctant to devote the financial and other resources to building skills among employees (i.e., women) who are perceived to come and go. Whatever the reason, the result is that Japanese women tend to be assigned to jobs that are less demanding and lower paying than those of their male counterparts. As a consequence, foreign businesswomen will not often find themselves seated across the table from a female Japanese executive, especially in a large Japanese firm.

The picture is not completely grim, however. As we mentioned earlier, women do more often hold managerial and executive positions in small to medium sized Japanese firms (Steinhoff and Tanaka, 1994). Japan is an economy dominated by small businesses, often family run. In many firms, the wife frequently takes an active management role; further, in some firms, women have begun recently to inherit the presidencies of family businesses from fathers and husbands. Thus, talented women unable to break into the larger corporations often find smaller firms more receptive. In addition, foreign firms also often hold promise for women seeking career opportunities. Perceived by male graduates of the top universities to be "beneath" them, foreign owned firms and international joint ventures have, for the last decade, eagerly hired talented Japanese women. Finally, women increasingly are their own bosses, acting as entrepreneurs opening businesses in growing industries such as travel and leisure (Steinhoff and Tanaka, 1994).

The Workplace Climate for Japanese Women

Despite the examples of women in managerial positions, most Japanese women working in business firms occupy clerical positions, in the offices of large Japanese firms. Their working environment is restrictive and dominated by culturally prescribed behaviors and expectations, for both men and women. Indeed, this group of Japanese working women performing clerical duties, typically called Office Ladies ("OLs"), are subject to a working environment that represents what many women face. The environment is characterized by a prevailing view of women as being subordinate, frivolous, weak, and expendable. We review each of these aspects in turn.

Women: subordinate to men. In a Japanese business firm, Japanese women are almost always subordinate to men working there. Three main factors contribute to this circumstance: position, age, and gender.

Position is the most critical reason why Japanese women tend to be perceived as being subordinate to men. In Japanese business, position in the hierarchy defines status, rank, and authority. People in higher positions command respect from those below. Japanese people are keenly aware of hierarchy, as anyone who has exchanged business cards will attest. The title on one's business card signals the position one holds in a company and, in turn, the rank. Once rank and position in the hierarchy are established, both parties know how to address one another and interact.

Since most Japanese working women occupy lower level positions, they are by definition subordinate to all those occupying higher level positions, who usually are men. Anyone, male or female, who is lower on the corporate ladder is expected to accept the superior status and authority of anyone above. Thus, women frequently find themselves in subordinate positions.

A second reason why most women, particularly office ladies, are subordinate to men stems from differences in age. Like position, age signifies a difference in hierarchy. As in other Asian countries, seniority and age command respect and deference. Since most OLs tend to be young women in their early-20s, they are usually younger than the majority of the males in business firms. Therefore, the women are junior and subordinate in the workplace.

Finally, gender itself clearly plays a role in women's subordinate roles in the Japanese working environment. Generally speaking, women are seen as the inferior sex in Japan, at least in business. The assumption is that Japanese women rarely have interest in the business or professional world, and thus lack business abilities and skills. Consequently, women will be subordinate to men, who are automatically assumed to have business interest and skills. As one successful Japanese woman put it, "[In Japan], the most stupid male is said to be equal to the brightest female" (Lebra, 1992: 388).

Apart from such causes for Japanese women's position in the workplace, it is nonetheless important to note that the Japanese, heavily influenced by Confucianism, consider rank and subordination to be part of the natural order of things. In Confucian societies, hierarchy simply exists: some person will *always* be lower or higher than another on the authority ladder. The Japanese consider such a situation to be right and proper.

Hierarchy and subordination translate into specific responsibilities on the part of the superior (as well as the subordinate). For example, usually the person in a superior position in Japan expects to protect and nurture subordinates. Many view this as a moral responsibility to the subordinate. Nevertheless, few men provide such nurturing to women subordinates, in part because they expect women will leave the company in a few years. The resulting perception is that women's development is less important, and hence there is less mentoring. In addition, mentoring would have a perceived sexual component that makes it uncomfortable for male Japanese bosses to undertake these duties (Carney and O'Kelly, 1987). Finally, Japanese men are also loath to accept a Japanese female boss because of the perception that she lacks necessary experience and contacts within the firm to offer mentoring to help further their careers (Carney and O'Kelly, 1987; Black, Stephens and Rosener, 1992).

Just as the responsibility extends downward from the superior, so too does it reach upward for the subordinate. Subordination in Japan means humility and obedience from the person occupying the lower position, meaning that Japanese women working in offices must be humble and obedient. In addition, men expect Japanese women to exhibit deference and attentive female "charms." Thus, while Japanese male managers are accustomed to receiving obedient and humble attention from *all* their subordinates, they expect even more deferential attention from their women subordinates.

In contrast to the Japanese approach to subordination and hierarchy, Western societies display greater ambivalence about whether differences in power or authority are "right" or fair. Rather than accepting (and respecting) higher ranking people because of their seniority or age, people higher up the ladder in Western businesses often must "prove" their competence more than those in a Japanese firm (Dore, 1987). Such thinking likely leads to greater acceptance by Japanese women of the workplace climate and their treatment.

Japanese women as frivolous. Many Japanese women in business are perceived as frivolous, not serious about their jobs and their companies. Women are seen as adornments. In fact, there is a Japanese term, *shokuba no hana*, that is applied to female employees, meaning "workplace flowers." Such a perception of a lack of seriousness may be somewhat self-fulfilling. Given the overt and covert discriminatory practices barring Japanese women from upper level positions in most firms, few incentives exist for them to form strong attachments to their companies or jobs. Since, often, the job content is severely below their abilities, they easily become bored. In fact, many younger Japanese women view working as a way to bide their time before they marry. As a result, many women see their work lives during their early-20s as a time for fun and travel before they settle down to the serious business of marrying and raising children.

Such attitudes have led office ladies to become an important segment of the Japanese who travel abroad. Indeed, young single Japanese women's vacation spots range from the beaches of Hawaii to the Alhambra in Spain. Unlike their male bosses and colleagues, they *take* their vacation days! Such behavior by the OLs means that most Japanese men feel their female subordinates lack a commitment to work and do not share the "all-out" drive of their male subordinates. In short, the women are viewed as "frivolous" because they appear to take their jobs less seriously than the men.

Women as weak. Another characterization of Japanese women in the work force is that they are weak, particularly physically. Various pieces of legislation help preserve this perception of weakness. Laws "protecting" women in non-agricultural jobs since World War II guarantee them time off with pay each month for menstrual discomfort. As mentioned previously, the Labor Standards Law prohibits women from working after ten o'clock at night. Another strictly limits the amount of overtime that employers require of women in non-managerial jobs. Further, in certain occupations, women may not work on holidays (Japan Economic Report 33A, 1991). Together, these laws provide a strong disincentive to employers to hire women, and have helped perpetuate the perception of women as physically weaker than men.

Interestingly, such a characterization contradicts the daily situation faced by many Japanese women. Traditionally, women shoulder much of the arduous physical labor in the agriculture industry, including rice planting, reaping, and field maintenance. Even in modern Japan, many women—often middle-aged—work on road construction projects, hired from local farming communities.

Women as expendable employees. Finally, in the workplace, Japanese working women are often viewed as "expendable" employees (Rohlen, 1979), regardless of job type. Women often hold either temporary or part-time positions and are among the key groups that Japanese employers use to absorb downturns in the economy. In 1986, for example, women held 74 percent of all non-permanent jobs and 81 percent of all part-time jobs (Japan Economic Report 33A, 1991). As holders of such jobs, women have become early—and easy—targets for Japanese firms that face cutbacks or "downsizing."

Even women who work full-time for large Japanese employers are considered expendable, easy to let go when necessary. Because firms invest little in training women, the skills and knowledge that women have are less crucial to firms. Holding no strategic or critical skills, therefore, women can be easily replaced when the economy improves. In short, while senior managers, particularly in larger firms, nurture and develop the abilities of their male employees, they judge women workers as somewhat fungible.

The work climate surrounding Japanese women described tends to carry over to women holding managerial positions as well. In fact, most Japanese expect even professional women to quit a few years after joining a firm to have children. In short, Japanese male bosses and colleagues do not strongly differentiate between Japanese women holding clerical positions and those in higher jobs. Finally, men expect the women to be deferential to all males, less serious than men about their work, not as strong in the work effort, and probably less intent on staying with a firm for a long term career.

CHANGES IN THE JAPANESE WORKING ENVIRONMENT

Despite the relatively inhospitable work environment for Japanese women in the past, several trends promise a more optimistic future for Japanese women who want a career rather than a job. Major recent changes include (1) the passage of an Equal Opportunity Law in 1985, (2) the transformation of the Japanese industrial structure and the composition of the labor force, (3) the breakdown of the permanent employment system, (4) the growing number of foreign firms in Japan, and (5) the changing attitudes of both male and female Japanese concerning work and women in the workplace. We discuss each of these next.

Equal Employment Opportunity Law

After considerable debate and consultation with industry and labor groups, the Japanese Diet passed an Equal Employment Opportunity Law in 1985. While similar to those in other developed economies such as the United States, the Japanese law has a major critical difference: it has very little power of enforcement. Sanctions for non-compliance are weak, more like slaps on the wrist than punishments. The strongest sanctions are for infractions in training, fringe benefits, retirement age, resignation and dismissal (Lam, 1992: 101). But for recruitment, hiring, job assignments and promotion, employers face only an "exhortation" to provide equal opportunity, with no legal ramifications for non-compliance. In short, the law is very management oriented.

Moreover, the short term effect of the law has been to push employers toward offering women more part-time jobs as a way to avoid providing the full range of opportunities offered to full-time (usually male) employees (Lam, 1992; Japan Economic Report 44A, 1993). In addition, the law has led many firms to force women who are hired into full-time jobs to choose at the outset whether they want a career-track or non-career-track position. If the women choose a career-oriented direction, they must also state they are willing to make the sacrifices necessary to pursue such a track within the company. The result is that few women pursue careers. As Lam (1992: 22) clarifies: "In practice men are almost automatically assigned to [the career management track], whereas women are selected for it only exceptionally. During selection interviews, women often appeared to be challenged with tough questions about mobility and potential sacrifices of family life. Despite the formal offer of opportunities, in reality very few women managed to pass the selection procedures."

Yet, in spite of the law's weakness, it represents a very "Japanese approach" to legal redress of social wrongs. Vague enough to allow considerable maneuvering by employers, it is also flexible enough to allow the government wide latitude in its application. Perhaps its greatest impact has been that it has forced extensive debate over the issue of equal opportunity, and has compelled the government to take a stand, albeit a weak one, against discrimination in the workplace.

Industrial Structure and Labor Force Composition Changes

A second major change in Japan affecting the workplace environment is the transformation of its industrial structure and labor composition. Like most advanced countries, by the year 2020, Japan will have a manufacturing labor force percentage that will mirror its farming labor force percentage—about 10 percent (Drucker, 1986; *Industries and Employment*, 1986). Even as labor shifts into tertiary industries, such as services, manufacturing itself has automated. Furthermore, in response to cost and trade friction pressures, Japan produces approximately one fifth of its industrial output overseas. In fact, Japanese firms have begun exporting their idle plants to developing countries (PSST, 1994).

The combined effect of such trends has been a much reduced need for blue collar workers and for supervisory personnel to manage them. The impact on jobs means that Japan is becoming an information society, in which knowledge industries predominate. People involved in the production of knowledge and its commercial uses—engineers; scientists in life sciences, chemistry and physics; lab technicians; and computer specialists—are highly sought after. This trend has led to a dichotomy in the labor market, between semi- and un-skilled workers and highly skilled ones. Rapidly disappearing are the relatively well-paid skilled heavy industrial jobs that were so prevalent, and where permanent employment could work so well.

Such professionalization of labor force jobs will work to the advantage of college educated women with degrees in high technology fields. In seeking employees with technical, immediately applicable skills rather than "generalists" with vague intentions to become managers, firms will increasingly pursue applicants with specialized expertise. Those professionals with specialized skills will, further, be more likely to integrate easily into a firm.

Such a trend should bode well for highly trained women with sought after skills. First, those with such specialized technical skills who maintain them when (if) they step out of the work force for childbearing will likely find good jobs awaiting them when they return to the work force. Some Japanese firms have in fact pursued such recruitment/retention strategies that include seeking and hiring talented Japanese women. For example, Toshiba has hired numerous women researchers, Mitsubishi Electric has engaged women engineers, and the Bank of Japan sought out female bankers in the mid-1980s. A final contributor to the trend is the rapid aging of the Japanese work force. As Japanese firms face a dwindling entry level work force source, they will likely pressure workers (including women) to remain in their jobs.

Changes in the Permanent Employment System

Japan's changing industrial structure and labor force composition also closely link to the changes in the permanent employment system so prevalent following World War II. This system has been one of the most stringent barriers to Japanese women in the work force. The concept of a "permanent employment system," which necessitated an uninterrupted career within one company, limited women's progress. As that system disintegrates, women may find more opportunities.

Since 1980, as Japan has moved toward a more knowledge-intensive industrial structure, the permanent employment system has evolved toward a more open labor market system. Seniority is slowly losing dominance as the primary criterion for promotion and pay raises. Instead, such decisions increasingly rely upon evaluations of individual skills and contribution. Other evidence of such a change include an increasing trend of mid-career hires. As firms move into high technology areas and change strategic directions, they find themselves forced into hiring (raiding) needed skills rather than developing them in-house.

Furthermore, Japan's economic recession in the early 1990s made it impossible for firms to continue such long used employment practices as "carrying" employees who were unable to contribute fully to the firm. Indeed, some firms were forced to fire core employees, a practice largely unheard of in Japan before 1990. With companies forced to modify many such aspects of the permanent employment system, the opportunities for women increase. Rather than being at a disadvantage because they are unwilling or unable to remain with a firm long term, professional Japanese women particularly now find that the breakdown of the permanent employment system allows them the flexibility to enter and leave the system more readily.

Increasing Foreign Firm Presence

A third trend enhancing the workplace climate for Japanese women seeking careers is the increasing presence of foreign firms in Japan. Foreign firms have always been at a disadvantage when hiring in Japan because of the perception that they are unstable and less prestigious than large Japanese firms. Unable, therefore, to hire male university graduates from prestigious Japanese universities, foreign firms have actively recruited Japanese women for many years.

Several other factors have contributed to the propensity of Japanese women to join foreign firms. First, women graduates of 4 year colleges, in particular, have often been shunned by large Japanese firms because they are "overqualified." Foreign firms, in contrast, have sought such women for those very qualifications Japanese firms shun. Thus, Japanese women increasingly have joined the much more hospitable foreign firms in Japan.

In addition, foreign firms have tended to be less stringent practitioners of the permanent employment system in Japan. They encourage, for example, more individualistic, merit-based employment practices. Such approaches are better suited to hiring graduates with the skills and talents the firms need, be they men or women.

Changing Attitudes

Finally, but significantly, the attitudes of both Japanese men and women are changing in ways that affect the career opportunities of Japanese women. Japanese women, blessed with the longest life expectancy in the world, realize that they typically have 30 years of healthy life once their children are in school. This recognition increases the pressure on them to pursue a meaningful job to fill those years. Thus, they view their jobs—and careers—more seriously and as long term endeavors.

In addition, Japanese women are increasingly marrying later than their counterparts 40 years ago. The average marrying age for Japanese women in the 1990s is 26 years old, rather than 23 in the 1950s. Further, Japanese women today bear fewer children (i.e., an average of 1.53 rather than 2.00) (Japan Economic Report 33A, 1991). Thus, women simply have more time to pursue jobs and careers.

The pattern of marrying later and having fewer children is also reflected in the emergence in the 1980s of the "*oyagi* gals," young women who have adopted "male" pastimes of playing golf, attending and betting on horse races, and keeping their own bottles of whiskey at their local bars (a Japanese businessmen's custom). These young women shirk from marriage and raising children partly because they have more options than their mothers. In short, therefore, for many young Japanese women, the dominance of marriage and children has diminished, both because they will spend less time in child rearing and because it holds less appeal than it did 40 years ago.

As Japanese women experience wrenching attitude changes, so too are Japanese men shifting. They increasingly accept, and, in some cases, encourage, women's participation in the work force. Hundreds of men, for example, have joined the "Ikujiren" (Child Care Federations) to demand child care time be given to male workers (e.g., to be excused from work to take their children to nurseries). The large supermarket chain Seiyu has been one of the employers adopting such practices (*JIWMP News*, 1986).

In addition to more liberal attitudes toward shared child rearing, male attitudes toward work and jobs are changing. The economic boom years of the late 1980s encouraged many skilled young Japanese men to leave unchallenging jobs in large firms where promotions had slowed as management became top heavy. At Sony, for example, one recruit reported that of the 47 graduates joining the elite managerial track this year, not one planned to spend his entire career at the company (Japan Survey, 1994).

Conversely, the Japanese recession, which led to layoffs or placement of older managers in small related firms, undermined the faith of the younger generation in the rewards for loyalty to a large firm. Such changes have led to greater mobility of young male Japanese workers and a greater emphasis on individual ability. These young men are more likely, as a consequence, to focus on their co-workers', subordinates', or bosses' skills rather than on their longevity and connections within the firm. In turn, they are more likely to accept talented women as equals as well. Finally, as a newer generation of managers moves up in Japanese firms, they may be more comfortable with hiring and promoting talented Japanese women.

The result of these pressures is a slowly adapting Japanese workplace, where Japanese women will have opportunities more equal to those given to men. Such continued change, however, depends greatly on Japan's economic health. The recent recession, according to the Minister of International Trade and Industry Eijiro Hata, forced Japanese companies to reduce the number of employees, and particularly women, they hire both for clerical and career positions. In early 1994, for instance, Nippon Life Insurance Company, the country's largest, reduced by 15 percent the number of women it hired for career positions. Its action was followed by two other large insurers (Job Seeking Women, 1994).

Thus, the tough economic environment has made Japanese firms risk-averse, and pushed them back toward a pattern of only hiring and developing male employees. As Japan emerges from its longest and deepest economic downturn in 50 years, it will be important to watch whether large companies in particular hire and promote women candidates.

JAPANESE WORKING ENVIRONMENT FOR FOREIGN WOMEN PROFESSIONALS

As we detailed previously, Japanese women face an inhospitable workplace environment. Clearly, since the perception exists that such difficulties may affect non-Japanese women, we next examine how much the difficulties encountered by Japanese women apply to foreign women professionals. Drawing upon the surveys and interviews we conducted, in the remainder of this chapter we consider two key issues relating to the Japanese working environment as it affects the lives of foreign women professionals. First, we examine whether foreign women are treated as the professionals they are, or whether they are affected by the inhospitability to Japanese women professionals. A related question is whether their experiences seem to be influenced by their Japanese language ability or the work groups with whom they interact.

Second, we explore whether foreign businesswomen in Japan, as contrasted to foreign businessmen, have any special advantages or any particular disadvantages, as some previous research has suggested (Adler, 1994). Understanding the issues embedded in this question should help decision-makers in multinational firms—as well as women contemplating working in Japan—determine the viability of foreign women professionals working in Japan.

How Hospitable Is Japan for Foreign Women Professionals?

The working environment that Japanese women face is without question less than welcoming. To some extent, it is reasonable to expect that such an environment would apply to foreign women professionals as well. Japanese men encounter few professional Japanese women in their workplaces, and generally perceive working women as subordinate, frivolous, and expendable. To understand how much such attitudes encountered by Japanese women apply to non-Japanese women, we examine the perceptions held by women in our study about the attitudes of Japanese bosses, co-workers, subordinates and clients toward them. Specifically, we examine the extent to which the foreign women are accepted as professionals in their fields. Next, we explore other aspects of their

Table 4.1

Average Responses to Questions Concerning Advantages and Disadvantages in Working with Japanese (Questions 48A–48L) (scale: 1 = strongly disagree to 5 = strongly agree)

Question	Mean	Standard Deviation	N
The Japanese people that I work with give me sufficient information and support to adequately perform my job.	3.7	(1.2)	91
I have a productive, trusting relationship with most of the Japanese I work with.	3.7	(.97)	91
I find that the Japanese I work with are curious about me.	3.7	(1.0)	91
I find that the Japanese I work with remember me easily.	4.5	(.79)	90
It is rather easy for me to get new business in Japan.	3.2	(1.0)	53
It is not difficult for me to get access to Japanese clients.	3.0	(1.2)	62
My communication with the Japanese I work with is open.	3.7	(1.0)	91
The Japanese people I work with seem comfortable working with me.	3.7	(1.0)	91
It does not seem hard for me to attract Japanese clients.	2.9	(1.7)	46
Generally speaking, the Japanese I work with seem to believe what I tell them.	4.1	(1.2)	91
I have found that the Japanese I work with accept me as a professional in my field.	4.0	(.91)	90
It appears that I have good credibility with the Japanese with whom I work.	4.1	(.76)	90

relationships with Japanese, particularly some of the perceived advantages and disadvantages they face, in comparison to foreign men.

Acceptance as a professional. To explore the extent to which foreign women felt they were accepted by their Japanese colleagues as professionals, we drew upon the survey findings, from Questions 48A through 48L (Appendix B). The women responded to a series of questions that dealt with how accepting they felt the Japanese (e.g., colleagues, clients) were of the foreign women as professionals (Table 4.1).

One statement (Question 48K) the women rated was a general one: "I have found that the Japanese I work with accept me as a professional in my field." The question required the women to think of *all* Japanese they work with, not only Japanese bosses, but their peers and subordinates as well. On average, the women responded very positively (an average of 4.0 on a 5 point scale, with 5 = strongly agree). In short, the initial reaction was that foreign women professionals in Japan, according to their survey answers, do not view professional status to be a problem. The skepticism about their professional status that Japanese women appear to encounter from colleagues and clients does not seem to transfer automatically to foreign women working in Japan simply because they are women. While at first blush this is encouraging, as we will see, the picture is somewhat more complex.

One issue of concern and interest for the study was the degree to which a foreign woman professional's Japanese language ability influenced her acceptability as a professional among Japanese colleagues. That is, does the ability to communicate linguistically garner greater respect and credibility for a foreign woman professional working in Japan? While the study suggests that there does seem to be some connection, it relates mostly to speaking ability: the greater a woman's ability to communicate verbally, the more she perceives her acceptance as a professional as positive. Women whose linguistic abilities are weaker reported that they felt more questioned as professionals. However, the relationship between ability to converse in Japanese and perception of professional acceptance was relatively weak statistically (a correlation of .17 at a .05 significance level). Thus, the results do not settle the question of whether foreign women gain greater acceptance as professionals as a result of their linguistic ability. Apparently, the ability to speak competently gives women a sense of being more accepted. Nonetheless, in interviews, several women did perceive that they felt more accepted professionally if they were able to communicate verbally.

A second possible influence on a foreign woman's acceptance as a professional is *whom* she interacts with most on a daily basis: boss, co-workers, subordinates, or clients. For example, if women interact primarily with *internal* constituents (e.g., boss or co-workers), will they perceive their professional acceptance to be greater than if they interact primarily with *external* constituents (e.g., clients, suppliers)? The argument for the former is that the internal groups have longer to get to know the women; as a result, the women have more time and opportunity to build credibility. Furthermore, the internal constituents will tend to know and understand that, in their home country operations, the women are accorded professional respect or they would not be working for the multinational firms.

To gain a sense of the impact on professional acceptance of the types of groups that women work with, the survey asked the women to estimate the amount of working time they spent daily with each of several groups (Questions 37 and 38). The women reported spending their working time primarily with Japanese nationals. Indeed, the women noted that they spent an average of 64 percent of their total work time interacting with Japanese nationals on the job: they spent an average of 6 percent of their work time with Japanese supervisors, 14 percent with Japanese co-workers, 11 percent with their Japanese subordinates, and 10 percent with clients and suppliers. The balance of their time was spent with "others," who were undefined.

The findings suggested a fairly strong connection (.32 correlation, significant at .00) between the amount of time foreign women professionals interact with subordinates and the extent to which they feel accepted as professionals. Several factors may contribute to this finding. Perhaps foreign working women who actually *have* (Japanese) subordinates by definition hold high level jobs. As a result, such women may naturally expect to be treated as professionals, and thus perceive themselves to be, regardless of whether they work in Japan or elsewhere.

Such an explanation would seem to fit with some of the comments from the interviews as well. The issue of holding a high level job—or at a minimum having a high sounding title—came up frequently. Indeed, several of the interviewees emphasized the need for their organizations to assign a foreign woman as high a title as possible to help her establish a professional presence in the Japanese workplace.

When that did not happen, the women felt frustration and inability to do their jobs successfully. Connie, for example, lamented that she had neglected to demand a clear and high enough title when she accepted the position in the Japanese branch of the non-profit organization for which she worked. Her unwitting ignorance of the importance attached to "position" in Japan led her to accept a vague title, which held little status. As a result, she felt greatly hobbled in her efforts to attain professional acceptance.

While most women experienced professional acceptance when they worked with internal groups, several noted that such a finding must be qualified. In addition to the comments from women whose subordinates bestowed credibility on them, we heard other comments from women who had the opposite experience with subordinates. A number of the women revealed that the greatest disrespect they had suffered came not from co-workers or clients, but from their *female* Japanese subordinates! For example, two young hybrids at American multinationals described secretaries who refused to answer their phones, do photocopying or do filing for them. They had to resort to doing their own or getting more sympathetic secretaries in other departments to help.

Both stated that the resistance was particularly strong among older female Japanese secretaries. The young women speculated that the *ages* of foreign women professionals and of their subordinates may affect foreign women's acceptance at least as much as gender may.

A fact that may support this conjecture is that the majority of foreign women professionals who encountered problems with female Japanese subordinates were also young, usually less than 30 years old. None of the expatriate women, and few of the women over 40, recounted any stories of difficulties obtaining compliance and help from their female subordinates. Perhaps, then, the young foreign women who were hired locally faced resistance because they were young rather than because they were female or professionals.

Interestingly, when the Japanese office of a firm actively promoted Japanese women to positions of authority, the problem of resistance to younger foreign women professionals seemed to dissipate. Sandy, who worked for an international household moving firm, found a very supportive environment among her Japanese female subordinates. She attributed this support to the pattern throughout the firm that Japanese women held many key positions of responsibility, such as chief accountant and inbound transfers manager. Such support of women generally, according to Sandy, led to an easy acceptance of her as a professional, because she was not seen as threatening.

The mixed acceptance by female subordinates was mirrored in women's comments about reactions of male Japanese subordinates. Several of the women reported resistance from their male Japanese subordinates as well. Jane, a local hire fluent in Japanese, gave an example of how Japanese men viewed a senior female expatriate at the foreign advertising agency where she worked. Her male subordinates acknowledged the foreign woman expatriate as hardworking, but thought her too aggressive and forthright. The Japanese male subordinates' way of resisting their female foreign boss was to be uncooperative, miss meetings and deadlines, and go behind her back to make decisions. According to Jane, the female expatriate senior manager was unaware of the source or depth of resistance, because of her lack of knowledge of the Japanese language and culture. While the female expatriate was still in her job, according to Jane, she was both performing below expectations and feeling frustrated.

A final example of the reactions foreign women professionals faced from their subordinates comes from Deborah. The manager of a data processing department of a large U.S. bank branch in Tokyo, Deborah found that whenever new Japanese engineer graduates were hired, their first reaction to her as their boss was surprise. After that, they spent time questioning her professional stature before finally acknowledging her skills and credentials. Indeed, due to her very high Japanese linguistic ability, strong management skills, and engineering expertise and excellent credentials, her subordinates have helped her build a very successful department. Interestingly, however, as she commented, her department comprises engineers from several national backgrounds, because of the shortage of engineers in Japan. As a result, such an environment, with its mix of Indians and Chinese and Japanese, may be more tolerant of diversity than is typical in Japan.

One of the surprising findings was the relationship (although weak) between the amount of time spent interacting with a Japanese boss and the women's perception of their acceptance as professionals: the relationship was negative ($-.17$ at .05 level of significance). Interestingly, however, women with American bosses did not report greater levels of professional acceptance. Indeed, there was no significant difference between the women with U.S. bosses and those with Japanese bosses with regard to how they perceived their acceptance and support as professionals.

In general, the women we interviewed supported this rather mixed finding. When Sandy, for example, worked in a Japanese firm, her Japanese boss reneged on a promise to sponsor her visa application and to pay her a certain salary. He attempted to get her to accept a lower salary to get the visa. Instead, she quit and found another job with a household moving firm. Eileen, a Japanese-American hybrid, had the choice of whether to work for a Japanese or an American boss. In the job interview, she found the Japanese boss to be much less accepting of her professional abilities; indeed, he said she would be given busywork for the first year while she learned the firm's corporate culture.

Despite such experiences, however, several women we interviewed had very supportive Japanese bosses. For example, Helen's Japanese boss, the CEO of the Japanese branch of a U.S. bank, was very aware of her experience and contacts within the home office, and was glad to benefit from them. To profit from her knowledge and contacts, he fully supported her career and activities in the Japanese office.

A related issue to general professional recognition was whether the foreign women perceived they were accepted professionally as readily as foreign men. Thirty-four women responded to survey questions that asked whether they felt they were "worse off, the same, or better off" than foreign men on several dimensions. The questions asked women for their perceptions of how their treatment would compare to that experienced by a foreign man holding the same job. With regard to professional acceptance, 11 women felt they were worse off than a foreign man would be, 20 felt their experiences were the same, and 3 felt that professional acceptance was easier for them than it would be for foreign men holding comparable jobs. In short, the women perceived it was somewhat harder—but not overwhelmingly so—to be accepted as professionals than it would be for foreign men.

Finally, findings from another survey question confirmed the perception that foreign women *can* gain acceptance as professionals. The question asked women to compare their present jobs with the jobs they held before coming to Japan with regard to their relationships with various groups. The groups included colleagues, subordinates, customers, and suppliers. Of the women who responded, the majority felt that their relationships with various groups were *as good as or better than* what they had with similar groups in the jobs they held before coming to Japan.

In sum, foreign women professionals in Japan seem to feel that gaining professional acceptance is not an automatic process and is somewhat tougher than it would be for foreign men. Moreover, if foreign women spend a lot of time with Japanese bosses, or are inept at speaking Japanese, then gaining professional acceptance seems to be more arduous.

Although women reported in the survey that acceptance was somewhat less onerous when they held jobs requiring much interaction with Japanese subordinates, the interviews revealed that much depends on the particular organization and women's personal characteristics. Nonetheless, the women we surveyed and interviewed generally felt they *had* gained professional acceptance. In short, they had to work hard at it, but felt it was feasible.

All of this is good news for decision-makers and for foreign women contemplating a posting to Japan. Professional acceptance is one of the most critical aspects of working in Japan. Without it, men or women will face huge hurdles. While such acceptance is admittedly difficult for Japanese women to gain, the women we studied reported that they were able to establish a strong professional presence. Furthermore, most of the women we interviewed repeatedly commented that they were not "unusual." In other words, these women suggest that there is every reason to expect that foreign women professionals in general can successfully gain acceptance as professionals in Japan.

Advantages and Disadvantages in Work Relationships of Foreign Women Professionals in Japan

Besides gaining acceptance working in Japan, foreign women professionals in Japan face other issues in their relationships with colleagues and others. Some of the most fascinating research on foreign women working overseas (Adler, 1993a, 1993b, 1994) has identified various advantages and disadvantages that such businesswomen working in Asia perceive they have. Interestingly, the women perceive these advantages and disadvantages to be different from those they may (or may not) experience when they work in their home countries. Furthermore, they are unlike problems faced by Japanese professional women. Through surveys and interviews, we explored how foreign professional women working in Japan felt about the advantages and disadvantages that had been identified by previous research.

In this next section, we discuss the perceived disadvantages and advantages reported by the foreign professional women, particularly as they influenced their relationships with colleagues and others in the workplace.

Disadvantages. One of the common perceptions (and fears) about foreign women working in Japan has been that Japanese clients and customers will not work with them, thus detracting from a firm's ability to secure business. Our study confirmed some of the difficulties that women face in this arena, but also pointed to some means for overcoming such challenges. Indeed, some women gave examples pointing to benefits of being foreign women professionals, which we discuss more in the next section.

In the survey, we asked women to rate the difficulty of attracting clients and doing business with Japanese outside their firms (a combination of Questions 48E, 48F, and 48I). Since not all women had external clients or worked with Japanese outside the immediate workplace, not all of them responded to the questions. Of those who responded, most rated the difficulty as "neutral" (i.e., 3 on a scale of 5). In other words, they saw neither advantages nor disadvantages to being a foreign woman professional when it came to finding and keeping business, although, in general, they rated their adjustment to these external Japanese relationships as lower than their adjustment to their other relationships (Table 4.1).

In general, the women we interviewed who had clients outside the workplace tended to confirm this finding. Jane, working for a well-known U.S. advertising agency, described the "offsetting impact" of being a foreign woman in Japan. She has found that Japanese clients are initially suspicious of her, particularly since they expect women to hold low level positions in firms. Nevertheless, because she is a foreign woman (and they are still somewhat rare in Japan), the clients often have strong curiosity about her. Often, Jane has been seated next to high ranking clients at social functions when her male counterparts were not, simply because of the novelty it represented to the Japanese. She has used these opportunities to build a personal rapport with clients and to allow her professional competence to shine. In many cases, her strategy paid off in business and, more importantly for her, wider credibility.

Both of us have had similar experiences. In conducting research for a doctoral dissertation, one of us found that vice presidents of leading Japanese companies often agreed to interviews, partly because the research interested them but also because they were fascinated that a foreign female Ph.D. candidate was looking into the management of innovation in large Japanese companies.

In short, some women have found that access to clients has been easier because Japanese businessmen are intrigued by the idea of professional foreign women. Unfortunately, however, many Japanese men approach such an encounter with curiosity as well as with skepticism, thinking that they are dealing with someone who may lack the authority or knowledge necessary to be a true representative of her firm. Thus, while such a disadvantage may be turned into an advantage, being a foreign professional woman clearly presents a challenge in dealing with clients and Japanese outside the workplace.

Also in the survey (Questions 49E, 49F, and 49I), we asked women to report on their perceptions of the ease or difficulty they face in gaining business from Japanese clients as compared to likely experiences of for-

Table 4.2
Respondents' Views of Their Work Relationships with Japanese Groups, Compared to Work Relationships in Previous Jobs (Percentages of Women Responding)

Variable	Less than previous job	Same as previous job	More than previous job
I have a trusting and professional relationship with my colleagues in Japan (N=76)	37%	38%	25%
I have a trusting and professional relationship with my subordinates in Japan (N=63)	27%	54%	19%
I have a trusting and professional relationship with my customers in Japan (N=62)	21%	44%	35%
I have a trusting and professional relationship with my suppliers in Japan (N=45)	29%	44%	27%

eign professional men. While most women responded by saying they perceived there were differences (i.e., more difficulties for them compared to foreign men), they were not overwhelmingly negative. The negative experience—as compared to their perceptions about what men encounter—likely reflected the initial resistance, discussed earlier, that women felt from Japanese clients and others. In our interview with the New York corporate lawyer, Amanda recounted the frustration she felt when new clients called the office and refused to speak to her if the senior partner (an American man) was out. Once she met the clients and established her credibility and competence with them, they were quite happy to work with her. That initial resistance, however, was hard for a successful woman to swallow. Overall, then, while the women perceived they held a slight edge over foreign men with regard to access to clients, they felt that, in the main, they faced some disadvantages in gaining new business, when compared with their foreign male counterparts.

We took the issue one step further and asked women to comment on the nature of the relationships they had with Japanese clients as compared to those they had in earlier jobs (Table 4.2). We also found that most of the women responding to the survey felt their relationships with clients were as professional and trusting as—*or better than*—what they had experienced in jobs they held prior to coming to Japan. Perhaps as in gaining professional acceptance, foreign women may have to work harder than foreign men, and overcome some additional obstacles, to gain credibility and deal effectively with Japanese clients. However, there was a solid consensus that foreign women professionals *can* and are doing it.

One unexpected, and tentative, finding from the interviews emerged in discussions with the two Japanese-American women. Both were second generation Japanese-Americans, from families who still spoke Japanese in the home and who had Japanese relatives in Japan. Both of these women worked in large, well-regarded American multinational firms. In the course of our interviews, each raised the issue of the difficulties she faced in dealing with Japanese women subordinates (i.e., secretaries), as we discussed earlier. Furthermore, they both experienced what they perceived to be much more difficulty with Japanese men, who viewed them more as "Japanese" than as "American" professional women. Thus, the attitudes that Japanese men hold about Japanese women in the workplace seemed to transfer to affect their interactions with these young Japanese-American women.

Advantages. Often, disadvantages and advantages are opposite sides of the same coin. While the women we studied turned many disadvantages (e.g., initial client resistance) into advantages, there were nevertheless some areas where they felt they had a distinct edge. First, the women reported one major advantage was visibility: they felt most positive (Question 48D: 4.5 on a scale of 5) about being remembered by the Japanese they interact with in their work. Moreover, the women felt their memorability was much greater for them as foreign women than it would be for foreign men.

Regarding credibility (Questions 48J and 48L), the women also felt quite positive: they perceived themselves to have excellent credibility with the Japanese they work with (4.11 on a scale of 5) and that their Japanese colleagues believe them (4.0 on a scale of 5). While they were positive about these dimensions, they perceived that they had no great advantages in these areas over foreign men.

On questions of the extent to which women felt trust, openness, and comfort in their work relationships with Japanese (Questions 48B, 48G, 48H), they were again quite positive. Further, as we have discussed, they felt the curiosity the Japanese have about them was something to be used in a positive way, rather than viewing it as a detriment. In all these aspects, they perceived that their situations were similar to those faced by foreign professional men.

In one area, however, the women were slightly less positive in their perceptions of their experiences in comparison to men's. Regarding the degree of information and support needed to accomplish a job (Question 48A), the women felt they received relatively less information and support (about 3.7 on a scale of 5), as compared to foreign men, in particular.

Such a reaction is not surprising, given the way the Japanese conduct business. In Japan, much exchange of information and, in turn, relationship building occurs after working hours. Many women we talked with mentioned that they only infrequently attended such after hours meeting. Indeed, several felt excluded from the after hours drinking so typical among Japanese co-workers and bosses in Japan. As a result, they felt "out of the [information] loop."

Interestingly, however, even more women mentioned that, as women, they had an allowable excuse to avoid such late night sessions. Furthermore, many women remarked that their foreign male colleagues often resisted being included in the after work sessions because of family pressures. The Japanese were less willing to accept the resistance from foreign men than from the women. Despite such exclusion from potentially valuable sources of information, on the whole the women felt they received sufficient support and information to do their jobs successfully.

The interviews revealed two other advantages of foreign professional women working in Japan: (1) the belief that they were better able to adapt to discriminatory conditions in Japan and (2) the perception that foreign women could more easily build interpersonal relationships than foreign men.

Dealing with being an "outsider" in Japan is one of the first shocks that any newcomer faces. Some people—women and men—appear to adjust more easily than others. Carol, a high level black expatriate working for a large American firm, offered an engrossing assessment of her ability to adjust. She felt better equipped than either foreign men or non-minority foreign women to deal with the ethnocentrism and exclusivity of the Japanese people. As a black southern woman, growing up in the United States and subsequently working for a mainstream U.S. corporation, she had many experiences that toughened her to discrimination. She endured slights as a child, as a student, and as an employee and learned to deal with them. Having been a member of a minority throughout her life, she was accustomed to prejudice and intolerance, common reactions of Japanese to non-Japanese. As she noted, "I've always been an outsider, dealing with crossing cultural borders. When a taxi in downtown Tokyo doesn't stop for a white foreign male, but picks up a Japanese man down the street, the white guy is incensed, hurt, confused. He's never been excluded before. Me, I just wait until the next time. I don't expect to be included, and these kinds of incidents don't get to me."

Hers was a surprising, and sobering, insight. While many corporate decision-makers may resist sending foreign women overseas because they *are* women, Carol's statement strongly suggests that foreign women, particularly black women, may have an advantage in adjustment that foreign white men will never have. Specifically, long experience with exclusion from the traditional cultural and corporate networks and activities that help white males further their business dealings is something that many professional women, perhaps especially minority ones, have faced. As a consequence, such women may be better able to handle Japanese ethnocentrism. Moreover, these women may have found alternative ways of dealing in the business world to help them perform their jobs. In short, a consequence of having to deal with racism and/or sexism in the United States may be a heightened ability to ignore (or at least survive) cultural exclusion and a greater skill at finding alternative routes to accomplishing job goals.

Finally, the interviews revealed another advantage: the perception that, in many cultures, women nurture human relationships. In Japan, developing personal relationships with business contacts is essential to building a solid business relationship. Several women felt that they were better at this process than their foreign male counterparts.

Indeed, the women we interviewed repeatedly commented on the relatively greater skills that women have in carrying out the tasks that help build personal relationships. Several women took pains to remember names or to inquire about a business contact's family, trips or hobbies. In fact, some of them took special care to bring little gifts for business acquaintances, or candy for business meetings. While an intriguing notion, this idea—like the previous one suggesting that foreign (especially minority) women may be better at adjusting in Japan—demands more systematic study before we can conclude anything.

SUMMARY AND CONCLUSIONS

In Chapter 4, we suggest that the environment for Japanese women professionals is rather unwelcoming. Furthermore, as yet, Japanese women play no substantial role in the Japanese business world. In spite of the inhospitality toward Japanese women in the workplace, however, foreign professional women perceive they are accepted as professionals by the Japanese they encounter in their work. The process has been anything but smooth, particularly when foreign women initially establish relationships with Japanese colleagues and others. Age, title, linguistic ability, and the groups with whom they interact appear to influence the overall acceptance the women experience. But the women in our study felt that ultimately they have been able to establish professional credibility in Japan.

Furthermore, the women report that they may, in fact, have some advantages over foreign men. Women feel they are more memorable or visible (because there are fewer of them), they may adjust more readily to feelings of exclusion since many have experienced it in their home environment, and they have better nurturing skills, which allow them to develop personal relationships.

In the next chapter, we examine a set of issues that follow naturally from questions about the extent of acceptance these women gain as professionals. Obviously decision-makers and women candidates for positions in Japan need to know whether foreign women professionals can be successful performers in the jobs they undertake. To address this issue, we will look further at the workplace environment and personal characteristics, as well as job aspects, that seem to influence the work adjustment and performance of the women in our study. Finally, we will confront women's assessments of whether the whole experience of working in Japan is worth it!

Chapter 5

How Do Women Fare?: Adjustment on the Job

In Chapters 3 and 4, we examined the forces behind the increasing numbers of women working outside their home countries and the particular workplace conditions facing foreign women professionals working in Japan. In addition, we examined how the women in our study viewed the relationships they experienced while working in Japan.

Now we turn to how the women view their adjustment and success in their jobs. First, we examine the extent to which women felt they adjusted to their work situations. Next, we examine the women's reactions to their jobs, in terms of their perceptions about their performance in the jobs, their satisfaction with their jobs, and their commitment to their jobs. Finally, we discuss how these women felt the work experience they gained in Japan would likely affect their long term career. Each of these factors contributes to an individual's overall ability to succeed, particularly in the unpredictable work world of Japanese business.

WORK ADJUSTMENT

A key to living and working successfully in a foreign culture is the ability to adjust to new ways of doing things (Dowling, Schuler and Welch, 1994; Black, Gregersen and Mendenhall, 1992). Women—and men—who are unable to adjust to working or living in a new culture often return earlier to their home country than they, or their organizations, planned. The cost of such "early returns" is not only a financial one for the firm but a large emotional toll on the returning expatriate,

Table 5.1
Work Adjustment of Respondents (Questions 16P, 16Q, 16R) (scale: 1 = strongly disagree to 5 = strongly agree)

Question	Mean	Standard Deviation
Overall work adjustment (sum of Questions 16P, 16Q, 16R)	3.8	(0.95)
Adjustment to specific job responsibilities	3.9	(0.95)
Adjustment to performance standards and expectations	3.7	(1.14)
Adjustment to supervisory responsibilities	3.8	(0.99)

who may feel like a failure. As a result, firms and individuals (should) spend much effort in increasing the chance of adjustment when they operate overseas. Thus, work adjustment is a *key* prerequisite to successful job performance in a foreign culture.

To assess the level of work adjustment of the women in our study, we asked a series of questions. First, we sought a general assessment of the women's perceptions of their adjustment to work. Next, we examined work adjustment as it seemed to relate to other key factors: work relationships, the nature of the job itself, and personal attributes.

For an overall sense of how well the foreign women professionals in our study adjusted to their work, the survey asked respondents to rate how they felt overall about their adjustment to their job responsibilities, performance standards, and supervisory responsibilities in Japan (Questions 16P, 16Q, 16R). The respondents rated their overall adjustment, on average, as "moderate" (i.e., 3.8 on a 5 point scale, with 5 being "extremely satisfied"). The women were generally—but not completely—satisfied with their adjustment to their jobs (Table 5.1). Of the three aspects, the women seemed least adjusted to performance standards.

To gain further insight into these overall reactions, we turn to three areas that may affect work adjustment and examine each. First, we will probe how work relationships may influence adjustment. Following that, we explore the nature of the job itself, in terms of how much autonomy or clarity it provides, as an influence on the adjustment a woman may feel. Finally, personal characteristics of the women themselves may influence their adjustment; we offer insights from the women on the impact that language ability, time spent in Japan and overseas in general, and age may have on adjustment.

Relationships with Work Groups

As we suggested in Chapter 4, the quality of foreign women professionals' working environment is in large part influenced by the quality of their relationships with various work groups. Just as those relationships affect women's perceptions about the extent to which they are accepted professionally, they also may affect their job adjustment.

The women who responded to the survey pointed to a clear and strong connection between their job and work adjustment and the quality of the relationships they have with their Japanese colleagues and others with whom they work (Table 5.2). Women who felt their Japanese bosses, colleagues, subordinates and clients had positive attitudes toward them (trust, belief in their professional competence, comfort, support, etc.) were more likely to feel they had adjusted well to their work. However, while this link exists, we cannot conclude cause and effect. In other words, the survey findings do not indicate whether positive attitudes on the part of the Japanese co-workers and clients help foreign women adjust to their work *or* whether well-adjusted foreign professional women tend to create such attitudes in those with whom they work.

While the survey results were tentative, some of the interviewees were more definitive with their responses, suggesting that the positive attitudes of the Japanese they work with may be a driving force of women's job adjustment. When we asked women to identify factors that helped women succeed and adjust to their work, three specifically mentioned their Japanese co-workers as a positive influence; one woman commented that her Japanese boss was a key influence. For instance, Jane spoke highly of her mostly male Japanese co-workers at the ad agency for which she works. Their patience and willingness to help her were a key to her learning and adjusting to her job.

Work Adjustment and the Nature of the Job

A key factor that previous research on male expatriates has suggested may influence expatriate adjustment to work or job is the nature of the job itself (e.g., Black, 1988; Black, Gregersen and Mendenhall, 1992). As we have mentioned, we sought to examine such assumptions as they applied to women. Thus, we asked women to describe, in the survey and interviews, the types of jobs they held. We explored three aspects: (1) the degree of ambiguity (or, the reverse, clarity) women had in their jobs, (2) the extent to which women faced conflicting job demands or expectations from various work groups, and (3) the range of autonomy or discretion women had in conducting their jobs.

Job ambiguity or clarity. Jobs overseas are frequently quite different from those held in home countries. Often, employees outside their home countries face considerable confusion over their job responsibilities, scope, or expectations. Such confusion may contribute to poorer or slower work adjustment, and in turn, inferior job performance.

Indeed, the women in our study strongly supported findings from earlier research on male expatriates in Japan (Black, 1988). Specifically,

Table 5.2
Correlation of Job Adjustment with Work Relationships, Aspects of the Job, and Personal Attributes

Variables	r	p
Work relationships		
Give me sufficient information and support	.44	(.00)
Have a productive, trusting relationship	.29	(.00)
Japanese seem comfortable with me	.35	(.00)
Accept me as a professional in my field	.42	(.00)
I have good credibility	.28	(.00)
Aspects of the job		
Job ambiguity	-.56	(.00)
Job conflict	-.31	(.00)
Job discretion	.62	(.00)
Personal Attributes		
Japanese speaking ability	.19	(.04)
Time in Japan (N=36)	.47	(.00)
Previous experience overseas	.28	(.02)

the degree to which foreign professional women understood the job expectations was strongly related to their adjustment to work (Table 5.2). The more ambiguous the expectations, the less well adjusted the women said they felt.

Given a situation of unknown demands or lack of clarity, many women took on the task of defining their jobs themselves. For instance, Terri, the hybrid who worked for a U.S. beverage firm, had to write her own job description. She claimed the initial lack of clarity was not a problem to her. Indeed, writing the job description allowed her to define exactly what she wanted to do. However, until her job was clear, she perceived that some of her co-workers and subordinates resented her being in the firm. She speculated that perhaps when foreign professional women have unclear jobs, those around them also experience this ambiguity and feel uncomfortable about their role. Terri further wondered whether her Japanese co-workers and others exhibited resentment because they were unclear on why *she* was hired rather than a Japanese.

While we may assume that job ambiguity causes trouble, another interviewee suggested that it may have benefits. Helen, a senior executive at a large U.S. bank, related ambiguity more to job level than to location (home or overseas country). She commented that foreign women in lower level positions need more job clarity to ensure their acceptance by others and their own adjustment to work. At upper reaches, according to Helen, job clarity could be a detriment to the flexibility that senior level expatriates need to accomplish their job goals. Thus, for her, the positive relationship between job clarity and work adjustment was somewhat dependent upon the level of the job.

Other women offered different perspectives. Amanda, the corporate

lawyer, explicitly linked her slow job adjustment to the ambiguity surrounding the role of the Japanese subsidiary itself, rather than to her job
in particular. The New York office, as well as the branch offices in Europe, often sent requests for information or work requested by their clients, and demanded that the Tokyo office respond immediately,
regardless of other work. Because of the lack of understanding (or respect for) the work done in the Tokyo law office, she and the partner
often felt compromised. They wanted to respond to home office requests,
yet such work meant they were less able to develop their own client base
(a key goal of the Tokyo office). As a result, she felt considerable ambiguity about her job tasks and had a difficult time adjusting to work.

   Conflicting job roles and demands. A second factor that may relate to
work adjustment is the extent to which employees face conflicting job
demands. Research on male expatriates has revealed mixed results concerning the effect of conflict on work adjustment (Black, 1988; Black and
Gregersen, 1991). The situation for women, however, may be somewhat
clearer. Particularly in Japan, where bosses, peers, clients, and subordinates typically have had little experience with businesswomen, many
different expectations may emerge for foreign women professionals. If
women experience serious conflicts because of these reactions, they may
delay job adjustment.

   Because of the paucity of women in managerial or professional positions in Japan (see Chapter 4), expectations for them are more equivocal.
Foreign women professionals would likely receive more conflicting signals about what is expected of them than male expatriates because of the
lack of consensus on appropriate behaviors for professional women. Our
survey results indeed revealed a negative relationship between amount
of job conflict and adjustment, although it was weaker than that between
job ambiguity and work adjustment (Table 5.2).

   The interviews offered more insights on how job conflict may affect
foreign women professionals' adjustment to working in Japan. Several
interviewees mentioned, for example, the conflict they experienced when
Japanese colleagues, bosses, and subordinates asked that they perform
duties below their professional stature. Connie provides one of the most
poignant illustrations. An expatriate with over 20 years of experience in
the non-profit organization where she worked, she was appalled that the
first training she received upon arrival in Japan was how to serve tea
and run the postal machine! Terri, the sports marketing manager working for a U.S. beverage firm, repeatedly found male Japanese colleagues
asked her to get tea. Her solution was to pretend she did not hear—or
understand—the request. In addition, the refusal of Terri's subordinates
to type her letters (meaning she had to do it herself or find a willing
secretary) created a major job conflict for her.

   Perhaps Japan is an unusual case, in that the lack of Japanese women in high professional and business positions may generate expectations that women in the workplace, including foreign businesswomen, should perform "women's" duties. Even so, such expectations on the part of Japanese businessmen can create a role conflict that likely delays foreign women's job adjustment in Japan.

Interestingly, *none* of the senior level foreign professional women (with the exception of Connie), mentioned such expectations and conflicts in the interviews. Evidently, when a foreign professional women is clearly in a high level position, the job conflict caused by cultural expectations of women's work roles decreases.

A second issue of job conflict that several women alluded to was sexual harassment. When they are sexually harassed on the job in Japan, foreign women receive messages that conflict with their own expectations about professional stature and role. Sadly, such experiences appear common among foreign professional women in Japan.

Several interviewees mentioned incidents in which they were sexually harassed by Japanese clients. Linda, working for a British advertising agency, was approached by a male client during a business related sailing excursion. She had to request that all future meetings with that particular client be held with a male colleague present. Eileen, working for a large U.S. telecommunications firm, recounted how she was sexually accosted at a client firm's party by two employees of the client's subcontractor. Several members of the client firm, who knew Eileen well, saw what was happening. They ran interference and apologized to her for the incident. Nonetheless, she felt the range of emotions common to harassment victims—shame, anger, fear.

Even interviewees who had not themselves experienced sexual harassment from Japanese men knew of and recounted incidents their friends had experienced at other firms. Even when the advances were not directed at them, interviewees had experienced considerable innuendo and sexual remarks from Japanese men that are offensive to Western women. Jane, another advertising agency executive, recounted remarks that her Japanese colleagues and clients made about women waitresses and entertainers during evening business entertainment sessions. Her clients have even complained about a translator's looks! For Jane, who had been editor of a feminist magazine in her U.S. college, the remarks caused considerable job conflict.

Clearly, many foreign professional women who faced a general atmosphere where potential sexual harassment was prevalent experienced a sense of job conflict that affected their work adjustment.

Job discretion. Finally, the amount of discretion that women have in their jobs appears to relate to work adjustment (Table 5.2). That is, the extent to which the foreign women were given the ability to decide what to do, when, and how provided the flexibility they needed to adjust to jobs in Japan. In essence, the more the foreign women had autonomy to make decisions about how to carry out their jobs, the better they were able to modify work roles to their skills. Further, such autonomy offered the women the leeway to identify and use past successful work behaviors and approaches (Black and Gregersen, 1991; Kahn, et al., 1964; Karasek, 1979). As can be seen in Table 5.2, there is a very strong and statistically significant relationship between job discretion and work adjustment.

In most of the interviews, many women acknowledged a wide range of flexibility and discretion in their jobs. Further, they cited autonomy as a major source of satisfaction with their jobs. Indeed, 8 of the 20 women we interviewed rated the degree of freedom they had in their jobs in Japan as "far more" than what they would have in comparable jobs in their home country.

Many women also mentioned in interviews that their jobs in Japan had much greater authority than jobs they might have in the United States. Terri, in charge of sports events marketing at the U.S. beverage firm, oversees a yen 1.1 billion budget (about $1 million). As she commented, few people her age (late-20s), male or female, would be given that degree of responsibility, and yet in Japan, she had that opportunity. Deborah, manager of a large bank's data processing department, directs all related purchasing decisions for the multimillion dollar operation. In sum, almost all of the women interviewed—expatriates, hybrids, and trailing spouses alike—felt they had much greater job discretion and responsibility in Japan than they would have in jobs in their own country with their present skills.

In addition to *more* responsibility, the interviewees also experienced *wider* responsibility. Amanda, the corporate lawyer, put it in context for her own situation: in the firm's New York law office, 300 lawyers carry out the work; in Tokyo, 2 people do whatever is needed. Consequently, she has worked with much more varied areas of the law than she would in New York. On the other hand, she also does tasks usually handled by paralegals in New York, such as ensuring that a document is notarized. In short, the lack of critical personnel gives many foreign women a chance for much greater and higher job responsibilities and authority than they would have in their home setting. Many women acknowledged this as a key reason they planned to remain in Japan in spite of frustrations with the job or with their social life.

A final point regarding job discretion and authority was the perception by women that their job in Japan afforded them greater access to people at higher levels in the organizational hierarchy. In several cases, the women noted they had become liaisons between their Japanese and American bosses. Particularly because the Japanese speaking women have the ability to understand what the Japanese management wants *and* they understand the foreign way of operating, they play a crucial liaison role. Furthermore, since most were admittedly not fluent in Japanese, their Japanese bosses tolerated their more direct (i.e., Western) way of stating ideas or suggestions. As a result, the women acted as linguistic and cultural translators between the Japanese and foreign contingents. To do this, though, they were granted relatively high discretion in their jobs.

Another outcome of this role was that the women had much higher visibility with upper management—both Japanese and expatriate foreign bosses. As such, the foreign women professionals felt they had greater impact than they would have in their home setting. Deborah, director of data processing in a bank, fully acknowledged the benefits of acting as a liaison between her Japanese boss and *his* (Indian) boss, higher up in the hierarchy. Her Japanese boss admitted to her that he was unable to deal well with the "emotionalism" of his Indian boss, nor was he able to present issues in a manner that was convincing to his Indian boss. As a result, Deborah frequently played the go-between or, at a minimum, counselor to her Japanese boss on how to deal more effectively with his boss. Such a position gave her much more power than someone in her rank would normally have had.

Foreign businessmen also experience wider job scope and discretion in Japan. However, it is interesting that in comparison to that of foreign males in one study (Black, 1988), the relationship of job discretion to work adjustment for women is much higher ($r = .29$ for the males in Black's study versus $r = .62$ for the women in this study).

Of the three aspects of the job, which is the most important contributor to the work adjustment of the foreign businesswomen in our study? When examined statistically (through regression analysis), discretion is the only aspect of the job that has a significant and strong effect on the work adjustment of the women in this study. In short, when looking at all three aspects of the job simultaneously, women appear to be most strongly and positively influenced in their work adjustment by how much leeway they are given in their jobs. While job conflict and ambiguity may have important effects on work adjustment, they are less important overall when viewed statistically.

Work Adjustment and Personal Attributes

A final factor affecting women professionals' ability to adjust to working in Japan was their personal attributes or characteristics. We examined four personal characteristics to determine their relationship to women's adjustment to working in Japan: (1) language skills, (2) time spent in Japan, (3) previous international experience (Table 5.2), and (4) age (Table 5.3).

Language skills. Earlier research discussed the issue of language ability as a factor in adjustment (Tung, 1990; Church, 1982; Torbion, 1982; Mendenhall and Oddou, 1985). On the basis of this research, we expected that the greater the woman's command of Japanese, the easier it would be for her to adjust to her job. Interestingly, the survey data do not strongly support this expectation. Language skills were not as strongly linked to foreign professional women's work adjustment in Japan (see Table 5.2) as one might anticipate. The only significant relationship was between speaking ability and adjustment, and even that was not particularly strong, in statistical terms.

The relationship between language and adjustment is apparently more complex than we initially thought. Indeed, the message from the survey data was borne out in interviews. When examined in more depth, the interviews suggested that, in general, the women noted two factors that apparently influence whether speaking Japanese is important. These included the extent to which jobs were focused mainly internally or externally to the organization and the degree to which the women had clear and highly sought expertise.

The extent to which their jobs were internally or externally oriented clearly affected the degree to which women felt the need to know and use Japanese. Helen and Marcy, in charge of internal auditing at a large U.S. bank and U.S. beverage firm, respectively, focused mostly on managing people dealing with internal accounting tasks; as a result, they could communicate clearly with colleagues using figures and data. Even though the women dealt with Japanese colleagues extensively, their jobs demanded less subtle expression because of their quantitative focus. As a result, neither felt the need to learn much Japanese and, indeed, expected their Japanese colleagues to know enough English for them to be able to work together.

Others felt quite differently about the importance of language to their effectiveness and ease of adjustment. In such cases, they used Japanese as a natural part of their jobs. Lorna, for example, perceived Japanese to be a critical tool. An entrepreneur running her own English language school, she has daily interactions with clients and government officials. The ability to communicate reasonably well in Japanese allowed her to build and maintain her business. On the other hand, she did acknowledge that for very intricate or extremely subtle negotiations or discussions, she drew upon a Japanese employee for help. Kiri, a consultant with an American based compensation firm, was the only native English speaker in her firm. In addition, a significant portion of her job dealt with finding and working with Japanese clients; thus she was forced to speak Japanese because of her interaction and the nature of her job.

In another case, Vicki was hired as a technical writer by a Japanese electronics firm in large part because she spoke Japanese, even though all of her writing and training were done in English. Although her work was internally focused, in that she trained company employees, they were still viewed as her "clients." Thus, as she commented, she had too much liaison work with Japanese co-workers for her *not* to speak Japanese. For women like Lorna and Vicki, a critical part of their adjustment, then, was being able to deal with clients or colleagues verbally. Thus, the extent of interaction with subordinates or clients determined whether most interviewees considered language skills a key to success.

In addition to the extent to which women's jobs required interaction with Japanese, a second aspect affecting the degree to which language seemed important was whether the professional women had clear, and highly valued, expertise. Many women who said their jobs required little Japanese language ability were high up in their organizations, or had some very specific expertise to offer Japanese clients. One women commented, "As the boss, I don't need to learn Japanese." As culturally insensitive as that may sound, several women firmly held to that argument. Others who made that comment cited their expertise as being one that the Japanese wanted and thus, *they* (the Japanese) were willing to learn English to gain access to it. Irene, a training consultant, had facilitation skills and training design and development skills that were in high demand. Her clients, as a result, accepted her inability to communicate in Japanese and used English to be able to take advantage of her knowledge.

In short, a more complex picture than we expected emerged from both the surveys and the interviews. Many researchers—and common sense—suggest that language skills facilitate expatriate adjustment to overseas assignments (Tung, 1990; Church, 1982). Our findings imply that, while there is a positive relationship between the two, it may be weaker than expected. The interviews exposed more subtle complexities regarding the extent to which language may bolster adjustment. Evidently, both the *nature* and the *level* of foreign professional women's jobs in Japan come into play when they—or their organizations—seek to determine how much emphasis to put on language skills. While knowing the local language may not hurt effectiveness, it may be less crucial in certain situations.

One final note is that, as we have seen, even when a foreign woman has excellent language skills, she may choose not to use them. As mentioned, certain interviewees revealed that they tended to "use" their linguistic ability (at least their Japanese *speaking* ability) under certain conditions. When they wanted to be "more direct" than Japanese typically are, when they wanted to avoid doing some task (e.g., serving tea), they tempered their use of Japanese to fit the situation.

Time in Japan. The notion of "culture shock" is discussed often with regard to expatriate adjustment overseas. Briefly, culture shock is a cycle of adjustment that many people experience when they move to a new culture. Typically, the cycle begins with excitement and stimulation in the early period, followed by disillusionment with the new culture during a middle period. Usually, after about a year, a person adjusts to living and working in a new country and culture. Thus, time in country plays a major role in the stage and degree of adjustment for people living outside their home countries and cultures.

Given such research, we expected that the longer foreign women professionals had been in Japan, the more they would understand and cope with the novelty and differences of the Japanese culture. In turn, that understanding would likely be tied to better work adjustment.

The survey and interview findings supported the notion that time in Japan related to adjustment (Table 5.2). Terri, for example, commented that it took several months for her to "find her way" in her job and begin to feel adjusted. She described how, as special events marketing director at a large U.S. beverage firm, she had slowly modified the ways she dealt with co-workers and suppliers. In the beginning, she showed her anger in meetings with suppliers who asked for exorbitant fees or conditions. She also confronted colleagues who tried to denigrate her professional stature in front of suppliers and others. After two years in the job, however, she learned how to cope and in the process became better adjusted *and* more effective. Even though she was Japanese-American, and thus well versed in Japanese culture, she faced an enormous learning curve regarding business practices. Until she achieved that level of competence—and comfort—she felt unsure about her job and usefulness.

Connie, working for the non-profit organization, also mentioned the immense gap she had in knowing how to do business in Japan before coming. She needed time to adapt, time to modify her expectations. While she felt she had failed to achieve full success in her job, at the end of her stay she was at least able to cope. Like Terri, she learned that confrontation gained her nothing. To adjust, therefore, she learned to find projects outside her main duties and reached a minimal level of work adjustment. She acknowledged that it had taken two years, however, to feel she was adjusted in any basic way. In sum, time spent on the job in Japan did seem to have a positive influence on the women's ability to adjust to work.

Previous overseas experience. Given the difficulty of adjusting to another culture, we expected that women with previous work experience overseas would adapt more easily to working in Japan. Having experienced culture shock and adjustment before, such women would likely be better prepared and more quickly adapt to the Japanese situation.

The survey results indeed indicated a connection between the amount of previous overseas work experience and work adjustment (r = .28, p = .02). Even so, the link between the two was rather weak statistically

(Table 5.2). Prior research also produced mixed results concerning relationships between the two (Black, 1988).

The interviews, moreover, did not overwhelmingly confirm such a link. Interestingly enough, none of the women mentioned that her adjustment or ability to function in Japan had been greatly enhanced by her previous overseas experience. Perhaps work experience overseas expedites adjustment to work in Japan but is neither sufficient nor necessary for successful work adjustment. The example of Carol, senior executive at a U.S. telecommunications firm, illustrates the point. A woman who had grown up in a small American town in the South and who had never traveled extensively even within the United States, she adjusted relatively easily to working in Japan. She expected conditions in Japan to be different; she had previously experienced feelings of being an "outsider," as a black woman in corporate America; and as a result, she adjusted with little trauma.

Another aspect may be that *where* women have lived and worked before is more critical than overseas experience per se. Some researchers (Mendenhall and Oddou, 1985) argue that when home and host cultures are quite similar, adjustment is easier. If, therefore, the women had lived in cultures not unlike their own (e.g., Americans in Canada or the United Kingdom), they may not have experienced fully the range of "culture shock" that they encountered in Japan. Thus, the previous overseas experience may have done little to enhance their work adjustment in Japan (Dowling et al., 1994).

Age. Finally, as we discussed in Chapter 4, age is an important aspect of hierarchy and status in Japan. A very Confucian society, the Japanese confer status on older people. Unlike in the youth centered West, in Japan older people are accorded respect simply because they have lived longer and have, presumably, acquired wisdom from their experience. Hence, we envisioned that older foreign women professionals would be accorded such status and thus more readily adjust to working in Japan.

Moreover, we anticipated that age would be particularly important for women professionals because of its association with organizational hierarchy in Japan. The Japanese assume that younger people hold lower level positions, since traditionally promotions are largely based on seniority rather than performance. Consequently, Japanese businessmen question whether younger people (perhaps especially women) have the competence or authority of a senior level person. Conversely, these businessmen may attribute *greater* competence or authority (or at least, appropriate authority) to older women. In short, being older may help foreign professional women overcome Japanese businessmen's initial expectations about competence or authority. Such women would presumably adjust more easily to working in Japan since initially they do not face the obstacles that younger ones do. Consequently, we expected that

Table 5.3
Average Work Adjustment of Women in Different Age Categories
(Percentage of Respondents)

Age category	Percentage of respondents	Mean	Standard deviation
Less than 25 years old	7	3.5	(.45)
25-34 years old	52	3.6	(.89)
35-44 years old	27	3.8	(1.2)
45-49 years old	10	4.5	(.58)
50-55 years old	4	4.3	(.82)

Note: there were no respondents over 55 years old

older foreign women professionals would adjust to working in Japan more easily than their younger counterparts.

According to the findings from the survey respondents, work adjustment seems generally to increase with the age of women (see Table 5.3). We are tentative about this conclusion, however, for several reasons. First, we had a limited number of older women in the sample group. A majority (85 percent) of the respondents were less than 44 years old, and over 50 percent were under 35 years of age.

Second, when we analyzed statistically (using an analysis of variance) differences across the five groups on average work adjustment, differences in scores were barely significant. In other words, while the survey findings *suggest* that age does relate to work adjustment for foreign professional women in Japan, the findings are not supported statistically.

When we assessed the interview responses, however, age did emerge as an important factor, particularly for women in certain jobs. Several of the younger women who dealt extensively with Japanese clients supported this notion. Kiri, for example, observed that in her work as a consultant to businesses on personnel matters, her youth worked against her. Her Japanese clients found it difficult to believe that a young woman in her mid-20s could have the experience and wisdom that a consultant should have. In her opinion, Kiri's youth was a greater obstacle to her adjustment and effectiveness than her gender. Sandy, working for an international household moving firm, echoed Kiri's comments.

Examples from the older women further strengthened the idea of age as a benefit for adjustment. Carol, the telecommunications executive, commented that to deflect any residual resistance to her due to her sex or race, she quickly conveyed to clients her age, both by discussing her extensive experience and expertise and by telling her age. Furthermore, she made sure that they learned early on of her high position in the organization. Being in her mid-40s was sufficient, in her opinion, to quell any lingering doubts over her competence or authority. In Japanese business, it is only when men reach 40 that they begin to wield considerable clout. Thus, she "used" her age to her advantage and, again, felt it helped her adjust to working in Japan as a result.

Lorna, owner of a language school, echoed Carol's view. In her view, a woman 45 or older who is poised and experienced will have fewer problems than a younger woman. Although gender will always be a handicap for foreign women professionals, Lorna still felt that age could compensate for some of the negative reactions to her sex. In fact, several interviewees recommended that women who had achieved a "respectable" age (in Japanese eyes) should "flaunt" it. Because many Japanese find it difficult to estimate a Westerner's age correctly, the women argued for letting Japanese colleagues *know* how old they are, particularly if their age is "advanced" enough.

Younger interviewees found the age issue more complex. On the one hand, they perceived that their youth was part of the "charm" they used to gain access to higher Japanese management levels than they would otherwise be accorded, given their relatively lower positions. Sandy, working for an international household moving firm, stated that "clients get a kick out of my youth."

Conversely, however, the women acknowledged that while youth was an advantage with regard to access and memorability, it had disadvantages as well. Many women felt that Japanese clients or co-workers assume that younger women tend to be more gullible and inexperienced in business. Sandy, for example, encountered clients who tried to avoid paying certain fees that they knew were legitimate moving expenses. She found they often asked her to provide "free extras" for which they knew they should pay, assuming that she was "too young to know better." She found it, as a result, challenging to settle into work before she overcame such expectations.

The younger women further commented that they were unsure whether their youth or gender was the driving force behind Japanese businessmen's attempts to deceive them. They nonetheless felt that together these attributes negatively influenced their adjustment.

As we have seen, foreign women professionals' adjustment to working in Japan relates to a number of factors: work relationships, the nature of the job, and personal attributes or characteristics. Unfortunately, our study provides only suggestions about which factors contribute to work adjustment and in what way. Like other research thus far, this project is unable to say conclusively which factor or factors are the most important. Doubtless, future research on professional women working in Japan and elsewhere overseas will help clarify the relative weight of each factor, just as research on work adjustment of male expatriates has explored these factors (Black, 1988; Black and Stephens, 1989).

Even so, our study does suggest that the work adjustment of foreign women professionals working in Japan correlates to some extent with the quality of their relationships with Japanese colleagues and with certain aspects of their jobs. On the other hand, personal attributes, such as age, seem to have a more mixed effect on work adjustment. Further, and perhaps initially surprisingly, linguistic ability and previous experience overseas seem less important. In addition, the interviews revealed that much seems to depend on the specific types of jobs women hold. Finally, with regard to the nature of jobs, job discretion and ambiguity seem most solidly related to work adjustment for most women and jobs.

Perhaps because of the still tentative nature of these results, however, both women professionals working in Japan and those who hire them should consider the factors discussed here to anticipate potential challenges women will find in Japan. Even if women professionals face none of the difficulties, they will nevertheless be prepared with ideas of how to be successful.

Work adjustment appears to be a necessary but insufficient condition for women professionals to perform successfully abroad. For anyone—male or female—contemplating an international job, an additional important issue stems from the question of whether he or she can perform the job. Corporate decision-makers are obviously concerned about the ability of any foreign woman professional they hire abroad to be successful in her job overseas. In the next section, we will explore the perceptions that the women in this study had about their performance and its relationship to work adjustment.

REACTION TO JOBS

A second area we studied was women's reactions to their jobs, in terms of how they felt about their own performance, their overall job satisfaction, and their commitment to their jobs. On the whole, most women were quite pleased with both aspects. Given that we assessed women's own perceptions about their performance and satisfaction, we were encouraged to find that most were so positive. Future research on foreign women professionals clearly needs to review perceptions of these issues by others as well (e.g., colleagues, bosses, clients). As a first step, though, we examined the reactions of the women themselves.

Job Performance

Several survey and interview questions addressed the issue of how women perceived their performance. The women, on average, scored their performance at 3.5, or just above "fully satisfactory" (on a scale of 1 = "unsatisfactory" to 5 = "clearly outstanding") (Table 5.4).

The survey, of course, was unable to capture the sense of achievement

Table 5.4
Job Performance: Percentage of Respondents Who Classified Themselves at Each Level of Performance

Level of Performance	Percentage
1 -- Unsatisfactory	2.4
2 -- Needs improvement	13.4
3 -- Fully satisfactory	33.0
4 -- Exceeds expectations	36.6
5 -- Clearly outstanding	14.6

and excitement that many of the women exuded when they talked in interviews about their performance. In the interviews, women usually perceived their job performance to be quite good. With two exceptions, the women we interviewed felt they had been "successful"; several felt they had been "very successful." Moreover, some women provided specific and measurable evidence of their success. Several independents, in particular, offered examples of high performance. Sandy mentioned the much higher than average number of bookings she had obtained for her international household moving firm. Linda cited the large number of new clients she had gained for the advertising agency where she worked. Vicki was so successful in her job as a technical writer that she decided to become a free-lance consultant, confident that she would receive a lot of work from the Japanese company for which she worked at the time. Two expatriates, Carol and Helen, also reported high levels of success in their jobs. They felt proud of their job performance, perhaps especially so because of the difficulties they had overcome to achieve it. Carol had baffled and ultimately won over her skeptical clients and co-workers. Helen, in fact, had begun internal organizational networking groups for women lower in the hierarchy to support them and help ensure their success. Indeed, the women frequently commented that they appreciated our doing the project because they wanted to convey the message that foreign women professionals *can* be successful in Japan.

Unfortunately, as we mentioned, in this study we lacked an independent, objective way to verify the perceptions of the women themselves regarding their success in their jobs. We had no opportunity to survey or interview their bosses, co-workers, clients and subordinates. We cannot say, then, whether information from others would dispute the women's conclusion that they—and others like them—were successful in Japan.

Nevertheless, we were impressed by the consistency of the *tone* of the women we interviewed when we asked about their job performance. These women were excited, proud, and confident about their accomplishments. Apparently, for many women good job performance is possible in Japan, and whatever challenges they faced in achieving success, they seemed capable of overcoming them.

Obviously not all the women felt successful. Connie, in particular, was the most discouraged. She felt she had failed terribly and called herself a "crash and burn" case at her non-profit agency. The day after we interviewed her, Connie was leaving her job and her career. She had decided to move to another country and take a year to consider her next steps. Clearly, not all women professionals in Japan succeed.

The statistical relationship between the women's perception of their job performance and their work adjustment was strong ($r = .47$, $p = .00$). This points to the necessity of ensuring that decision-makers consider the factors related to work adjustment when hiring foreign women professionals for jobs in Japan.

Job Satisfaction

The foreign women professionals in our study held a wide variety of jobs, from lawyer to technical writer, from owner of an English school to manager of a group of data processing technicians. Their comments and insights suggest that most felt they were performing their jobs successfully and that they were relatively well adjusted to working in Japan. We were also interested in learning how satisfied or happy they were in their jobs. Clearly these women could do their jobs, and do them well, without being fully satisfied with the jobs or conditions under which they worked. We were curious, then, about the extent to which they felt fulfilled with their jobs and work.

The survey results showed moderate levels of satisfaction with overall job situations (Question 33L). The women rated their satisfaction an average of 4.4 (on a scale of 1–7, with 7 being "very satisfied"). To probe further, we asked other questions (Questions 33A–33K) about satisfaction with particular aspects of their jobs: their pay, their level of autonomy, the extent to which they felt recognized for their efforts, their working relationships and the long term career implications of the jobs. Table 5.5 summarizes their reactions.

Job and Organizational Commitment

A final area we investigated regarding women's reactions was their commitment to their jobs and the organizations for which they worked. Such issues are especially important for corporate decision-makers. Research on American male expatriates has consistently shown that they quit their organizations in alarming numbers after returning from an overseas assignment (e.g., Black, Gregersen, and Mendenhall, 1992). Researchers have offered many reasons for the dissatisfaction returning ex-

Table 5.5
Average Satisfaction Scores for Different Job Components (scale: 1 = very dissatisfied to 7 = very satisfied)

Job Aspect	Mean	Standard deviation
Satisfaction with pay	4.8	(1.8)
Satisfaction with autonomy	5.1	(1.8)
Satisfaction with responsibility	4.6	(1.8)
Satisfaction with way managed	4.0	(1.9)
Satisfaction with way recognized	4.0	(1.9)
Satisfaction with relationships with co-workers from home country	5.0	(1.9)
Satisfaction with relationships with Japanese co-workers	4.8	(1.3)
Satisfaction with longer term career implications	3.8	(1.9)
Satisfaction with overall job situation	4.4	(1.8)

patriates experience. Several cite poor (or no) corporate repatriation programs to absorb expatriates into the system (Napier and Peterson, 1991). Another common reason is the discontent that expatriates feel with the typically "smaller jobs" they receive upon return: reduced job scope, autonomy, and discretion. Because, as we have seen, expatriates often have much greater authority abroad than their home office colleagues, they resent being forced to rein in their autonomy once back in the parent company. Unfortunately, the loss in talent to corporations from expatriate defection makes overseas positions even more costly. Thus corporate decision-makers need to consider what will happen to employees when they are assigned in the home country, even as they take jobs abroad. Since existing research leaves unexplored the issue of whether women expatriates have a similar level of job or organizational commitment to male expatriates, we wanted to assess the applicability of existing findings in our sample of women.

Furthermore, in our study, of course, most of the women professionals were *not* traditional expatriates. Instead, most were independents (hired in their home countries for jobs in Japan or hired locally) or trailing spouses who sought jobs once in Japan. Nevertheless, many worked in multinationals which could theoretically use their skills in the home country. Thus, it behooves corporate decision-makers to consider the commitment their people feel even when they work, or are hired, outside the home country.

In general, we expected independents (i.e., hybrids and local hires) to show less commitment to their companies than expatriates. Since the independents were hired by a Japanese branch of a foreign company, or by a Japanese firm, they accepted that the parent company made no promise to offer them jobs if and when they returned to their home countries. So unless the women intended to stay indefinitely in Japan, we expected them to show little commitment to their firm. Likewise, as trailing spouses would be expected to follow their husbands to the next assignment, we expected very low commitment to the organizations.

The survey results confirmed our hunch. We assessed commitment to organizations by asking women the extent to which they expected to be working for their present firms in 3 years (Question 35). Their average response rating was 3.3 ("unlikely"). The rating scale ranged from "not likely" (1.0) to "extremely likely" (7.0). Next, we asked women to estimate how long they planned to remain at their companies. Less than 50 percent expected to remain fewer than 2 years with their present firm, and 85 percent planned to stay no more than 6 years. Among the six expatriates, all but one indicated that she would likely leave her present company within 4 years.

Clearly, most women felt little overall commitment to the companies they worked for in Japan. The interviews strongly confirmed those results. In particular, the younger independents consistently commented that after a few years in Japan, they intended to quit and return to their home countries. The reasons that independents wanted to return were as varied as their reasons for taking jobs in Japan. Many planned to pursue master's degrees in business; one envisioned establishing her own human resource management consulting firm; one even foresaw a career in politics! Kiri, who worked for an American compensation and management consulting operation, was married to a Japanese engineer; they anticipated moving to the United States so that their children could be educated there rather than in Japan. Finally, several single women mentioned the dearth of potential marriage partners as a reason for returning home after a few years! We discuss in more depth such personal issues in Chapter 6.

Interestingly, some women were zealous in their commitment to remaining in Japan, regardless of the organization for which they worked. The factors driving that commitment were often personal as well as professional. These tended to be independents, rather than expatriates or trailers. A manager of a data processing unit deeply committed to remaining in Japan, Deborah had created a full life for herself. An accomplished martial arts student, she was the only foreigner allowed to work with one of the aikido masters in Japan. As such, she felt a strong sense of duty to her teacher, and to the discipline the sport instilled in her. Consequently, she intended to remain in Japan, at least as long as her instructor was alive.

In a very different way, another independent reached a similar conclusion. Donna, who initially moved to Japan as a "trailer" of her fiancé, had remained after the breakup of the relationship. Working for a British office location service firm, she had been in Japan 10 years, in large part because of her child. She arrived when he was 4; at 14, he had been completely educated in private schools in Japan and she felt his education—and his personal safety—were at a level unattainable in her U.S. West Coast hometown. She had developed a vast network of friends in Tokyo and built her involvement in a number of organizations. As she said, her life *is* in Japan, not in the United States.

Even these women, with their deep commitments to remaining in Japan, held lower commitments to their particular jobs or firms. Indeed, most perceived Japan as a temporary residence. The only way for most of the foreign women professionals to remain with their firms was to become part of the worldwide organization.

Some sought that route. Jane, who worked for the British advertising agency, was hoping to remain with the firm and transfer to its U.S. office. Helen, the senior manager expatriate at a large U.S. bank, intended to return to the United States with her bank but more for personal than career reasons. Her husband had returned to his job in the United States and they had wearied of such a long separation.

In short, however, it is unrealistic to expect long term commitment to their organizations from many of the independents or trailing spouses. While the women viewed their time in Japan as a time to be productive and learn, most tried to be realistic about the career payoff. We now turn to this in the final section.

Implications for Long Term Career

During the last part of the interviews, we asked the women a series of questions designed to assess their future expectations. First, we asked about what type of work they expected to do in the future. Next, we questioned whether their firms had any plan for their return to the home office. Finally, we queried them on their perceptions of the effect (benefits and drawbacks) the time they spent in Japan would have on their long term careers. For this last question, we asked specifically about whether and how they had enhanced their existing skills, how they had grown personally, and whether their Japan experience would likely have any financial effect on their careers. On the survey, we asked about their overall satisfaction with the long term career effects of their job in Japan (Question 33K) (Table 5.4).

Little knowledge about "what next." Our first finding, driving other comments, was that most women were uncertain about their next career steps. Even among the expatriates, who at least intended to remain with their firms, the majority of women appeared to have done little career planning. The exception was Carol (senior manager in the telecommunications firm). Before she accepted the job in Japan, she had negotiated—and been assured—a job at the same level as her Japan job. Interestingly, none of the others had made such negotiations or received such guarantees. While Amanda (the lawyer) knew she would have a job with her law firm when she returned to the United States, she had little idea of what level she would move into. Indeed, she commented that moving to Japan had probably hurt her career in terms of making partner at the same pace as those with whom she entered the firm. Even Helen, the senior manager in the Japanese branch of a major U.S. bank, had no certainty of a job in the home office that was appropriate for her skills. If she found no such job, she intended to move to another bank upon her return.

Such a nebulous situation about future jobs within their organizations when or if employees return to their home countries is certainly common—and well documented—among traditional expatriates. The vagueness stems from the firms as well as the employees. Many companies do not do sufficient planning when it comes to employees returning from posts abroad. Firms often are unable to tap fully the talent, knowledge and skills that those employees offer. As a result, employees sometimes take the initiative of forcing a discussion about their futures, as Carol did, if managers in their firms do not.

For many employees, jobs abroad represent major risks. The greatest is trying and failing, and *then* lacking a safety net of a guaranteed job. If employees and their managers in the parent firms fail to plan for the return *and* the employee fails in an overseas job, a real disaster can occur. Unfortunately, Connie's situation may not be atypical. She admitted that she was more excited about finding a job in Japan than in considering what she would do upon completion of her stay. As a result, she negotiated no guarantees regarding her career or jobs upon completion of her assignment.

When her two year commitment was drawing to a close, she began applying for posts in the United States. She applied for 33 jobs, had one interview, and received no offers. All this occurred within an organization where she had worked for almost 20 years, where she had been the "first woman" to do many top jobs and had a long record of successful performance prior to her Japanese experience. Accordingly, she left the organization for good. In sum, even expatriate women who work for global organizations and were sent by their home offices to Japan have little real security that their organizations will provide for them in the future.

Yet, despite the uncertainty about their future and a common feeling that organizations in general recognize only marginally the value of international work experience, the women were fairly positive. Certain groups felt more optimistic about the effects of their working in Japan on their long term career; all reported benefits of the experience in their lives in general. We classified the effects into three categories: job skill enhancement, personal growth, and financial impact.

Enhancement of job skills. Most of the younger independents, in particular, were quite positive about the impact of their experiences on their job skills. Some, such as Jane, Kiri, and Linda, commented that their jobs in Japan allowed them to develop specific job expertise, such as human resource management consultancy or advertising. Others, including Terri, felt their learning centered more on general job skills such as managing large budgets.

Still others, particularly those who had studied the Japanese language, used the experience to reinforce and perfect their language skills. While they expected their sharpened language ability would interest firms in the United States, few expected to find jobs solely on that skill. Even over the few years from the time that several of the independents arrived, they perceived a shift in what firms in the United States sought in their new hires. Linda, for example, who worked in a Japanese branch of a worldwide public relations firm, spoke only Japanese all day. While she acknowledged that her language skill had improved dramatically, she noted that "just being good in Japanese isn't enough to get a good job anymore." On the basis of her perception, she anticipated that firms would be more concerned about her knowledge of how Japan and Japanese business work than her language ability.

Other women mentioned enhancing business skills. In particular, they noted they had learned how to make and maintain contacts in Japanese business and how to conduct international business more broadly. Finally, several women mentioned raised awareness of the importance of the interpersonal side of business, including how to entertain and how to negotiate. They hoped that such skills would make them attractive to potential employers in their home country.

Personal growth. By far, the most frequently cited benefits to working in Japan related to personal growth in the women. Expatriates, independents and trailers alike repeatedly commented on being forced to new depths of "flexibility" as a consequence of working in Japan. Catherine, a former non-profit executive who followed her husband to Tokyo, eventually found work in a conference planning organization. During her move and early months in Japan, she had to learn to think about herself and her skills in an entirely new way. She spent several bitter months trying to find a position like the one she had left in the United States. Ultimately, however, she became creative about how to view her skill set and fashioned several jobs into something she found fulfilling.

In addition to looking more creatively at their job skills and job goals, several women learned to be flexible on their jobs. Mastering the Japanese way of doing business stretched their tolerance, openness and endurance! As Vicki remarked, working as a technical writer in a Japanese company taught her that she could work in *any* kind of corporate environment. While she hoped to avoid that fate by starting her own consulting business, she had developed the confidence to know she could endure—and succeed in—conditions she had previously abhorred.

Women also gained flexibility from dealing with Japanese attitudes toward women professionals in general. As they experienced sexual bias and harassment, they cultivated the ability to recognize and understand another cultural perspective. By grasping that perspective, the women also said they learned to concentrate on the important aspects of their jobs and to avoid being pulled into peripheral frustrations. In her work for a large U.S. beverage firm, Terri initially bristled at several behaviors that were quite different from her American habits. Learning to sort out the unimportant ones (e.g., letting Japanese men precede her onto elevators) had taught her to focus on the essentials of relationships rather than on surface behavior.

For many, working in Japan had been broadening on several levels. When she worked in her New York law office, Amanda confessed to being on a treadmill. She concentrated fully on her career within that organization. Amanda further observed that her New York law office was quite provincial: most of its lawyers discounted happenings outside New York as being of secondary importance. Indeed, she admitted that she had a similar attitude before joining the Tokyo office. As a consequence of stepping out of New York geographically—and psychologically—Amanda began to question her firm's values and how much she wanted to remain with the company. After a year in Japan, she found her New York firm no longer dominated her outlook or was her "whole world."

In another way, Deborah experienced a liberation from her firm. She noted that the U.S. computer firm that first sent her to Japan had been, till that time, her whole life. She had known only that firm and was fully committed to it and the project she worked on. As she matured and as she became more interested in Japan and Japanese martial arts, her awareness of and confidence in her options increased. Thus, when her expatriate assignment was complete, she left the company rather than return to the United States with the computer firm.

Such "shaking up" or reexamination of how much their firm or corporate career meant to them was uniform across the expatriates we interviewed. All referred to the tremendous personal growth they experienced in Japan and how their development had affected the way they would approach their companies and careers in the future. Working in Japan helped them set priorities and determine what was important to them and made them more skeptical about corporate demands they face. Several explained that they felt more "present oriented"—rather than always looking to the next career or life move, they were learning and enjoying their present circumstances. Others commented that they were more willing to take risks than before going to Japan.

Such questioning and increased confidence in themselves may help explain some of the poor success firms have had with repatriation in general. Perhaps all expatriates, male or female, are susceptible to personal growth abroad, which in turn causes them to question and become less committed to their companies when they return to their home countries.

An interesting, as well as optimistic, result seemed to occur even for Connie, who had such poor performance and overall work experience. Even though her job performance was a disappointment, she noted that her experience in Japan may yet have a positive long term effect on her career. Connie acknowledged that she was unable to successfully complete the job for which she felt she had the skills. Nevertheless, her failure to integrate into the Japanese branch of the agency had provided an excellent learning experience. Never having failed before, she became both more humble and flexible as a consequence of her situation. Both of these attributes, she felt, would serve her well in future endeavors.

SUMMARY AND CONCLUSIONS

Despite particularly challenging work settings, foreign women professionals in our study appeared to adjust quite well to work in Japan. They anticipated challenges (which indeed existed!) but found ways to overcome or adjust to them. Moreover, the foreign women professionals were generally satisfied with their overall performance and various aspects of their jobs. The group we studied relished the discretion, responsibility and latitude their jobs offered and were adamant that women can be successful in a wide range of workplace locations.

While adjustment, performance and satisfaction on the job are extremely important, much of what affects these features of jobs relates to life outside work. In the next chapter, we will examine how the women and their families dealt with living in Japan.

Chapter 6

Women's Lives Outside Work

Neither men nor women spend all of their lives working. A job in Japan demands adjustment not only to the working world but also to a strikingly different, for most foreigners, daily life. Learning to live comfortably comprises adjusting to the mundanes of life, among them food, climate, and simply getting around. The challenge of building a satisfying life outside the workplace can be tremendously draining yet exhilarating for foreign women professionals and their families in Japan. Success in these aspects is so important, for both the women and their families, because it can contribute greatly to women's success in their work.

In Chapter 6, we explore how the foreign women professionals assessed their adjustment to the non-work elements of their lives in Japan. The chapter comprises three sections. First, we review overall adjustment of the women and key parties in their lives. Next, we discuss how the women dealt with daily life in Japan. Finally, we examine the foreign women professionals' social lives in Japan, another crucial contributor to their overall adjustment. Within the discussion, we note how adjustment to life outside work relates to other factors, such as Japanese language ability or time spent with Japanese nationals off the job.

GENERAL ADJUSTMENT

Adjustment for foreign women professionals to life off the job in Japan has several ingredients. Besides their own adaptation to Japan, that of their husbands or partners, and that of their children, are important. Finally, women's adjustment may also be affected by reactions of family and friends outside Japan (e.g., the family "back home"). We address each in turn.

General Adjustment to Life in Japan

On the whole, the foreign women professionals were fairly satisfied with their adjustment to life in Japan. The survey showed that most women felt fairly well adjusted to general living conditions in Japan (Question 16A—self). They rated their adjustment an average of 4, on a 5 point scale where 5 meant "completely adjusted." At the same time, they acknowledged that irritations such as small apartments, crowds, and expensive food are part of the reality for everyone—foreigner and Japanese alike—of living in Japan.

Adjustment of Spouses and Partners

About a third of the women we surveyed were married or had long term partners. The 33 married women rated their husbands' general adjustment as slightly lower (3.8 out of 5) than their own (Question 16A—spouse). In addition, it became clear through the survey results that the women's adjustment to living in Japan was strongly related to the husbands' or partners' adjustment (correlation = .69, p < .00). These results are not surprising and in fact mirror those from earlier research about male expatriates.

The interviews provided more perspective about just how and under what conditions spouse or partner adjustment related to the woman's adjustment. Several of the married women had been the impetus for a move to Japan. When the men transferred without jobs, adjustment obviously was more difficult for them. Helen, a traditional expatriate who took a top job at an American bank, had faced a grueling decision on whether to return earlier than she had expected. When she accepted her initial overseas assignment, her husband had taken a leave from his job. Two years later, it had expired and he returned to the United States to resume his position. While he was in Japan, he had been quite unhappy about his opportunities and, in fact, was ready to return to the United States. As a result of his dissatisfaction, Helen was finding her own situation less attractive as well.

While Helen's circumstances were not uncommon, some women experienced quite different outcomes with their partners and spouses. Amanda, the corporate lawyer, moved to Japan with a man she subsequently married. A software engineer, he quickly secured a good job with the branch of an American investment firm. While Amanda had instigated the move, he had relished the chance for doing something different and, in fact, thrived in his position. Furthermore, he enjoyed studying Japanese, learned about the Japanese way of doing business and was making numerous Japanese friends. She commented that, in fact, he was better adjusted to life in Japan than she. His satisfaction helped her adjust as well. Indeed, at the time we interviewed them, they had recently decided to remain longer in Tokyo.

Although several women noted the strain of finding satisfying work for their husbands or partners, many felt their experience in Japan actually strengthened their relationships. Amanda's husband, for example, was instrumental in her learning to cope with the questioning of her competence that she encountered from skeptical Japanese clients. Because the two of them were geographically so far from family, they were forced to rely on and communicate better with one another.

Likewise, Connie, despite her failure at work in the non-profit agency, felt her marriage was stronger as a result of the time she and her husband spent in Japan. Furthermore, her disillusionment with her work performance had clarified for her the importance of her non-work life.

Adjustment of Children

Very few women in the survey had children living with them in Japan. Even so, the eight who did reported strong positive adjustment by their offspring. Indeed, the average rating was 4.6 (out of a possible 5) in terms of how well the women perceived their children to have adjusted to life in Japan. We also had one interviewee whose child was living with her in Japan. Raised there from the age of four, Donna's teenage son had spent his most conscious years in Japan. Donna felt her son was completely comfortable living in Japan. He was capable of traveling alone all over Tokyo, spoke Japanese fluently, and accepted Japan as "home."

Such responses confirm research (Black, 1992) that younger children often adapt better and faster than do their parents to living abroad. Even so, we can draw no firm conclusions from such a small survey sample or from the comments of the one mother among our interviewees.

Adjustment of Family in the Home Country

Some of the interviewees raised the issue of their families "back home" and how their reactions influenced the women's own adjustment. Two women reported that their families in the United States were *very* unhappy with their being in Japan. Amanda, the lawyer, recounted her parents' displeasure that she had adjusted so well (after a year); further, they were apparently "horrified" that she and her husband had agreed to stay another year. Linda, working for a worldwide public relations firm, conveyed her family's irritation that she had sought (and found) a job in Japan. Her conservative U.S. family considered her decision to be "weird" and pressured her to return. Evidently, their pressure worked to some degree. Linda commented that part of her rationale for returning to pursue an M.B.A. degree was her parents' urging her to return.

In a somewhat different vein, April faced internal pressures relating to family. A trailer and former consultant, April followed her husband to Japan and commuted back to the United States for several months finishing up consulting jobs. Once she settled in Japan, however, she felt uncomfortable not being in the United States as often because of her aging parents. Before moving to Japan and even while commuting, she had been "accessible" to them, had they needed her for medical or other advice. In Japan, she felt quite disconnected. Thus, she and her husband faced a decision about how long to remain in Japan as her parents became older and more frail.

In sum, family (particularly parental) reaction and concerns about relatives in the home country appeared to weigh heavily on women's overall adjustment.

ADJUSTMENT TO EVERYDAY LIFE IN JAPAN

Japan is, without a doubt, a country where living conditions differ markedly from those of most industrialized economies. Its geography, with arable or habitable land representing only 13 percent of total land mass, means that the approximately 130 million inhabitants must content themselves with small houses and gardens.

In addition, historical and perhaps cultural factors led post–World War II Japan to subordinate the needs of individual Japanese to the economic growth goals of the society. As a consequence, the Japanese have fewer public parks, fewer houses on sewer lines, and much higher consumer prices than their counterparts in the United States or Western Europe. Public transportation is plentiful and reliable, unlike in the United States, but also extremely crowded and uncomfortable in most urban areas. Housing—both rental and purchased—is expensive, forcing most middle-class urban families to purchase homes in remote suburbs. The businessmen breadwinners, then, must accept long daily commutes.

In short, North American or European women professionals moving to Japan typically encounter a dramatic change in life-style, usually for the worse. They must tolerate smaller apartments, costlier goods, longer commutes, and fewer urban green spaces than they may be accustomed to. On the positive side, they have no fear of crime. For several reasons, Japan enjoys one of the lowest violent crime rates in the world. As a result, it is far safer (although never entirely so) for foreign women professionals to move freely within urban areas. On almost all other dimensions, however, daily life in Japan is much tougher and offers more hassles. Successful adjustment to the mundanes of daily living is thus important for foreign women professionals to feel at home in Japan.

To learn more about their reactions to general living conditions in Japan, we asked the women how they felt about several aspects. We also asked them to rate their perceptions of how well their family members had adjusted. In most areas, such as living conditions, social norms, food, shopping, transportation, weather, and recreational facilities, they reported that they and their families had adjusted fairly well (Table 6.1). The women rated their adjustment to these areas between 3.5 and 4.5 (with 5 = "completely adjusted"). The women rated their families' adjustment likewise as "moderate" in these areas.

Adjustment was not altogether positive in all areas, however. The women faced significant adjustment problems in two key areas: health care and housing. We address each in turn.

Health Facilities

Contrary to their generally positive responses about most aspects of living in Japan, the women were more concerned about health care in Japan. As a result, they rated their own adjustment to Japanese health facilities to be only "average" (3.0 out of 5).

Such a reaction likely stemmed from several factors. First, Japan's health system is a strongly government controlled system. Waits in doctors' offices are long and the system emphasizes basic services rather than specialty care. Since a majority of the foreign women professionals in the study came from the United States, they were probably most accustomed to the U.S. health care system. If these women were used to a system that seeks to provide more "consumer orientation," a full range of medical services, and access to the latest medical technology, it is little surprise that they found it difficult to accommodate to the Japanese system. Japan does have private hospitals, including some specifically for foreigners, which in facilities and orientation more closely resemble those in the United States. Unfortunately, we did not ask women to indicate whether their dissatisfaction was with traditional Japanese or foreign sponsored facilities.

Another reason why the women may have had more difficulty adjusting to health care facilities may relate to their language ability. Clearly, inability to communicate in fluent Japanese with a health care provider who speaks limited English could affect the women's reactions to health facilities or providers. Being in a situation where the women or their family members were sick or injured made them particularly vulnerable and helpless. Being unable to understand completely what

Table 6.1
**Adjustment to Living Conditions in Japan of Respondents, Husbands/
Partners, and Children (scale: 1 = not at all adjusted to 5 = completely
adjusted)**

Adjustment areas	Mean	Standard deviation
Living conditions -- Respondents	4.0	(0.68)
Husbands/partners	4.1	(0.72)
Children	4.3	(0.71)
Social norms -- Respondents	3.6	(0.74)
Husbands/partners	3.7	(1.13)
Children	3.9	(0.80)
Food -- Respondents	4.4	(0.80)
Husbands/partners	4.6	(0.87)
Children	4.8	(0.71)
Shopping -- Respondents	4.0	(1.1)
Husbands/partners	4.0	(1.2)
Children	4.0	(1.7)
Cost of living -- Respondents	3.8	(1.0)
Husbands/partners	3.6	(1.0)
Children	--	--
Transportation -- Respondents	4.2	(0.97)
Husbands/partners	4.0	(0.92)
Children	4.6	(0.76)
Weather -- Respondents	4.2	(0.85)
Husbands/partners	4.0	(1.0)
Children	4.7	(0.76)
Recreational facilities -- Respondents	3.6	(0.88)
Husbands/partners	3.3	(0.88)
Children	4.1	(1.1)
Health facilities -- Respondents	3.0	(1.1)
Husbands/partners	3.0	(1.1)
Children	3.6	(1.1)

transpires or to communicate needs and symptoms doubtless increased
the anxiety that illness provokes in the first place.

When we statistically tested this assumption, that women with less
Japanese language ability were also less comfortable with Japanese
health facilities, we found, not surprisingly, that indeed there was a relationship ($r = .38$, $p = .00$). Evidently, women who are more comfortable expressing their physical needs and problems in Japanese are best
able to adapt to differences in health care practices and facilities. It thus
lends more support for the idea of providing language training, since

adjustment to health care seems to be the most difficult aspect of adjustment to Japan.

Housing Costs

The second major area that some women reported caused them difficulty in adjusting was the cost of housing. Long the most expensive city in the world, Tokyo has rents that astonish nearly everyone who moves there. Indeed, many women commented that until they lived in Tokyo, they also were unable to fathom the prices. Tokyo real estate, in 1994, was the most expensive worldwide, followed by that in Hong Kong.

The survey asked no specific question about costs of housing but many interviewees raised the issue of housing subsidies as important elements of their job negotiations. As we anticipated, widespread differences existed in terms of what the various groups of women received in housing support. In short, the expatriates and most trailers (because of their husbands' or partners' subsidies) were not dissatisfied with their housing arrangements, in contrast to many of the independents, some of whom had elaborate "roommate arrangements" to afford housing.

All expatriates received liberal housing allowances. Indeed, because of exorbitant rental rates, expatriates would not be able to afford apartments without substantial financial support. Many had large (by Japanese standards) modern apartments in fairly central Tokyo neighborhoods. Consequently, the expatriates we interviewed expressed little discontent with their housing.

Interestingly, two of the independents we interviewed also received housing subsidies. In fact, Sandy, who worked for a worldwide moving company, received the most generous compensation package of any of the non-expatriates. Her perquisites comprised a housing subsidy, a car, home leave every other year, and language study support. Another independent, a manager with a British commercial office leasing and management firm, also received a housing subsidy.

Aside from these exceptions, other independents received little housing support. None of the "hybrids," hired in the United States for positions in Japan, and none of the other locally hired women had subsidies for housing. In general, they were expected to pay for their own housing. In a sense, they received less equitable treatment in the large Japanese firms than did their Japanese colleagues, many of whom had access to company sponsored housing. Those working for smaller Japanese companies faced more similar conditions to those of their Japanese counterparts, who also receive no subsidies or company housing.

Finding and renting housing, therefore, represent an expensive proposition, particularly for women who plan to work only a few years in Japan. To rent an apartment, most people must prepay up to 6 months' rent; usually 3 months of that rent is non-refundable. Moreover, many Japanese apartments are completely unfurnished, requiring renters to buy kitchen equipment (e.g., refrigerator and stove) in addition to furniture. In sum, housing, especially when it is not subsidized, represents a large expense in foreign women professionals' budgets.

Several interviewees, frustrated with their lack of housing subsidies, recounted unsuccessful attempts to gain greater support from their companies. In one case, the woman felt that the housing subsidy had been a source of either miscommunication or manipulation by her Japanese employer. Vicki, the technical writer, was hired in the United States by a Japanese firm to work in Japan. Her understanding, based on a verbal agreement with a company representative, was that it would pay 20 percent of her rent, up to a certain amount. With this understanding, Vicki rented a two-bedroom apartment in an upscale apartment complex. Although by U.S. standards, the apartment was rather small, in Japan it was considered quite comfortable. However, after she had signed the lease and paid enormous initial fees, she learned that the company would only pay 10 percent. Despite her protests, the firm representative denied having promised more; as a result, Vicki was forced to accept the situation. Yet, even after 2 years, the incident continued to rankle her. She learned—and advised—that such agreements should always be in writing before coming to Japan.

SOCIAL LIFE IN JAPAN

A key aspect of non-work adjustment for foreign women professionals working in Japan is their ability to create satisfying social lives. Feeling comfortable in Japan means, among other things, being content with networks of friends and the pattern of social activities that women develop in Japan.

Because many of the women we studied had little experience living in Japan before, we were curious about how they created their lives, particularly since many had to build them "from scratch." We were, therefore, interested in several aspects of building a satisfying social life: (1) the extent to which women interacted with Japanese outside work, and, related to that, the extent to which their language abilities (or lack of abilities) seemed to influence those interactions; (2) the importance, and difficulty, of socializing with expatriate men; and (3) the ways in which they created networks of friends.

Interactions with Japanese Outside Work

We examined interaction among the women and Japanese outside work through questions in both the survey and interviews. We sought to understand the amount of time the women spent with Japanese, the extent to which they felt their adjustment to living in Japan related to their interaction with Japanese friends, and the degree to which their language abilities seemed to help their social lives.

Amount of time spent with Japanese. Several survey questions probed the extent to which the women professionals made contacts and friends among the Japanese. The survey asked how much non-work time, during an average week, the women spent with Japanese. They reported that, on average, they spent 32 percent of their time outside work with Japanese friends. This average response is influenced by several women who spent almost all their free time with Japanese, thus skewing the average upward. Nevertheless, this average still appears surprisingly high, given that a third of the respondents were married and presumably spent much time away from their jobs with their families. In fact, however, when we compared non-married and married women, in terms of the amount of time they said they spent with Japanese, the results were ambiguous. While married women, on average, spent less time outside work with Japanese (24 percent of their time) than non-married women (39 percent), the difference was only moderately significant (t-value = 2.24, p = .03). Even so, apparently unmarried women do tend to have more non-work contact with Japanese.

Adjustment in relation to time spent with Japanese outside work. We also queried the women on the extent to which they felt they were comfortable socializing with Japanese outside work. Their level of comfort averaged 3.5 (on a 5 scale), or "moderately comfortable." Given the apparent wide divergence of experience levels in Japan, such a fairly moderate response is unsurprising. We also found a strong positive relationship between the amount of time off the job that the women spent with Japanese and the degree to which they were comfortable socializing with Japanese (r = .46, p < .00). Furthermore, as expected, the women who were most at ease socializing with Japanese outside work also felt they had adjusted well to living in Japan. Clearly, the more time women spent with Japanese in non-work situations, the greater their adjustment seemed to be to the nuances of Japanese culture, and in turn, to living in Japan. The difficulty, however, is in determining in which direction the relationship flows: do women who socialize with Japanese outside work feel more comfortable with living conditions or do women who are better adjusted tend to socialize more with Japanese outside work?

Such a question has important implications for cross-cultural training. The two are likely interconnected and reinforcing. That is, women who are more flexible will accept changes in living conditions easily and will be more open to forming non-work relationships with Japanese. These relationships, in turn, help them better understand life and living in Ja-

Table 6.2
Adjustment to Socializing with Japanese: Relationship to Time Spent off the Job with Japanese, Language Ability, and General Adjustment

Adjustment to Socializing with Japanese and...	r	p
Time	0.46	0.00
Japanese speaking ability	0.51	0.00
General adjustment to Japan	0.39	0.00

pan (for a complete review of acculturation, see Mendenhall and Oddou, 1985).

Importance of language skills. Language ability clearly influenced whether one is likely—or able—to be comfortable socializing with Japanese. The relationship between the foreign women professionals' confidence in their Japanese speaking abilities and comfort in socializing with the Japanese was indeed quite strong ($r = .51$, $p < .00$). True for expatriates in any culture, the ability to enter into the social world of the native population depends greatly upon the expatriate's linguistic ability. The same held for the foreign women professionals in our study. Both the survey and interviews showed a consistent pattern in this regard (Table 6.2). Women who had good Japanese language skills, such as Linda (the public relations expert) and Kiri (the human resource consultant), most often reported having a large network of Japanese friends. Those with little or no Japanese language ability, including Amanda (the lawyer) and Carol (the telecommunications executive), commented that they spent most of their social lives with other expatriates.

What difference does it make whether women do or do not socialize with Japanese outside work? The importance rests primarily with whether such socializing seems to contribute to the women's general adjustment. As the survey results revealed, the women who were comfortable socializing with the Japanese reported higher levels of general adjustment to the Japanese culture ($r = .39$, $p < .00$). Such adjustment to living in Japan should, in turn, ease women's adjustment to their working lives.

Indeed, several women we interviewed—particularly those with Japanese language skills—composed their social lives largely around friendships and networks with Japanese people. For Eileen, the Japanese-American woman working in a telecommunication firm, developing a social life in Japan was relatively easy; her large network of relatives gave her a natural entry into Japanese society. She spent much time with cousins, and, through them, made other Japanese friends as well. In addition, Eileen shared an apartment with a Japanese roommate and met others through her. Because of her Japanese language ability and her family ties to Japan, Eileen was able to create a social life full of both Japanese and American friends.

Jane, working for an American advertising agency, grew up in Japan and spoke fluent Japanese. She socialized outside work with some of her male Japanese colleagues from the ad agency and had developed comfortable relationships with them. Linda, with the public relations firm, also spoke Japanese and had mostly Japanese friends, whom she knew from a previous visit. She had lived in Japan years earlier as a student. At that time, she had a serious relationship with a man who subsequently died. Before his death, however, she met many of his acquaintances and friends. Deborah, the data processing manager, found a strong network of Japanese friends through her deep involvement in aikido. She became so committed to martial arts and to Japan that she chose to live in a Japanese neighborhood and develop primarily Japanese friends. In each case, the women felt quite well adjusted to living in Japan, in large part because of their capability to communicate with Japanese people. These women all spoke Japanese very well, if not fluently, and pointed to that as a key.

Socializing with Foreign Men

We expected that foreign women professionals would be more likely to adjust to living and working in Japan if they had the ability to make friends with Japanese people. While the interviews supported this basic idea, some women raised another element that many considered to be as—if not more—important. Interestingly, some interviewees suggested that the issue was not whether women were well networked with *Japanese*. The group we interviewed, which overwhelmingly consisted of single women, felt instead that the lack of opportunities to meet eligible men was a more important influence on their non-work adjustment.

Indeed, nearly every woman had an anecdote that supported this supposition. For example, Carol, the telecommunications manager, divorced and uninterested in remarriage, reported that she was having the time of her life. Because Tokyo is large and cosmopolitan, it attracts world class entertainment, which she had previously never had the chance to enjoy. Further, her business position and African-American background have accorded her opportunities to meet people she never would have in the United States. She has received invitations to embassy functions; when world renowned reggae bands visited Tokyo, she attended parties in their honor. Carol seemed to have a highly satisfactory social life, spent almost entirely with expatriates. Interestingly, other women who also networked only with expatriates, such as Helen and Irene, reported being satisfied with their social lives, thus casting some doubt on the criticality of socializing with Japanese to adjust.

One area of great frustration to many women was the lack of male friendships and potential partners. Most single interviewees consistently complained about the paucity of eligible males. Few could envision becoming romantically involved with a Japanese man, primarily because of the large gap in marriage role expectations between foreign women and Japanese men.

On the other hand, single expatriate men seemed in short supply, largely because they found Japanese women so attractive! Terri, the young, nice looking woman in charge of special event marketing at a U.S. beverage firm, stated that many foreign men were overwhelmed by the attention they received from Japanese women. Indeed, contrary to their image as passive retiring women, many of the Japanese women were quite aggressive in their pursuit of potential foreign mates. This unusual, and flattering, experience for male expatriates was in stark contrast to the more egalitarian, complex relationships demanded by women in the United States. As a result, according to Terri, many foreign men found the Japanese women a welcome relief. Echoing Terri's frustration was Linda, an advertising agency employee. The day we interviewed her, she told us, with some excitement, that she would be having drinks that evening with a foreign man she had met on the subway. This was the first date she had had in months! Given Linda's stunning beauty and vibrant personality, it was hard not to credit her viewpoint that the lack of eligible men had created a gap in her social life.

Terri's viewpoint on the attention that foreign men sometimes receive in Japan was verified by other women we interviewed. In addition, various authors have documented and analyzed it. One of the most insightful was Pico Iyer, in his 1991 book *The Lady and the Monk*, the story of a year he spent in Kyoto, during which he developed a friendship and affair with a Japanese woman.

None of these women, all in their mid- to late-20s, was seeking a mate. Nonetheless, they each commented that a reason for returning to the United States in the coming 5 years was the hope that they might find someone to marry. In short, foreign women professionals can create fairly satisfactory social lives for themselves in Japan. Even so, young, single women interested in meeting and socializing with foreign men faced some barriers to totally adjusting to Japan. Clearly an issue for any single woman contemplating working in Japan, building a satisfying social life with expatriate men is conceivable but apparently rather difficult.

Building networks. The women in the study used several avenues to find friends in Japan, particularly foreign friends. For many, the organization of foreign women professionals (Foreign Executive Women) in Tokyo that cooperated with our study was a key venue for meeting other foreign women professionals. An organization started by expatriate women in the early 1980s, FEW provides women with professional support to meet the challenge of working in Japan. In addition, the regular monthly meetings offer women the chance to meet and make connections that turn into friendships. Six of the women we interviewed identified FEW as an important source of both connections with and support from other foreign women professionals.

Interviewees mentioned other organizations that offered opportunities for them to meet other expatriates. For those who could afford it, or whose organizations paid the membership fee, the American Club was cited as an excellent place to meet expatriates. Donna mentioned the College Women's Association of Japan, as well as the American Chamber of Commerce, of which she was a Board member. Eileen, the young Japanese-American woman working for a U.S. telecommunications firm who has strong political aspirations, was chair of the local group of a U.S. political party. Connie, at the non-profit organization, had founded a Celtic dance group which she described as a major place where she socialized. Carol, the black vice president at a U.S. telecommunications firm, joined a group of other black expatriate professionals living in Tokyo who participated in many social activities together.

Many women commented that friendships they made in Japan were deeper than those at home. The lawyer, Amanda, mentioned that, for the first time in her life, she was unable to spend important holidays with her family. Instead, she and her husband celebrated Thanksgiving and Christmas alone or with new-found friends in Japan. She felt the bonds they forged by creating their own traditions together or with friends made these connections very special and more intense than those in the States. This sentiment struck a chord with us as well; one of us, who lived in Japan for 8 years, found that the friendships made there with expatriates, as well as some Japanese, have lasted more than 20 years.

SUMMARY AND CONCLUSIONS

Generally speaking, the foreign women professionals in the study appeared to have adjusted well to living in Japan. Their main areas of concern or complaint were health care and housing costs. Further, single women in particular perceived limited opportunities to meet eligible foreign men and noted it as a frustration that somewhat hindered their satisfaction with life outside work.

Overall, however, most women expressed satisfaction with their lives in Japan. In many cases, they seemed genuinely stimulated by the variety of people they encountered, as well as the many cultural events and entertainment opportunities. A few, such as Donna (working for the office location firm) and Deborah (working for the data processing department of a bank), considered Japan to be their "homes," and they had little intention of returning to the United States in the near future. Even those who expected to return within the coming 1–3 years acknowledged that they had created a life outside work that gave them the basic emotional sustenance they required. Yet, as we have noted throughout the chapters on home and work adjustment to Japan, the women suggested several ways that they, as well as organizations hiring women, could help ensure success off the job for women working in Japan. In the last two chapters, we discuss these recommendations.

Part III

Piercing the Bamboo Wall

As previous chapters repeatedly affirm, foreign women professionals can successfully work and adjust to living in Japan. Such success bodes well for businesses and organizations seeking human resources for global operations. To ignore women as a potential staffing source of Japanese operations, in particular, makes little sense for business firms.

Obviously, not all foreign women will succeed in assignments in Japan, just as not all foreign men do. Nonetheless, organizations need to identify those women likely to succeed *and* offer assistance, where possible, to heighten the chances of success.

Previous chapters have suggested that several factors may contribute to or hinder likelihood of success. Such factors rely upon attributes and actions both of the women themselves as well as of their organizations. Chapters 7 and 8 identify and offer some recommendations both for organizations and for women on ways to more fully use the pool of foreign women professionals available to work in Japan, *and* to increase the likely success of those hired or sent. In Chapter 7, we focus on recommendations for companies. The recommendations, which stem from the current study as well as previous research on expatriates in general, pertain to selection, recruitment, preparation, support and repatriation or return of foreign women professionals working in Japan. Some of these recommendations apply to male expatriates as well.

Part III closes with Chapter 9, which proposes suggestions for foreign women professionals. These recommendations comprise ideas from the research done for the present study, as well as our own experiences and others' past research.

Chapter 7

Recommendations for Firms

To gain full benefit of using foreign women professionals for positions in Japan, business firms can take several actions that will enhance the opportunity to find and support such women. In Chapter 7, we discuss several actions firms can take in selecting, recruiting, preparing and providing support to foreign women professionals. In addition, we provide other recommendations for firms that can reinforce a supportive work environment for women, such as hiring Japanese women professionals for appropriate jobs.

SELECTION OF WOMEN

Decisions about what type of employee to hire obviously depend greatly upon the position or job requirements that a company needs to fill. In fact, firm managers should first conduct a careful analysis of the position and attributes required for it (Black, Gregersen and Mendenhall, 1992; Ettorre, 1993; Solomon, 1994; Tung, 1988). In many cases, jobs that need to be filled by foreigners are strategic; sometimes, however, they are technical, "troubleshooting" or even developmental (Black, Gregersen and Mendenhall, 1992; Dowling, Schuler and Welch, 1994; Tung, 1981, 1988). Job requirements clearly will influence the type of person a firm seeks.

For example, many jobs held by foreigners in overseas subsidiaries are seen as quite strategic. As liaisons between the home and host operations, such jobs often involve coordination and control, information and technology exchange, or management development for succession planning (Black, Gregersen and Mendenhall, 1992: 59; Mendenhall, Dunbar and Oddou, 1987). For those positions, firms may in fact need to find someone from the home office with sufficient company experience to address and fulfill the strategic purposes of the job.

Conversely, other positions in subsidiaries have more technical content, and, as a result, demand less direct links with the parent operations. In some cases, jobs may require some understanding of host country business practices but less specific knowledge of the company. For example, the job may require interaction with other foreigners, as clients or suppliers, rather than Japanese. Many of the locally hired women we studied found their positions because their firms needed someone to interface with other foreign firms or customers in Japan. Sandy, for instance, secured her position in an international moving company because it required someone who could work with both the foreigners who were moving in and out of Japan, *and* with their (mostly) foreign employers.

In other cases, a job in Japan may require interfacing with a department in the parent company, such as the production department, but not entail extensive, in-depth firm knowledge. Finally, some jobs may require technical skills available, but in short supply, in Japan (e.g., software design). These types of jobs might, therefore, be inappropriate for most host country nationals, but be quite apropos for "independents." Thus, a crucial question for decision-makers in any firm is the type of people various positions require in overseas operations: in essence, could some jobs that are unsuitable for Japanese be adequately filled by a foreigner who is not a current member of the organization (i.e., could the subsidiary hire an "independent"?)? Such thinking breaks a traditional pattern that has assumed "foreigners" in jobs meant "transferees." Evidently, job requirements may not always warrant an expensive transferred expatriate, but instead be filled satisfactorily by a foreigner already living in Japan.

RECRUITMENT

Once organizational requirements are clearly established for jobs in overseas operations, the recruitment process should match that need. Obviously, recruiting approaches will hinge upon whether a job necessitates an expatriate or whether a locally hired foreigner will fit the needs. The approaches to recruiting each type of employee differ, as we discuss later.

Recruiting Expatriates

Much research has focused on issues relating to recruiting, and selecting, expatriates for overseas positions (Black, Gregersen and Mendenhall, 1992). The recruitment of personnel to fill key positions overseas depends on a firm's overall staffing approach. Several researchers (Dowling et al., 1994) have classified staffing approaches into four categories. An ethnocentric approach emphasizes use of parent country nationals in all key positions of overseas subsidiaries, where parent country refers to the firm's headquarters country. A polycentric approach uses host-country nationals (i.e., hires locally), while a geocentric approach ignores nationality and simply chooses the best person for the job. Finally, a regiocentric approach is geocentric but is limited to a single region. Obviously, *where* a firm looks for people to staff a Japanese subsidiary is partly a function of its overall strategy. Thus, recommendations we make concerning recruitment must be considered in light of a firm's particular approach to international staffing.

Broaden the pool. The first recommendation involves increasing the number of women candidates for positions in Japanese subsidiaries. Given our predictions about future needs for employees who are capable of dealing effectively in a global environment (Chapter 1), many firms will be forced to expand their selection pools for employees for such overseas operations. This study suggests that firms operating in Japan consider more closely labor pools they have traditionally overlooked or neglected. In particular, trailers and independents who seek work once they are based in Japan often represent an untapped, yet quite talented pool of potential employees.

Our study uncovered numerous examples of these "on-site" potential employees. Irene, former vice president and marketing manager from a U.S. bank in Chicago, had left her job to try "something new"—consulting on her own in Japan. Although she sought her own projects, she was also open to job offers from firms in Japan. Deborah, an electrical engineer with a master's degree from a prestigious U.S. university, went to Japan as a traditional expatriate. When her assignment finished, she became an "independent," resolving to remain in Japan, rather than return to the United States. April, an expert on quality improvement processes, went to Japan as a trailer. After several months of settling in, she began looking for ways to use her skills in Tokyo. These women are representative of the highly skilled foreign women professionals already in Japan whom foreign—or Japanese—companies could hire. The existence of such a potential pool takes some pressure off firms that face the difficulties of finding appropriate transferees.

With regard to recommendations that fit recruitment of women more specifically, the study helped to identify several. First, a firm can take several key steps to ensure it has a sufficient number of women in its candidate pool. Foremost is opening the recruitment process so that qualified women receive information about specific jobs overseas (Taylor and Eder, 1994). Often the method for generating a candidate pool can be haphazard at best, as pressured decision-makers rely on established internal networks to find potential expatriates (Hixon, 1986; Miller, 1973). In the past, such environments have worked against women in part because of (often unfounded) notions about whether they can succeed in foreign assignments (Adler, 1994; Black, Gregersen and Mendenhall, 1992). Particularly for countries like Japan, firms must counter possible bias against assigning foreign women professionals. Indeed, in Adler's (1984a, 1984b, 1984c) early research, home country managers' reluctance to send women abroad was the greatest hindrance to their success!

By openly posting foreign assignments or otherwise ensuring all potential candidates are aware of a position in Japan, firms increase candidate pools, circumvent the influence of erroneous preconceptions about candidate requirements, and ensure (in the United States) legal compliance. In 1991, the Civil Rights Act was broadened to cover overseas assignments of U.S. employees explicitly (Taylor and Eder, 1994). Unless a local law, as opposed to a cultural custom, is clearly violated, a U.S. firm cannot exclude from consideration any candidate for overseas assignment on the basis of gender, race, religion or ethnic background.

Link assignments abroad to career development. Besides opening the recruiting and selection processes, firms may examine other staffing activities. Increasingly, firms are reviewing their career development procedures to assess the role that experience or assignments abroad may play for employees. As firms *anticipate* international staffing needs, they can build training and experience into employee career paths (Black, Gregersen and Mendenhall, 1992).

Moreover, if international experience is a criterion for higher level positions, then it behooves management to foresee such needs for women employees to avoid adding another layer to the "glass ceiling." In short, incorporating international experience into career development for employees is simply good corporate practice. Additionally, it may force firms to consider women employees as viable candidates for overseas assignments.

In our study, Carol was illustrative of the value of identifying high potential employees for whom international experience is important. Her telecommunications firm had selected her as a "fast tracker" several years earlier. She had, as a result, completed several posts designed to advance her knowledge and move her upward. When she reached the appropriate career stage, she received the opportunity to undertake an assignment in Japan. Because of the extensive career development and planning, the offer was not a surprise to her. Consequently she was better prepared psychologically, as well as professionally, for the challenge.

Let the women decide! Finally, firms should avoid excluding women from consideration for possible jobs in Japan, even if they have characteristics that firm managers may assume will make them decline overseas posts. Being part of a dual career couple, for instance, should play no role in whether a woman is considered for—or offered—a position abroad. Firm decision-makers may erroneously prejudge a male spouse's willingness and ability to move overseas with his wife. Dual career situations indeed present special challenges, to men as well as women. Nevertheless, earlier research has indicated that male expatriates who are part of a dual career couple are just as successful at adjusting to overseas assignments as those who are not (Black, Gregersen and Mendenhall, 1992: 68). Our study would support such findings; in several cases where the spouse or partner "followed" the woman, the adjustment was quite favorable.

On the other hand, especially for overseas jobs, family adjustment is important for an employee's adjustment. Thus, assessing family situation is legitimate in recruitment and selection decisions. Nevertheless, rather than categorically dismissing women who are part of dual career couples, firms should include them, when their job qualifications merit it, in candidate pools.

To ease the dual career challenge, firms may offer a range of assistance. Some provide the spouse access to an on-site network to help in job searches. Others offer "employment dislocation allowances" to help pay for training or to compensate the loss of a job. For instance, 3M offers a dislocation allowance of up to $5000 for the spouse of an expatriate (Black, Gregersen and Mendenhall, 1992: 72).

Recruiting Women Already in Japan

Much research has focused on issues relating to recruiting and selecting expatriates for overseas positions (Tung, 1988). Recruiting women who live in Japan (i.e., trailers and independents who go to Japan on their own) presents special challenges for firms, beginning with simply finding and identifying potential candidates among such a dispersed pool. Several recommendations for this process emerged from the interviews.

Use foreign firms' networks. First, foreign firms in Japan may identify trailing spouses through their own transferred expatriates (i.e., the spouses/partners who accompany expatriates). As each firm creates its data base, it can then share that information through a network with other firms in the area. Through the network, firms may circulate data about spouses' backgrounds, qualifications and job aspirations. Many interviewees commented that such a process exists in Tokyo but occurs only informally, through word of mouth. A more formalized system, coordinated by an organization such as the American Chamber of Commerce, would enhance the spread of information about trailing spouses—male or female—seeking work in Japan.

Use local headhunters. Another potential avenue is local headhunters whom firms use to locate qualified Japanese candidates. Catherine, herself a trailing spouse, said such headhunters have in the past favored Japanese over foreign (especially trailing spouse) candidates for their pool of human resources. She recommends that foreign firms that use headhunters pressure them to help the trailers of the firm's own expatriates. Urging such headhunters to create a labor pool of trailers streamlines the process of identifying potential talent firms could hire locally. Moreover, it offers foreign women professionals the chance to communicate their qualifications to more potential employers.

Tap local professional organizations. Another recruitment avenue to help foreign firms identify both trailing spouses and independent women professionals is FEW, the Foreign Executive Women organization that comprises over 200 members in the Tokyo area. FEW's monthly meetings as well as its newsletter provide ways to advertise for positions best staffed by non-Japanese, who need not be transferred expatriates. Indeed, several interviewees mentioned FEW as one of the first organizations women join when moving to Tokyo. Many women have found it to be a valuable networking source through which they have learned of potential positions.

FEW encompasses all types of women professionals working or living in Tokyo. Other organizations specialize in certain groups of foreigners. For example, another key professional organization is Kaisha (the Japanese word for "company"). With over 400 members, the Tokyo-based Kaisha group embraces foreigners with various professional backgrounds who primarily work for Japanese firms.

Some of Kaisha's members were recruited in their own countries (i.e., "hybrids") to work in Japan; others were independents who went to Japan to seek jobs on-site. Interestingly, as a group, Kaisha members seem more committed to being in Japan, and sometimes less concerned about whether they work for a Japanese or a foreign firm. Many of Kaisha's members are foreigners who have encountered a "bamboo ceiling" in Japanese firms and may be seeking opportunities in foreign companies. Others may be nearing the end of contracts with Japanese firms but want to remain in Japan. Also, on average, they often have more sophisticated and higher level Japanese language skills as a consequence of working in Japanese firms. Such a group, therefore, represents another pool of potential candidates for foreign firms.

Use the local media. A final recruiting avenue is advertising in the major English language publications such as *The Japan Times.* While this represents more of a shotgun approach, it may reach a different group of potential foreign women professional candidates. For example, because such publications circulate throughout Japan, firms may attract potential recruits living outside the Tokyo area who are, consequently, not part of the professional networks discussed earlier.

Recruitment Frustrations and Discrepancies

Firms that recruit women already living in Japan (i.e., trailers and independents) or that hire women in their home countries specifically for jobs in Japan (i.e., hybrids) typically offer positions and packages quite different from those expatriates receive. Interestingly, the interviewees had perspectives on what firms could do in this regard.

Many interviewees in the independent, hybrid and trailer groups remarked that they received much lower compensation packages than expatriates. Indeed, most strongly resented the discrepancies. One trailing spouse, for example, hired at the Tokyo branch of a U.S. bank, received a salary commensurate with her qualifications. She received no other benefits, however, such as housing support, home leave support or pension. Her firm's rationale was that her expatriate husband (working for another organization) received such benefits and thus her bank need not provide them for her. Her resentment at being treated as a second tier employee eventually led her to quit the job. Another trailer said her boss explicitly sought to hire trailers because they "came with an expatriate package" (through their husbands), including access to expensive expatriate enclaves, like the American Club. He boasted of gaining benefits so "cheaply."

Some interviewees voiced similar frustrations, particularly single women who received no housing support. While none expected to receive a full expatriate package, all felt some housing and basic language support was reasonable. As they observed, most full-time Japanese employees of larger firms receive housing support, through either company provided apartments or low interest house mortgage loans. Finally, to do their jobs effectively, many of them needed Japanese language skills; while many were competent, all felt they could improve.

In short, trailing spouses and partners, independents and hybrids increase firms' pools of qualified candidates for positions in Japanese operations. While they tend to be less costly than expatriates, most women suggested that firms offer a compensation packages that strikes a balance between a bare bones, "take it or leave it" approach and the full blown set of benefits commonly provided to expatriates. Most women wanted to have challenging work but also wanted to feel appreciated for it.

In sum, firms that seek foreign women professionals for their Japanese operations—both transferred expatriates as well as women hired locally or for Japan based jobs—should benefit from the decision. Companies that restrict their recruiting and hiring horizons to men, particularly to male expatriates, pursue a costly path. Not only will their candidate pools be smaller, but they may fill some positions with expensive expatriates whose talents may be "wasted" in an assignment better filled by qualified "on the scene" candidates.

PREPARATION

A third critical area in which firms may enhance likely success of foreign women professionals, particularly transferred expatriates, is their preparation for assignments. Research over the last two decades has shown that cross-cultural training, both pre-departure and on-site, enhances expatriates' adjustment to the culture, their job performance and their cross-cultural skills (Black and Mendenhall, 1991; Lanier, 1979). Black and Mendenhall (1991), for example, found that 11 of 15 studies of the relationship of cross-cultural training to performance reported a positive significant connection.

Interestingly, in spite of evidence that such preparation helps managers, most companies provide no or inadequate cross-cultural training to expatriates. According to one survey (Oddou, 1991), only 35 percent of U.S. firms gave expatriates any cross-cultural training at all, a result confirmed by other research (Black, Gregersen and Mendenhall, 1992: 92). With such low odds, such firms likely provide even less training to foreigners hired in-country. But this is penny-wise, pound-foolish behavior. Adequately preparing people, whether expatriates or locally hired staff, for overseas assignments can enhance success. Firms providing little cross-cultural training support run the risk of expatriate failure and potential "damage" in lost productivity for their firms. Disillusioned expatriates, for example, may return home early, at enormous cost; or locally hired employees may leave to join a competitor. The loss to firms, therefore, is more than monetary; it can lead to loss of morale in the Japanese subsidiary and to wrecked customer relationships (Adler, 1991; Oddou, 1991; Black, Gregersen and Mendenhall, 1992).

For firms that do seek to prepare employees, especially women who will work in Japan, prior research and this study offer recommendations of what training to provide. Black and Mendenhall (1991) offer a useful way to analyze the issue through a set of questions:

- How different is Japanese culture from Western cultures?

- How much interpersonal interaction will foreign women professionals expatriates have with the Japanese, both within the workplace and outside?

- How different from previous jobs, and how difficult, are the jobs the women will hold?

In the next section, we review each of these points.

Japan: A Culture Apart

Most people from industrialized Western cultures, even those with some experience living in Japan, find its culture "very different" from their own. Japanese culture has few similarities with Western cultures, despite its superficial adoption of many American and European styles, music, and food. At the deepest level of assumptions about how the world works, the Japanese are the product of a history, religion and way of life that translate into a set of values and norms that most Westerners find unfamiliar.

Given such a pronounced difference between Western and Japanese cultures, expatriate women transferred to Japan may require in-depth cross-cultural training before their assignments. If a woman has extensive previous experience and knowledge of Japan, this aspect of training clearly may receive less emphasis.

Extent of Likely Interaction with Japanese

The amount of interaction with Japanese that foreign professional women encounter may also influence the type and extent of training to deliver. Many positions for foreigners require little direct contact with Japanese supervisors or subordinates, and frequently those Japanese have good English ability. In such cases, pre-departure cross-cultural training can be less rigorous because there will be fewer occasions that will necessitate cultural adaptation by expatriate women. A typical example was Marcy, controller for a subsidiary of a U.S. consumer goods firm. She has contact primarily with the non-Japanese vice presidents of the subsidiary; in addition, she has few Japanese subordinates. Her pre-departure training was shorter than that of Carol (the telecommunications executive), whose job focused often on extensive negotiations with external, Japanese customers. For Carol, an understanding of such issues as Japanese history, culture, and ways of doing business was also critical.

Novelty and Difficulty of Positions

Finally, the "newness" or "toughness" of women's positions in Japan may drive the nature and extent of pre-departure training. Situations requiring more rigorous training emerge when jobs in Japan entail duties and tasks that differ substantially from those in previous positions. Moreover, women who are likely to confront special obstacles in accomplishing their tasks will likely need more extensive and perhaps very specific preparation. Tasks such as leading a firm's entry into the Japanese market or working with Japanese government agencies rarely have clear paths on how to accomplish them. Adding such trials to situations where firms have constrained resources or rapidly changing environments further complicates women's jobs. All add difficulty to jobs that are already taxing because of their newness. For example, Terri, hired as a special events marketing director for a U.S. beverage firm, assumed a job in which she had no direct experience. Her background, including her knowledge of Japanese, appealed to her employer and led to her recruitment and selection. Given the newness of the job *for her*, however, she could have used additional training. On the other hand, the job was not particularly "tough," since a predecessor had developed the basic infrastructure and job tasks.

Pre-Departure Training: Options

Pre-departure training can differ in its length, methodology, and content. The greater the need for pre-departure training the longer it likely should or will be. Some researchers recommend that total training, both before departure and in the country, should reach a maximum of 180 hours (Black, Gregersen and Mendenhall, 1992). The method or approach to the training itself will vary, depending upon the extent of need or rigor. Training rigor is the "degree of mental involvement and effort that must be expended by the trainer and trainee in order for the trainee to learn the required concepts" (Black, Gregersen and Mendenhall, 1992: 97). More rigorous training demands active trainee participation and experiential learning techniques, such as role plays and simulation. Low-rigor training relies more on passive techniques such as films, lectures and books. Finally, the training's content will hinge upon the needs of the women receiving training. Those anticipating high interaction with Japanese require more language training and cultural understanding; those facing new or very difficult responsibilities will need job-specific training.

While much of the pre-departure training recommended for firms applies equally to male and female expatriates, certain aspects demand special attention for women. One of those pre-departure training areas likely to be useful for Western women expatriates who work in Japan is how to deal with sexual harassment. As discussed in Chapter 5, many foreign women professionals had encountered such harassment; we repeatedly heard about the negative effects of such breaches of sexual and professional respect by Japanese customers, colleagues and bosses. Given the prevalence of sexual harassment and its impact on women's self-esteem, Western firms, in particular, should anticipate that it will be a problem and equip women expatriates with the skills they need to cope effectively.

In addition to readings and lectures on Japanese attitudes toward women, and how these attitudes can result in unpleasant behaviors, women may need specific training in how to deal with likely situations. Role plays, cases, simulations of typical breaches of professional and sexual courtesy may help brace them for possible awkward confrontations in Japan. Effective training can help women identify and practice coping skills that allow them to respect the Japanese culture but also to retain their sense of self-esteem and professionalism. For example, women might engage in a role play in which they face some of the typical "sexist" remarks common among male Japanese clients. Women may experience comments such as recommendations that (single) women be married or comments on the physical attributes of female servers in restaurants. Hearing such comments in training would prepare women and give them practice in dealing with their emotions and how they will react to those making such comments. Such role plays could be easily generated through experiences of women currently working in Japan. Finally, training should include an identification of how to obtain support and understanding outside work to help face these situations productively.

Many of these recommendations for expatriate training are fitting as well for foreign women professionals hired *in* Japan. Clearly, training needs will depend on the specific situations of those foreign women hired in Japan. For example, trailers may have had some pre-departure training through their spouses' or partners' organizations. Independents may have extensive prior experience in Japan as students in high school or college. Because they often have more comprehensive background knowledge and language skills, they may require less thorough training on-site.

Our interviews found that most firms refrain from providing training to foreign women professionals hired in Japan. The argument against offering training is that the women hired specifically for jobs in Japan are unlikely to remain long term with the firm, since most are less likely (than expatriates) to work for the company once they return to their home countries. Such thinking, however, may save money only in the short term. Even if the women remain with the firm only in Japan, the quality of the work they do there clearly affects the firm's performance. Firms pay significantly less to hire independents or trailers than they do to send and maintain expatriates. In a sense, then, the training cost is negligible for those hired in Japan.

ON THE JOB SUPPORT

Once foreign women professionals, whether sent as expatriates or hired in-country, assume positions in Japan, their firms can take numerous steps to increase their chances of success. The activities include, for example, providing ongoing training; supporting women's memberships in outside organizations; granting a clear, high level job title; and clarifying, as much as possible, their job responsibilities and performance standards.

On-Site Training

If foreign women professionals receive pre-departure (or pre-job) preparation, why would they need additional training? More importantly, if women receive little or no preparation, how could in-country training help? Perhaps the most poignant example of the need for on-site training emerged during our discussions with Connie. An expatriate sent to Japan by a non-profit organization, she received essentially no pre-departure training. Much to her surprise, Connie discovered an extremely hostile work environment in Japan. The receiving branch, Connie, and her office in the United States had miscommunicated (or not communicated at all) about expectations or the nature of her job. Soon after arrival, she began to experience what to her were serious professional slights. In response to those affronts, she used tactics that had served her well in the United States: directness and assertiveness. For example, she felt her job in Japan lacked real responsibility and, furthermore, that the branch was not fully using her talents. To address this issue, she drafted a list of the needs of the Japanese subsidiary (as she perceived them) and identified how her skills and knowledge could help meet them. Her boss ignored her suggestions and repeatedly disregarded her attempts to change her job tasks; in fact, over time, he reduced her responsibilities even further.

Connie was also challenged by a male Japanese colleague, who tried to have his desk placed "ahead" of hers. She had enough knowledge of Japan to understand what desk placement meant, but her response was unproductively direct and assertive. He tried to have her desk moved while she was away from the office, but she countermanded his orders, saying that her desk was "too big" to be moved. She eventually lost the battle, and much credibility with the staff.

During our interview, Connie acknowledged that she had learned too late that her direct, assertive approaches were inappropriate in Japan. She lamented that only recently had she met a cross-cultural consultant. Indeed, she had hired the consultant (and paid personally for the consultant's services) to begin understanding the environment she lived and worked in. Finally, in her last year of a three year assignment in the Japanese subsidiary, she was gaining insights into how to work in Japan. The consultant had helped Connie understand the events she experienced and how her behaviors had exacerbated rather than helped the situations. Sadly, Connie admitted that by the time she began working with the consultant, it was far too late to remedy her situation.

As Connie's experience illustrates, training or access to a cross-cultural consultant during the early stages of working in Japan can be, for some people, highly necessary. For most, it is often very effective. One benefit of on-site training is its ability to cement the theory learned in pre-departure or "initial" training. The realities of adjusting to working and living in Japan are much more complex, and difficult, than pre-departure training can demonstrate.

Indeed, others have suggested that on-site training can be quite effective. Black, Gregersen and Mendenhall (1992: 106) offer four advantages for cross-cultural training in the country of destination: (1) given its relevance, trainees are usually more highly motivated to learn; (2) once trainees are on-site, they have baseline experience with the local culture as a foundation for learning deeper cultural values, norms, and ideas; (3) on-site training offers an environment where trainees can immediately apply what they learn; and (4) the environment itself makes the training content real.

Foreign women working in Japan face unusual challenges. They encounter complexities of establishing and maintaining their professionalism in an environment where their credibility may be more frequently questioned. They also need to learn how to use the advantages they have as women. The situations they experience may demand interpretation, which good cross-cultural consultants or trainers can offer. Such assistance can be invaluable in decreasing the emotionalism that surrounds these issues.

Little clear guidance exists on how much training should be given before departure, upon arrival, or on the job. Much depends on the particular job and individual woman. Women with a great deal of Japanese experience and language ability may need training before departure and upon arrival that focuses more on job specific tasks than culture. Novices to Japan, likely to have much interaction with Japanese in their jobs, may need most of their training after beginning the job, with escalating focus on cultural aspects as time in Japan increases (Black, Gregersen and Mendenhall, 1992).

For all, but particularly for women with extensive Japanese interaction, language training will be valuable on an ongoing basis, as well as prior to departure for Japan. Although the links between Japanese language ability, job performance and other aspects of adjustment were somewhat mixed in our study, learning the language certainly cannot hurt. Indeed, it should be supported for foreign women professionals who wish to improve their performance, particularly when their jobs require a high degree of interaction with the Japanese.

Organizational Memberships

In addition to providing ongoing cross-cultural and language training, firms can help foreign women professionals by covering membership costs in professional and social organizations in Japan. An organization like FEW, for example, offers an avenue for foreign women living in Tokyo to meet other women professionals living and working in Japan. The monthly meetings usually combine a social hour with a talk on some aspect of adapting successfully to Japan. Furthermore, the organization is an excellent forum for meeting and networking with representatives of other foreign firms in Tokyo. Thus, membership in FEW affords women a way to share and understand their experiences of working in Japan, but, more importantly for firms, it offers a potential source of business.

Several women we interviewed belonged to the American Club, for American expatriates and their families. Membership is more diverse than that of FEW, so the American Club provides an excellent place to meet a variety of others living and working in Japan. Further, it offers a valuable way to network with male expatriates in business. Likewise, the American Chamber of Commerce affords women another way to meet other Americans in business in Japan.

Other organizations provide means for women to meet and socialize with Japanese. Many of these groups revolve around some interest or hobby, such as flower arranging or aikido. Deborah, the data processing manager, for example, was a foreign woman professional who became quite well adjusted to living in Japan and friendly with several Japanese through her aikido club.

Job Titles

One of the most important actions firms can take to increase foreign women professionals' likely success is to grant job titles that are significant and as clear as possible. Japanese in general, and businessmen in particular, are much more sensitive to status and differences in hierarchy than are Westerners, particularly Americans. Thus, firms can greatly enhance foreign women's credibility by ensuring that their titles signal the companies' confidence in their abilities and competence. Obviously, titles should be accurate. If there is a choice of titles to bestow, however, firms should adopt higher ones, which in turn increase the bearers' (in this case, foreign women professionals') status. This relatively small cost to firms can yield high potential payback in helping to increase foreign women's effectiveness.

Women in the study provided several examples of the importance of titles. Donna, in charge of office leasing with a large foreign firm, began her job with the title of "manager." An English term, the word *manager* was phonetically rendered into Japanese on her business cards. While most Japanese, particularly those who spoke English, understood the term, it conveyed little specific information. As it does in the United States, the concept "manager" covers a wide spectrum of possible jobs within an organizational hierarchy in Japan. Thus the title communicated nothing about Donna's status within her organization. Indeed, the very vagueness of the term seemed to imply to the Japanese that her position was unclear to the firm. In short, her title did little to enhance her credibility with Japanese business contacts. Donna eventually lobbied to change her title to one more specific and meaningful to Japanese with whom she worked.

Conversely, Carol, as a "vice president" of a major U.S. telecommunications firm in Japan, found her title was invaluable in establishing professional credibility with clients. Japanese clients and colleagues questioned neither her competence nor her authority to make major decisions. Because her title clearly indicated her position as a member of top management, her professional competence was never questioned. In sum, foreign firms should consider implications of the job titles they confer on foreign women professionals working in Japan, particularly for those who are not part of the top management of the Japanese subsidiary.

Job Clarity

A final action to increase the chances of foreign women professionals to be successful in Japan is to guarantee their jobs are as clear and well defined as possible. As we discussed in Chapter 5, the more ambiguous the expectations are about women's jobs, the less likely the women are to adjust well to their work. Thus, one way firms can enhance likely success is to provide much information about anticipated and actual job responsibilities and performance standards. While such practices make generally good sense, they are particularly significant for people who are simultaneously adjusting to challenging work and living situations.

To help foreign women understand job expectations, some firms arrange for the person taking a job to overlap with the person leaving it. Assuming there is a job predecessor, many women commented on how useful it was for them to learn the ropes directly from someone who had been performing it. For many, the predecessors were able to smooth the transitions for key constituents (e.g., introduce the job taker to Japanese clients and suppliers). Particularly critical in a country where business depends upon personal relationships, such introductions helped both the incoming women and their new clients adjust to the change. Finally, some women noted that working closely with previous jobholders allowed the predecessors to "hand over," figuratively, their credibility with subordinates. In so doing, the incoming women professionals avoided some of the time typically spent establishing basic credibility.

While ideal, such overlap between job leavers and takers is not always possible. Sometimes predecessors leave quickly; sometimes, the position itself is new and thus there is no "predecessor." Regardless, incoming foreign women professionals need to spend time with their direct supervisors at the onset of the job to clarify expectations for the position.

OTHER ACTIONS TO ENHANCE SUCCESS

Beyond providing support to the foreign women professionals themselves, this study generated other recommendations for what firms can do to make the Japanese subsidiary environments more sensitive to foreign women's specific issues. In our interviews, the women identified several actions their firms had taken, or could take, to improve the Japanese subsidiary as a workplace supportive of foreign professional women. Three frequently raised recommendations follow:

- To hire qualified Japanese women for career track positions in the subsidiary;
- To instill a corporate culture that condemns sexual harassment and discrimination;
- To train personnel who work closely with foreign women professionals.

We review these actions in turn.

Hiring Career Oriented Japanese Women

Most of the foreign women we met argued that foreign firms could greatly help their situations by making the work environments better for Japanese women professionals as well. Indeed, they repeatedly called upon firms to hire Japanese women for career track positions in Japanese subsidiaries as a crucial step in creating a work environment that is supportive of women in general.

As we described in Chapter 4, most Japanese firms resist hiring women for anything but clerical positions. Yet as the world's "oldest" population, facing a potentially devastating shortage of talent in the next 20 years, Japan may be forced to consider hiring women for other types of positions. Moreover, significant numbers of qualified Japanese women are increasingly available (Japan Economic Report, 41A, 1994), for several reasons. One of the most important is that Japanese parents no longer refrain from providing a 4 year college education to their daughters, as they had until only recently. In fact, many of these young women are as talented as their male counterparts, graduating from the top Japanese universities in increasing numbers. As a result, the pool of qualified Japanese females will only grow (Japan Economic Report, 41A, 1994). Finally, many talented young Japanese males still hesitate to join non-Japanese firms (Black, Stephens and Rosener, 1992; Huddleston, 1990).

Such trends bode well for foreign firms in Japan. Because qualified young women are largely excluded from blue chip Japanese firms, they often seek jobs at joint ventures or with foreign companies. Consequently, Western firms can significantly advance two goals by hiring Japanese women for career track positions. First, they raise the quality of their own job applicant pools by including talented young Japanese women. Second, they can help build a work environment that supports foreign professional women by creating a place where both Japanese and foreign women's job abilities are taken seriously.

An interesting by-product can also emerge from such an organizational approach. In several cases, the foreign women professionals worked jointly to develop the Japanese women who were hired by their firm. For instance, Helen, as part of senior management at the Japanese branch of a U.S. bank, had set up monthly luncheon meetings with Japanese women managers in the subsidiary. While the subsidiary actively recruits Japanese women for its career track positions, few had reached upper management. In her position as a senior manager, Helen was a role model of a woman who dealt with Japanese men as both peers and subordinates. In her discussions with the Japanese women managers, Helen drew out their frustrations and fears about climbing higher in the organization, and provided insights and guidance. Even though Helen was *not* Japanese herself, she nonetheless felt that, at a minimum, she provided an example of a woman in a powerful position with some ways of thinking about the challenges of rising in the company.

Eileen, working in the Japanese subsidiary of a U.S. telecommunications company, offered another example of a foreign woman professional acting as a model for younger Japanese women. In fact, one of her senior managers had asked Eileen to "take under her wing" one Japanese woman in particular. Evidently the Japanese woman, although well qualified and on a career track within the company, behaved in "girlish" ways considered feminine and attractive in Japan, but inappropriate for professional situations. Eileen helped the woman understand that her behavior was off-putting to male peers and superiors. Once the woman understood this, Eileen assisted the young woman in developing a more professional demeanor.

For Eileen (as it would be for many women), this task was a challenge. She had to be very careful in how to discuss these behaviors, given the

Japanese sensitivity to loss of face. Fortunately, Eileen's own background as a Japanese-American, and her extensive knowledge of Japanese culture and language, helped her in the effort.

Censuring Sexual Harassment and Discrimination

Hiring qualified Japanese women into foreign firms represents only a start. Firms must also create organizational cultures that do not condone sexual harassment or discrimination against women, Japanese or foreign. To do so is, of course, extremely complicated from several perspectives.

Obviously, transferring organizational norms wholesale from the West to Japan will fail. Such thinking applies to sexual harassment and discrimination as well. Particularly foreign firms based in the United States may well have norms that are stringent and very culturally based regarding sexual harassment and discrimination. For example, Americans value directness of speech, which results in norms concerning how to deal with sexual harassment. Women are encouraged and learn to deliver clear, explicit communication that sexual overtures are unacceptable in the workplace.

While direct approaches may work well in the American work environment, they may fail in Japan. Such directness, for example, would doubtless lead to tremendous loss of face for any Japanese male rejected in this manner. Several women used more indirect ways of discouraging unwelcome advances. Some, for example, mentioned (possibly fictional) fiancés back home, accompanied by a firm "no" that avoided direct censure of the men's conduct. While it is impossible to delineate precisely *how* a foreign firm should "translate" its organization's stance on sexual harassment and discrimination for the Japanese subsidiary, it is important that it be done carefully and thoughtfully. Cross-cultural consultants as well as senior level Japanese management should be utilized to create an approach to achieving the goal of a work environment that is intolerant of sexual harassment and discrimination, yet is culturally acceptable to Japanese employees. This is a challenging but not impossible goal, as more and more international firms are discovering as they create global corporate cultures (Trompenaars, 1993).

Foreign firms and their professional women employees, therefore, face challenging situations in deciding how to deal with such issues in culturally acceptable ways. For example, one woman who encountered flagrant overtures from clients at a social dinner, quietly enlisted the support of her male Japanese colleagues to ward off the unwanted approaches. Another woman tactfully told a Japanese man she was flattered but uninterested by his advances. In both situations, the women were less direct and confrontational than they would have been in the

United States. Also, in both cases, their approaches worked and the men refrained from bothering them again.

Training Colleagues Who Work with Foreign Women

A final recommendation for firms to help foreign professional women be successful in Japan is to train personnel, in the subsidiary, who work closely with the women. The people who should receive training fall into three key groups: other foreigners, particularly non-Japanese expatriates; Japanese subordinates (where appropriate); and Japanese peers and supervisors.

Other foreigners. Non-Japanese personnel, such as male expatriates, can play significant roles in helping women professionals establish and maintain credibility. Several women in our study commented on the critical capacity their male bosses and peers had to ease the acceptance of the women. Many women—as well as one American male we talked to informally—commented that success in Japanese subsidiaries depends upon the performance and accomplishment of *all* employees, men and women alike. Thus, the senior male executives realize that not supporting their foreign women employees could only hurt the operations' achievements.

Training for such foreigners, as a result, should focus on learning how they can help the process of establishing and building women's credibility with Japanese inside and outside the firm. As Amanda so tellingly explained, even her impeccable legal background and credentials helped little until she had been accepted by Japanese as credible. The senior partner in her law firm's Tokyo branch assisted greatly in building her acceptance by clients with his actions. His judicious and laudatory introductions, remarks about her legal acumen and insistence that clients work with her when he was unavailable proved invaluable for her. A training course could help other foreign men do what Amanda's partner did naturally. Such a course could focus on how colleagues and bosses could use culturally appropriate ways to achieve acceptance of foreign women professional colleagues. Amanda's colleague, for instance, well aware of the importance Japanese attach to university background, used the prestige of Amanda's alma mater to build credibility and establish her competence. He knew enough about Japanese culture to use that hook to craft her credibility. Familiarity with culture, and how to use such knowledge tactfully, could help male colleagues and bosses enhance the success of foreign women working in Japanese subsidiaries.

Japanese personnel within the firm. The Japanese personnel within subsidiaries who interact with foreign women professionals are also good candidates for training. As women reported in Chapter 5, some Japanese subordinates, particularly older female secretaries, may resent foreign women. In the worst cases, such subordinates may try to sabotage foreign women; at a minimum, many make work life difficult. Moreover, Japanese male subordinates may have trouble adjusting to working with foreign women. They may view them as powerless and question their professional competence (Black, Gregersen and Mendenhall, 1992; Lebra, 1992). Women need to be aware of and address such concerns to prevent their subordinates from trying to undermine them.

Thus, training for such groups should emphasize the legitimacy of firms' choosing foreigners, and particularly foreign women, to occupy posts in the subsidiary. The training may need to state explicitly that foreign selection decisions typically ignore sex and age, as compared to Japanese company systems. In addition, just as foreigners need to understand Japanese culture, Japanese subordinates may need to grasp the cultural foundation for work behavior of foreign women professionals. Japanese may see foreign women's behavior, for example, as abrasive and unfeminine. Particularly Japanese women subordinates may need to realize (even if they cannot accept) that such behavior is more common in other cultures.

Finally, given a penchant for Japanese women to be more "nurturing," training for female Japanese subordinates might draw upon this dimension. Specifically, training may focus on their inclination toward caring for others by showing that foreign women professionals do need help and support. Some of the foreign women professionals we interviewed, for example, were able to tap the nurturing instinct among some of their Japanese female subordinates. Terri, for example, frustrated by her own secretary's unwillingness to answer phones or do copying, eventually found a more sympathetic secretary in another department who helped her. Indeed, the woman was so enthusiastic to see a younger woman pursuing opportunities denied her (as an older Japanese woman) that she was very amenable to assisting Terri.

Japanese peers and superiors. A final group who could benefit from training on how to deal with foreign women professionals is the Japanese peers and bosses of those women. Japanese peer colleagues, in particular, can be difficult obstacles, as we saw with Connie in the non-profit firm. Like their foreign counterparts, Japanese peers and bosses need to understand the benefits to supporting all employees in a subsidiary, including foreign women.

Also, since such groups can be instrumental in dealing with clients or suppliers, some training should focus on involving the participants in identifying ways to help establish foreign women professionals' credibility. By thus vesting in the process, Japanese bosses and peers would become more accepting of their responsibility to help the foreign businesswoman be successful.

GOING HOME

Foreign firms have obligations to enhance the success of all employees in their Japanese subsidiaries, certainly during the time the employees work in Japan. Foreign women professionals who have been successful in Japan represent unusual (because there are simply so few such women working in Japan) and valuable resources to foreign as well as Japanese firms. Recognizing that value should lead firms to act proactively regarding repatriation. Firms can do more to ensure the success of women while they are still in Japan by considering what will happen when they leave. Such planning applies to expatriates and independents alike.

Expatriate Return

When firms send foreign women professionals on assignments to Japan as expatriates, the obligation and planning for repatriation are obviously easier. Yet, even for transferred expatriates, many firms lack repatriation programs for expatriates, male or female (Adler, 1991; Black, Gregersen and Mendenhall, 1992). The most common complaint from returning expatriates is that firms have no ready or appropriate positions for them, or that the positions they receive make little use of the skills and knowledge gained overseas. In one survey of American expatriates, 40 percent of the respondents said that on their return to the United States there was no specific job for them (Oddou, 1991). Furthermore, many repatriated employees claim that the jobs they receive upon return have narrower scope and less autonomy than their jobs overseas (Napier and Peterson, 1989). Lastly, even when employees received some predeparture training, they almost never receive "repatriation preparation," which often entails more traumatic shocks. Adjusting to being "home" rattles many expatriates and their families in more profound ways than they experienced moving abroad (Black, 1992).

As a consequence, many expatriates leave their firms within their first year after returning. Black (1991), for example, reported that 26 percent of the American repatriates he surveyed reported they were actively looking for a different job after they returned to the United States. In short, most firms fail at integrating returning employees.

Losing foreign women professionals who are transferred as expatriates may have further negative consequences than the admittedly steep cost of losing a successful, globalized manager. First, successful women expatriates represent scarce resources. Given their small numbers, successful women who repatriate can be powerful models to other women considering high level corporate careers. Returning successful women exhibit to others that it *is* feasible to do well in countries like Japan. Equal employment opportunity pressures to open up selection processes for overseas positions (Taylor and Eder, 1994) will force U.S. firms to proactively seek out women candidates for overseas positions. One way of increasing the attractiveness of assignments abroad is to demonstrate that other women have been successful.

Successful returning foreign women are also invaluable sources of information and insights on how to adapt to living and working in Japan. Potential women candidates can readily identify with them and thus view them as very credible informants (Black and Mendenhall, 1991). Their advice on how to form good working relationships with clients and subordinates, how to develop a satisfying social life, and how to deal with distance from family and friends can provide information for other women who are deciding whether to accept—or pursue—overseas posts. Given the general lack of information about what women experience, involving them in pre-departure training for potential expatriates could help validate what cross-cultural trainers impart.

Given the importance of retaining women repatriates, what can firms do to increase the likelihood of their staying with the firm? On the basis of our interviews, as well as earlier research in the area (Black and Gregersen, 1991, 1992; Black, 1992; Tung, 1988), the most critical step firms can take seems to be to plan for the return well in advance. Some women recommended that women and their managers discuss the return *before* the assignment begins! At a minimum, the women advised that returns be discussed and planned at least 6 months in advance; research in this area supports this policy (Black, Gregersen and Mendenhall, 1992).

The reasons for such planning are tied directly to the women's ability to perform in their jobs in Japan. The uncertainty of what would happen post Japan distracted many from their ongoing jobs in Japan; this finding correlates with prior research on the negative effect of uncertainty on the job performance *after* repatriation (Black, 1992). Moreover, such apprehension seemed to make them receptive to other alternatives, weakening their commitment to staying with the organization. Amanda demonstrated these tendencies. Being in Japan, she had begun to feel distant from her law office's New York base. Not only did she feel far away geographically, she began questioning its norms and values. The further lack of clarity regarding what her position would be when she returned to the United States undermined her commitment to staying with the law firm. If she indeed leaves, her firm will lose a valuable liaison with Japanese clients, and a role model for other women lawyers who might consider working in the Japan branch of the firm.

Given the impact of their performance in Japan, firms should likely give attention to planning for the expatriates' return. Clearly, one of the most critical aspects is the nature of the jobs that returnees will have in home operations. Unfortunately, the expatriate women we interviewed noted that most of their companies had made few provisions for their future positions. Only Carol had an idea of the job she would have in the United States in her telecommunications firm. She commented that, before she took the Japan post, she insisted her manager discuss and set tentative guarantees about her future opportunities. Few women—or men—expatriates are as forward thinking in urging their firms to plan ahead.

Independents

What about foreign women professionals working in Japanese subsidiaries who are *not* expatriates? We focus here on the independents (both locally hired and "hybrids" hired in their home countries for posts in Japan). Because trailers' location decisions are likely to be heavily influenced by their husbands' or partners' careers, firms may find it more difficult to incorporate them into the home operations.

Many independents in our study expressed interest in continuing to work for their firms once they returned to their home countries. Yet none reported any system to help her—or her firm—identify appropriate positions in the parent company. If they sought employment with their firms in the home operations, the women expected to be treated as any new applicants would be, despite their knowledge of the firms' Japan operations.

Such apparent lack of planning on how to use such women is disturbing. Many of them had a good command of their firms' global challenges from on-the-job experience in one of the important subsidiaries. Firms wishing to increase globalization would be well served by finding ways to identify independents, both male and female, who work in overseas branches and encouraging them to continue work for the firms once they return to their home countries. These "candidates" have been tested; the firms already have information about their job skills and performance. Why waste such invaluable resources? A global human resource planning data base would be one avenue firms could use to help locate and develop such independents.

SUMMARY AND CONCLUSIONS

Chapter 7 has suggested that firms can do much to increase the probability of success of women professionals working overseas. Some recommendations apply equally to male expatriates. Firms truly wishing to globalize and use their human resources as wisely as possible should carefully consider these suggestions. In addition, foreign women expatriates themselves can do a great deal to enhance their own success in Japan.

In sum, firms have many options of ways to improve the chances of

finding talented women professionals for overseas posts as well as enhancing their success. An intriguing aspect of working to improve foreign women professionals' situations is that firms may enhance the
overall work environments of Japanese operations for other groups, most
critically for Japanese professional women.

We turn in Chapter 8 to recommendations for the adventurers themselves, the professional women who work—or want to—in Japan.

Chapter 8

Recommendations for Women

No one can understand why I'm doing this after all the problems I had adjusting, but I've just agreed to stay in Tokyo for another year.
Surprised foreign woman professional

Despite—or perhaps because of—the challenges, the women adventurers we studied often surprised themselves by wanting to remain in Japan longer than they initially intended. We have profiled the engineer who came for 2 years, remained for another 2 years beyond that and then ultimately decided to stay at least "until her aikido instructor dies." The woman quoted was one who had a particularly difficult adjustment, having never lived outside the United States or had any interest in doing so before her Japan assignment. Even she admitted that she was captivated. Clearly, working and living in Japan as a foreign woman professional not only are viable, but for many women provide an environment in which they thrive.

To understand what conditions help women do well in Japan, we asked our sample group for recommendations they would offer to women considering working in Japan. Their comments fell into four general categories: (1) how to prepare for and seek a job in Japan, (2) what to do (or not do) on the job, (3) what to do (or not do) off the job, and (4) how to prepare for the return to one's home country. We discuss findings and insights for each category of recommendations.

FINDING AND PREPARING FOR A JOB IN JAPAN

As we have noted throughout this book, the approaches women took to various issues often diverged, depending upon the ways in which they found their jobs. Nonetheless, several common themes emerged on the issues that foreign women professionals should consider in seeking to work in Japan.

Three areas were of particular interest. First, the women had several comments on attitudes toward finding a job in Japan. Next, several offered suggestions on how to get settled, including assuring they received a fair compensation package and building in key perquisites where possible. Finally, many women had advice on the nature and type of preparation they thought were useful before moving to Japan.

Finding a Job

Several women noted that the economic environment changed dramatically in Japan between the late 1980s (when many of the women we studied had found their positions) and the mid-1990s. Many initially went to Japan because of the slow economies in their home countries. The younger American independent job seekers saw Japan as a way to bypass limited opportunities in the United States. Thus, several mentioned that assessing the economic environment of their home and target countries (in this case Japan) offered a way to determine employment opportunities. Indeed, some women commented that looking for positions in Japan in the mid-1990s would be quite difficult, compared to the conditions they encountered 3–7 years earlier. Because of the tight conditions currently facing job seekers, some women suggested that it was even more important to have a job in Japan *before* arriving.

The expatriates faced none of the uncertainty regarding having a job in Japan; some of them, however, made suggestions for how to reduce ambiguity about their returns after completing an assignment. Several suggested that women hold discussions (about the nature of the job they would have upon reentry into their home countries) *before* taking a job in Japan. In one case, a woman admitted making a grave mistake by assuming there would be *any* job for her, let alone one with greater responsibility. Thus, to reduce stress later during the overseas assignment, several women advised building into the transfer some assurance about their situations upon finishing the assignment.

For those who choose to go to Japan and search for work on-site (either as independent seekers or as trailing spouses or partners), the women had several suggestions. Their advice tended to focus on developing the willingness to be flexible and creative. Several women commented on the difficulty of moving into a job like the ones they had left. Others noted how disappointed they were to find no jobs that completely ful-filled their expectations. Catherine, a trailer, described extensive "soul searching" that she and her "trailing" acquaintances experienced upon arriving in Japan. Having left fulfilling careers to follow a spouse or partner, and unable to find work easily in Japan, she and many others sought refuge in returning to school or in doing volunteer work, to main-tain a sense of self-esteem. Trying to stay busy and productive was the key, even if it meant doing something outside their traditional disciplines or career areas.

Thus, in seeking work, many women sought jobs that were comple-mentary to their professions, particularly when they were unable to find jobs that exactly matched their goals. For instance, being willing to do marketing *and* advertising would open more avenues for women than just seeking employment in one or the other area.

Related to this, numerous women commented on the importance of using networking to discover opportunities. Traditional sources of net-working included the groups open to women professionals, many of which we have mentioned. The principal such group was FEW, Foreign Executive Women in Japan. In addition, several women urged job seek-ers to use contacts at traditional business sources, such as the American Chamber of Commerce in Japan. Still others mentioned Kaisha, the group for foreigners who work for Japanese firms. Finally, Emily, a Jap-anese-American working in a telecommunications firm, suggested seek-ing out and networking with Japanese women as well, rather than depending solely upon foreign women. For her, members of branches of American political parties in Tokyo, such as the Young Democrats, were especially important.

Often women suggested using more innovative networking ap-proaches. The woman who sought a position with a European consumer products firm did not receive the job there, but, because she so impressed the man who interviewed her with her enthusiasm and persistence, he recommended her for a job he knew about at another firm. She got the second job, although it was very different from what she had expected.

As women uncovered job opportunities, their emphasis and sugges-tions shifted to how they assessed their potential employers. Several women recommended considering the ownership of firms and men-tioned disparities between Japanese and foreign owned firms. In general, the women we interviewed considered the foreign owned firms (even subsidiaries that had mostly Japanese employees) to be more open to the idea of hiring foreign women professionals. Moreover, they felt those firms were better prepared and willing to give women "true responsi-bility." As we mentioned earlier, at least a quarter of the women we spoke with had been frustrated at the expectation that they would "serve tea" or act as a "token foreigner" in their jobs in Japanese firms. Thus, assessing the likelihood for genuine responsibility and a chance to learn was critical.

Finally, as we discussed in Chapter 7, firms appear to differ in the level and type of training and support they offer foreign women professionals. That extends to the networking within firms as well. Helen, one of the senior managers, remarked that foreign companies typically support networks for foreign women and women in general. Indeed, she was active in the Foreign Executive Women's network. In addition, within her own bank, she was encouraged to act as a mentor to younger Japanese women as well.

Getting Settled

A second aspect of finding and preparing for a job in Japan focused on issues of "settling in." The experiences of traditional transferees and independent job seekers differed, in some cases dramatically. As one independent seeker commented, the expatriates are typically shielded from some of the "red tape" related to becoming settled in Japan. Nevertheless, expatriates and independents alike offered advice.

They stressed two areas in particular: (1) having the organization provide various types of support and (2) gaining a fair compensation package.

Cross-cultural advice and support. One traditional transferee commented that she should have built into her compensation package some ongoing consultant assistance for understanding and working with the Japanese, once she arrived in her job. She had found and was working with a local consultant to gain such knowledge but had to pay for it herself. Interestingly, given the general lack of formal company sponsored training that appears common among firms transferring expatriates overseas, the idea of ongoing on-site assistance may be a better solution, as we proposed in Chapter 7. Several of the traditional expatriates, particularly those with little overseas experience or in-depth knowledge of Japan, initially discounted the value of cross-cultural training. Indeed, only after they had been in Japan for several months did they begin to see its usefulness. Perhaps if future expatriates request such ongoing corporate support, it will become more common.

Fair compensation package. Some women had advice on how to "get a fair compensation package" from their employers. Unfortunately, in those cases, they had learned from experience—they were not receiving such a package. We discussed in Chapters 3 and 5 the case of Emily, the independent "hybrid" who was hired under the local staff office, at a "secretary level" designation. Her male American counterparts, conversely, were hired through the international human resources office.

The result was that she received a much lower pay and benefits package than did the men.

In another case, as we mentioned earlier, Sandy was hired by a Japanese firm with what she considered to be a generous compensation level. The firm also promised that it would sponsor her work visa application. Under time pressure to secure the visa, Sandy discovered after several months in the job that her employer would only sponsor her visa application *if* she agreed to a drop in her compensation. The firm's intention was to take advantage of her position (i.e., needing the work visa). The strategy backfired, however. Sandy left the firm and joined another, but not without hassles (including having to leave the country and reenter on her visitor's visa while her work visa was processed by her new employer). Her suggestion to other women was to be wary of deals that "look too good" and get the agreement you reach with a potential employer in writing.

Finally, seeking information to know what *is* an appropriate level of compensation is a way to counteract the potential for misunderstandings. Terri, working for an American consumer products firm, developed a network of alumni from her university who were living in Tokyo—other young people who worked in Japan, both for foreign and for Japanese firms. Before negotiating her initial and subsequent compensation packages, she queried fellow alumni to gain a sense of what the pay and benefits range was in a given year.

Preparing for Working and Living in Japan

Once women decided to look for jobs in Japan, they tended to prepare for the adventure in different ways. Their suggestions for doing so fell into two categories: (1) what women could do themselves, such as having strong technical expertise, learning the language and culture, and preparing themselves emotionally and psychologically for Japan; and (2) what women could do to strengthen their credibility and ease in doing their jobs.

Technical competency. Regardless of the way the women found their jobs or went to Japan, they consistently noted that having some technical expertise that was in high demand was fundamental to success, no matter what type of job or firm. The expertise could be supported by having a particular type of degree (e.g., graduate degree in international management) or coming from a well-known university (e.g., the engineer/manager who went to M.I.T.). Once the women showed their competence, their credibility was established and, with those people who knew them, subsequently unquestioned. Such suggestions support Adler's (1994) earlier findings on the importance of competency.

Some of the expatriates also commented that although technical competency was indeed necessary, they started with an advantage if they came from well-known or highly reputable firms. In essence their Japanese counterparts, superiors or subordinates—or external stakeholders (e.g., customers or suppliers)—assumed that their firms had transferred the women because of their competence. As a result, establishing credibility was faster and easier for them. The independent job seekers, since they were hired locally, faced a greater challenge establishing themselves internally but could also trade on the firms' reputations (particularly if they worked for well-known foreign firms) with external groups.

Language and cultural skills. Many of the women in the study advocated that women working in Japan have at least some knowledge of Japanese language and culture. While not all of the expatriates considered learning Japanese necessary to be successful in their jobs, most acknowledged that having "taxi Japanese" made living in Japan more workable. Other women did need it for "basic survival" in the workplace as well. Others found Japanese useful for gaining the "real information" needed for their jobs, much of which was available only from subordinates who spoke no English.

Interestingly enough, even women fluent in Japanese do not always exercise the option of using it. One woman commented that she never "showed" the extent of her Japanese language fluency. Remaining humble about her true language expertise allowed her to "surprise" the Japanese and, moreover, she gained an advantage in negotiations because she could eavesdrop on discussions.

Several women recommended learning about Japanese culture, and offered myriad means of achieving such knowledge. Some gained insights and perspective through working with local cross-cultural consultants; others learned from predecessors or became friendly with Japanese whom they could use as "sounding boards" to understand the events of their work lives. Still others learned "on the job," gaining experience by making cultural mistakes.

The combination of technical expertise with knowledge of Japanese culture and language was unbeatable, according to several women. Traditional expatriates often arrived with high technical qualifications but little in the way of language and culture knowledge. The less successful independent job seekers, on the other hand, sometimes came with language skills but limited technical expertise areas of interest to firms. Blending the two sets of knowledge was the key to succeeding. Deborah, the data processing manager, for example, was confident of her ability to remain indefinitely in Japan because she had highly developed skills in both areas, which according to her was still a relatively unusual combination. Thus, finding ways to blend technical expertise and cultural and language skills, regardless of which came first, repeatedly emerged as a strong recommendation.

Lastly, as we have mentioned in Chapter 5, women frequently commented on how to "use" maturity and age to one's advantage. Given Japan's emphasis on respect for age and wisdom, Lorna saw benefits to being older—including the poise and maturity that age typically bring. From her perspective, she felt that younger women faced greater obstacles because of their age than their gender; her advice to older women was "If you've got it, flaunt it!"

Guarantees or help from their firms. Finally, several women offered ideas of what to ask from their firms that would smooth their adjustment to working and living in Japan. In tandem with the importance of establishing credibility through technical expertise, several women noted the value of having a title that reflected responsibility and status. A consultant whose firm wanted her husband's expertise in Japan negotiated to be transferred herself as an expatriate. As part of the package, she received a promotion and a higher title sooner than she would normally have so that she would command higher respect in Japan. Tying in with the Japanese culture's attention to hierarchy, a higher title gave the woman a slight boost in her dealings with Japanese employees as well as clients and others outside her firm.

Finally, some women suggested that, given the rigors of life in Japan, anyone considering working there might consider shorter assignments (particularly for expatriates) before assuming a multiyear post. Women with little previous overseas experience, in particular, felt they spent their first year simply adjusting to living in Japan. Thus, having a chance to work for shorter periods in Japan might have prepared and eased the transition, particularly for expatriates.

WHAT TO DO, EXPECT AND KNOW ON THE JOB

The adventuring women we studied also had numerous recommendations regarding what foreign women professionals should do (or not do) once they were working in Japan. Their ideas clustered into four subgroups of recommendations. The women had suggestions about what kind of behaviors women should have on the job. Next, they offered advice on how to manage relationships with colleagues at work (i.e., peers and subordinates) as well as individuals and groups out of work, including clients, suppliers, and customers. Related to both of the first components, the women had suggestions about knowing how far to push one's ideas or goals and when to quit or back away from them. Finally, they offered several general thoughts on aspects of work that newcomers should be aware of and prepared for, from sexual bias and harassment to stress.

On-the-Job Behaviors and Attitudes

The women had six general suggestions regarding behavior on the job. We discuss each in turn: (1) exploiting gender where appropriate, (2) being flexible and entrepreneurial, (3) learning humility and toughness, (4) using time rather than fighting it, (5) supporting other women, and (6) trusting oneself.

Exploiting gender where it helps. Our research supports other work (e.g., Adler, 1984c) in arguing that, for foreign women professionals working in Japan, life is not "all bad." In fact, such women have definite advantages. Aside from simply acknowledging that their gender has benefits, several women maintained that women should go further and capitalize on that advantage.

Because foreign women professionals remain somewhat unusual in Japan, the women in our sample found that they were often the first or one of the first *"gaijin* women" Japanese men had worked with. Since the men appeared to find the women so unusual, their behavior was perhaps less traditional or programmed than it might be with foreign men. For instance, Terri, one of the independent job seekers who dealt with many clients, commented, "Japanese men don't know how to say 'no' to women." As a result, she used this weakness to great advantage in her sales position. She predicted that, as more foreign women professionals work in Japan, she will be unable to exploit such an advantage in the future so she was seeking all the gain from it that she could.

Further, the women we studied argued for going beyond the advantages accorded *women* and focusing on ways to learn to "charm" the Japanese in general. Several women said they had learned much from the Japanese about the importance of trying to enchant and charm. Many of the women had recommendations in this area.

First, they consistently commented that, while they do not recommend women flaunt their femininity, they should not hide it. Dressing professionally, yet femininely, was completely acceptable. Wearing suits or dresses that were colorful and tasteful but not "copying men" was the appropriate mode. One senior level woman also allowed the "softer" side of her personality to shine through tactics like taking candy to meetings. Her comment was that men clearly could not behave in such a way and she used such actions as a way to disarm and soften her Japanese counterparts. We note, however, that this woman held a high position in her firm, which may have permitted her to use these particular tactics.

Other women went further in their suggestions. Several of the younger independent job seekers, for example, noted that because foreign women are still a peculiarity in Japan, they could use their rarity to play on the Japanese men's sense of "whimsy." Specifically, several mentioned that they agreed to lunch with Japanese men as a way to build business relationships and take advantage of the curiosity that the men had toward them and their work. If women can accomplish more business or make more sales this way without compromising themselves, went the reasoning, they should take advantage of it while they can.

Some women mentioned that learning what "charms" the Japanese people should be applied to groups other than businessmen. The "true buyers" of services, for example, are often women. Given the nature of Lorna's business—running an English language school, catering largely to children—she had discovered what attracted customers. In her case, she found that if she charmed children and pets (!), the mothers, who were the real decision makers, would become loyal customers.

Being flexible and entrepreneurial. As we have discussed before, the attitude of flexibility, as well as willingness to look for and take advantage of opportunities were repeatedly stressed by the adventuring women we met. The idea of flexibility emerged in terms of learning new disciplines or work areas as well as *how* to comport themselves at work.

Regardless of how women found their jobs—through traditional transfers, through on-site seeking, through "hybrid" arrangements—they underscored the importance of taking on and learning how to tackle new areas in their work. Earlier we commented on the significance of moving beyond proven skills to be entrepreneurial in the tasks and approach to work. This attitude applied both to finding work as well as to designing and shaping a job, once gained.

We described previously some of the creative ways that women found work. In other cases, women also discussed the importance of being creative in designing their own jobs. Since many Japanese employees—their subordinates, peers or superiors—were less comfortable with changing existing approaches to their jobs, the women felt they had more freedom to develop their own niches. For example, Kiri, the only American in the Japanese branch of a human resource consulting firm, commented that most of her Japanese colleagues were reluctant to use the telephone for business, particularly with their American counterparts in the United States. As a result, Kiri took on the responsibility of doing most of the "phone business." As such, she became the key liaison with the home office, allowing her greater access to higher level managers than she would normally have had. Her experience was typical of several independent job seekers working in subsidiary offices where they were the only foreigners.

For these women, the need to be flexible extended beyond the way the work was done on the job. Many mentioned that one advantage of being a woman was that there was no expectation of after work socializing (i.e., drinking) with the Japanese employees. Late night drinking and partying are not uncommon among men working in Japanese firms, but as women, they were not required to participate on a regular basis. On the other hand, one woman mentioned that she had to be flexible enough to go out drinking and socializing periodically, as a way to cement good working relationships.

Finally, several women talked (again) about the importance of language in providing more flexibility and autonomy. One manager commented that her fluency allowed her to take on more responsibility because she was able to gain knowledge and understanding of a situation more easily than her expatriate counterparts who depended upon middle level Japanese managers. She could, in essence, "skip" levels and go directly to the first line employees who were aware of problems, needs, or progress on tasks. Such access increased her power and autonomy on the job.

Being humble, gracious . . . and tough. Several of the women who knew little about the Japanese or their culture before arriving in Japan were startled by certain features. Typically aggressive in their home country environments, many of these dynamic women were forced to learn to accommodate themselves to "Japanese approaches" in various ways.

One woman commented that she was at first baffled by the apparent humility and frequent "apologizing" that she encountered from the Japanese. Once she understood the cultural context better, she became comfortable with the idea of humility and refrained from putting herself in the limelight. Indeed, she learned that humility about her competence and skills could be an effective tool for gaining psychological advantage in negotiations. While maintaining her own goal in mind, she was able to be accommodating enough to meet Japanese expectations, giving her an edge over foreigners who were unable to subsume some of their aggressiveness.

Related to humility was the emphasis women placed upon learning to be gracious. Again, Carol, the senior telecommunications manager, commented on how much she had learned from the Japanese about the methods and importance of entertaining guests. She mentioned simple actions such as escorting customers or peers to the elevator following meetings, or offering tea and carrying on social conversation. Rather than viewing such activities as a "waste of time," as she did right after her arrival in Japan, she came to understand the significance to the Japanese of carefully constructed graciousness and its meaning for business.

Other women talked of having to learn "humility" in other aspects of their jobs. Terri, a young woman who initially was angered and showed it when she was ignored or asked to pour tea in meetings, eventually learned how to deal with such situations. She overlooked the offense and ignored the requests to get tea. Further, she found that eventually she became used to such behaviors as letting (Japanese) men enter elevators first.

Finally, each of these examples suggests that the women learned to balance patience with persistence. The humility, graciousness, and patience were consistently counterbalanced with a clear sense of the goals the women wished to achieve. Showing patience, not revealing their weaknesses or emotions while pursuing goals, exhibited "toughness." That, according to the women, earned them enormous respect from the Japanese.

Indeed, several women provided examples of cases where their patience and persistence ultimately helped them gain their goals *and* the respect of the Japanese. For instance, Eileen's 2 year struggle to maintain composure while fuming about her inequitable treatment in compensation and Lorna's struggle to build a business in the face of initial government challenges reflect the gracious persistence that emerged in the successful women we studied.

Using time rather than fighting it. Tying closely into the ability to develop patience was an understanding of the use of "time." Particularly the women who were active negotiators with the Japanese had learned that the sense of time differs between task oriented Europeans and Americans and more "process oriented" Japanese. Once the women realized that their efforts to "accomplish a goal" could work against them in gaining the best outcome, they began to recognize how they could use time as the Japanese do.

Related to the use of time, many of the women commented on the importance of knowing "when to push and when to quit" (discussed more later). They were unable to give firm "rules" on how to know how far they could push an idea or goal before they lost the ability to achieve it. Most said that such a "feel" came with experience. Nevertheless, they acknowledged that a critical component was being able to see "timing" as a strategic tool, one used effectively by the Japanese and, with seasoning, by foreign women professionals as well.

Supporting other women. One of the most enjoyable aspects of getting to know the women in our sample group was realizing how remarkably supportive they were of other women—women who were already working and needed support as well as women who were seeking work. Particularly the more senior level women commented about the importance of providing a network and of acting as a mentor to other foreign professional women working in Japan. In some cases, such as Helen's, senior women formed support groups within their work settings or acted as mentors. Some foreign professional women even found themselves acting as mentors for younger Japanese women. Eileen, the young "hybrid" in the telecommunications firm, worked with a Japanese woman on everything from how to dress to how to present ideas to management.

Trusting oneself. A final recommendation from women, regardless of the type of job they held, was that other women going to Japan must learn to trust themselves. Many women, particularly the trailers who arrived without work and often without enthusiasm for being in Japan, found themselves rudderless for several months. They were angry, frustrated, and questioning their competence and self-worth. Moving beyond those feelings was difficult yet necessary for emotional well-being. Catherine, a trailer with a high level position in New York, followed her investment banker husband to Japan. Throughout the first frustrating year, she blamed her husband, her husband's firm, and the Japanese for her dissatisfaction. Eventually, however, she realized she could control her life and her career. She reassessed and "repackaged" her skills and expertise and found a part-time job in Tokyo.

Trusting oneself was also important in finding a balance between adapting to Japan and learning from it without "becoming Japanese." Some women commented that once they were on the job, it was tempting yet dangerous to take on too many Japanese characteristics. While most agreed with the value of learning patience, graciousness, or humility, they also conceded that "becoming Japanese" was risky.

If any of our interviewees had the potential to "become Japanese," it was Deborah, the data center manager who studied aikido, spoke fluent Japanese and chose to live in a totally Japanese neighborhood. She acknowledged the likelihood that she could "go native." Instead, she used the assignment in Japan as a time to question assumptions about how a job or task should be done. Seeking to blend what she learned from both the Japanese and American approaches to doing business, she merged them into approaches that were comfortable and appropriate for her. In essence, Deborah developed her own "new" style. The benefit of her position was that she understood enough of the Japanese and American approaches to appreciate and use what aspects were appropriate, but being a foreigner in Japan, she was also allowed the freedom to develop a style that was neither Japanese nor American.

Managing Relationships

Japanese are known as people for whom relationships are critical in the harmonious functioning of society. The adventurers we studied recognized that importance and created their own approaches to developing and managing relationships, both with Japanese and with other foreigners.

The power of networks—inside and out. As mentioned, some of the senior women used networks such as FEW to offer support to the younger or newer foreign women. The discussions included cross-cultural issues, such as ways to handle various typical problems that arose in dealing with Japanese peers, superiors, or clients. Other women used the networks to gain intelligence about their compensation or benefits packages before negotiating initial or annual changes.

Many women talked about the value of building networks outside their workplaces. Many drew upon the foreign community (both men and women) for developing business. As we discussed in Chapter 3, several women were members of such groups as the American Club of Tokyo and used that as a place from which to conduct business. Others became active in the ACCJ; indeed, one woman was a member of the Chamber's Board of Governors (i.e., Board of Directors), giving her access to key foreign businesses and managers in Japan.

Look at situations with "Japanese eyes." Much of our discussion throughout this chapter has an underlying theme—the successful women we met tried hard to understand the Japanese perspective on events and to remain non-judgmental. As one person put it, she tried to use "Japanese logic" to understand events, comments, or reactions made by Japanese colleagues at work or clients, suppliers or others outside the organization.

The women described how they tried to envision situations or themselves from the perspective of the Japanese. In some cases, for example, the younger women feared that the Japanese would view them as even younger (i.e., less credible) than they in fact were. As a result, at times, they were explicit and straightforward with the Japanese about their ages or their backgrounds and competence.

Yet, even the women who had spent several years living in Japan, either working or as students, admitted the difficulty of truly being able to comprehend situations "with Japanese eyes" without some help. The approaches that women used to gain more access to "Japanese logic" were quite varied. Many drew upon the wisdom of other foreigners who had worked in Japan longer than they. Others identified "mentors" within their firms to whom they could go with questions or frustrations.

Still others sought advice from Japanese friends or, in the case of the Japanese-American women, relatives—both in Japan and in the United States. Terri, working for an American beverage multinational, frequently sought advice from her executive mother based in the United States. Also typical was Deborah, the data center manager, who used her aikido instructor as a sounding board and mentor. When she faced a baffling situation at work, she would describe it to him and gain his interpretation of the events.

Indeed, we have also used such approaches. In the early 1980s, one of us was researching Japanese compensation and performance appraisal practices. The days were spent listening to the "official responses" about how firms handled poor performance, and how they evaluated and rewarded executives. The evenings were spent with a Japanese friend, who also happened to be a senior executive at another of the Japanese blue chip firms. He would listen to what the Japanese managers had said and then "interpret" what they had "really" meant. His interpretation went beyond the language to the unspoken messages that were being sent. Clearly, his cultural interpretation bridged the gap between an American researcher's lack of sensitivity (as a non-Japanese) to a full understanding of what was being said and deeper insights from the interviews.

Nurturing relationships. Creating and nurturing relationships are fundamental to conducting business in most of Asia. While they acknowledged the importance of relationships even in Western settings, the women saw a fundamental difference in the reverence with which relationships are nurtured in Japan. The women we interviewed consistently commented on how important it is to build and maintain good relationships with people they encounter in their work. One woman commented that having strong relationships (*ningen kankei*) with everyone, including people she thought were "jerks," was a major part of her job.

Interestingly, although the women stressed the importance of having good relationships, they also relished the freedom they had in *how* they nurtured and worked within those relationships. For example, several of the women who worked for Japanese bosses noted that, because they were foreigners, they were "allowed" to be more direct in their opinions with their bosses than their Japanese counterparts. This links back to earlier comments about ways to "use" fluency in the language—when the women chose to, they ignored the subtleties of the Japanese language. These women could "choose" to be more direct with their superiors and were given such license because they were foreigners, and thus not expected to understand the Japanese culture fully. In fact, some women noted that their Japanese bosses likely appreciated the directness. As a change from the unfailing cautiousness that Japanese typically apply to their speaking, the bosses may have found it refreshing to have subordinates who were less circumspect when they talked!

Finally, several women discussed the importance of maintaining relationships with subordinates because of their ability to buffer the women from various tasks. Some women developed close relationships with their secretaries, who could help them accomplish the "mundanes" of life, from getting a telephone and other appliances installed in their apartments to arranging for business meetings or purchasing office equipment.

Yet, at the same time, the women were adamant that directness in dealing with conflict was less successful. In particular, they agreed that expressing anger or frustration, especially with groups such as clients or suppliers, was never appropriate. Terri, at the U.S. beverage firm, learned this lesson after a reprimand from her boss when she became outraged at a supplier. Nurturing relationships in Japan, then, particularly for foreign women professionals, often requires "unlearning" some behaviors such as assertiveness. The women's comments about learning to deal with conflict validate earlier research (Abe and Wiseman, 1983; Hawes and Kealey, 1981).

Being the liaison with the "home office." A final "relationship" encountered by many of the women we studied was that between the local Japanese subsidiary office and the home office of a multinational firm. This, of course, applied to women employed by non-Japanese firms. In several of the cases of independent job seekers, as we have mentioned, they were the sole foreigners in their offices. As a result, by default they often became the main liaison person with the firm's domestic head-quarters office.

Many women acknowledged that being such a liaison meant that the job demanded very long hours. Simply because Tokyo and New York or San Francisco were on dramatically different time zones, the women were forced to work late hours to be able to talk by telephone during the headquarters' daytime hours. While this was a drawback, most of the women saw their roles as inherently valuable and useful for learning more about the firm. Indeed, several of the locally hired women anticipated being able to transfer to their firm's domestic offices in the future, because of the experience they had gained working for the firm in Japan.

Other women, particularly the transferees, viewed the relationship with headquarters from another dimension. They too were sometimes the key liaison for transmission of information. But, further, they were also the "interpreters" of the organization and its politics for the local office. The senior bank auditor was in large part recommended for the job because of her long association with the bank and knowledge of internal politics and workings of the organization.

Knowing When to Hold and When to Fold

Just as in a poker game, the foreign women professionals in Japan advised that knowing when to push ("hold") and when to back off ("fold") is crucial in dealing with Japanese in a work setting. As in the art of "using time," the women frequently commented that they needed to understand when to push and when to back off of issues. As one woman, active in negotiating with potential and current clients, commented, "I can never 'out-negotiate' the Japanese; I can only start high and come down."

The bulk of the counsel that women offered in this regard was to learn patience and to control emotion, to learn when to react, and to know how far to push. The engineer who later became the manager of a data processing center for an international financial institution noted that she used a "gentle approach, with no 'table pounding' " but was nonetheless direct, something the Japanese were unable to do. She could make requests, saying, "Here's what I want and why," and could get results from her Japanese and foreign subordinates alike with such an approach.

Interestingly, for many of these women such a "gentle approach" was feasible yet stressful. Used to being assertive and direct in their American or European contexts, they had to alter their behaviors on the job in Japan to achieve goals that would normally be accomplished in a very different manner (including some "table pounding!"). Because of the need to take a more delicate approach, withholding emotion, several women said they needed an outlet—off the job—to relieve stress they would otherwise vent by ranting on the job. We discuss more fully such outside work releases in the next section.

"Be Prepared"

A final aspect of on-the-job advice offered by our sample women relates to various issues that surprised them and that they see as important for other foreign women professionals to be aware of. The issues include ones that affected women in all the groups (from expatriates to trailers) as well as some that were of concern only to certain groups (e.g., Asian-Americans).

Sexual bias and harassment. Heading the list of issues that foreign women professionals should be prepared to encounter were sexual bias and sexual harassment. By sexual bias, we mean the range of affronts, insults or misunderstandings women face doing business in Japan. Several women recounted situations, for example, where they were ignored in business meetings, where clients refused to deal with them without a foreign male present, or where they were treated as oddities. While such events irritated the women, they eventually learned to deal with them.

Other women, particularly those in senior management positions, learned they had to make their positions known early in discussions with clients or counterparts in other parts of the firm. If they did not, their Japanese colleagues would address comments and questions to the men (often the women's subordinates) in the meeting, ultimately leading to embarrassment for all concerned. They learned to gracefully make their high ranks clear, preventing future misunderstandings.

Sexual harassment, on the other hand, was sometimes more serious and disconcerting for the women we studied. Furthermore, unlike sexual bias, it was a topic that did not emerge during earlier research on foreign women overseas. Nonetheless, it was clearly an issue for several of the women in our sample.

Overt sexual advances by Japanese men were not uncommon among the women we interviewed, particularly among the younger women who held positions of less power than their transferee counterparts. Because it was an issue so frequently mentioned, we sought ideas on how the women did or should deal with sexual harassment.

The first suggestion women had was simply to be aware that it occurs and will likely arise, especially for the younger women. Most of the independent job seeker women had experienced harassment from Japanese men, most often from their colleagues or clients. Nonetheless, the women typically were able to deal with it and move forward without major incident. The women advised against getting into situations where harassment was likely to occur, most commonly during after work drinking sessions or on company sponsored outings.

When women did encounter harassment, they were usually able to handle it effectively by indicating total lack of interest. In almost all cases, the harassment ended. In only one situation, of a young Japanese-American woman, did the offender, who happened to be a major subcontractor of a client, continue to pressure the young woman. With help from some client firm members, the woman was finally able to cajole the man into halting, but she felt the incident affected her ability to work with the client on future business dealings.

Adjustment stress. A second area of surprise for several women was the degree to which they encountered culture shock and related adjustment stress. As we have described throughout the book, the majority of our sample of women were independent job seekers, women who had sought jobs in Japan because they had some previous experience or knowledge of Japan and the Japanese culture. Many of them had been exchange students; one had begun to study aikido seriously and saw her move to Japan as a natural way to learn more about the culture. Despite such preparation and desire to be in Japan, and despite their overall satisfaction with their situations in Japan, many of these same women did experience much stress during their first 1–2 years. Indeed, one woman was amazed to undergo a serious bout of culture shock after she had been in Japan for 13 months. Others who moved to Japan more reluctantly also faced serious adjustment stress. The "trailer" women particularly encountered periods of self-doubt, loss of self-esteem because they had gone from being employed and contributing members of a family unit to being dependent financially and emotionally on one or a very few people. Typically they eventually decided to become more proactive, to seek and find jobs and ultimately "move on."

Others experienced stress on the job because of the nature of Japanese management and business practices. One woman, used to having a clear goal and getting periodic (if informal) feedback from her managers, was at a loss when she received neither in her job in Japan. In Japan, bosses typically give their subordinates little overt positive praise. Realizing that such external encouragement is uncommon in Japan, she finally recognized that she would have to monitor—and reward—her progress herself, rather than depend upon the corporate structure. Thus, being prepared for stress and culture shock became a critical learning point for several women.

Being a "curiosity." Several women commented that they felt they were viewed as oddities or curiosities by the Japanese. One African-American woman "expected" (and felt) discrimination everywhere—on the job, and on the street. Since she was prepared to be considered unusual, she was not surprised that it happened.

Expectations for Japanese-Americans. Finally, the two women who were Japanese-Americans experienced a different form of "discrimination" or treatment as oddities. Since they looked Japanese, and could speak fluent Japanese, they felt they were subjected to harsher standards in their behavior and performance than were their Caucasian counterparts. Whereas Caucasian Americans were excused if they made language errors, the two Japanese-American women were not.

They felt that their actions and behavior were scrutinized more closely and that, in some respects, they were expected to "act Japanese." Having been reared as assertive American working women, they found such demands unreasonable and unfeasible. Again, while they had no clear solutions, they felt being aware of such likely expectations for Japanese-Americans could lessen the surprise future women would face.

WHAT TO DO, EXPECT AND KNOW OFF THE JOB

Life in Japan for foreign women professionals is challenging enough in the workplace. It can be as demanding, if not more so, off the job. The main areas of recommendations for dealing with life outside work focused on the types of relationships women had (or did not) and ways to maintain equilibrium in a society very different from the ones they left at home.

Outside work, the women we studied all commented that they needed some outlet for socializing. Their comments regarding socializing focused on (1) the extraordinary female friendships they developed, (2) their interactions (or lack of them) with the Japanese, and (3) their relationships with men.

Friendships with Other Women

Several of the women in our sample were pleased and astonished at the extent to which they were able to create and build solid friendships with other foreign women in Japan. Since many of the women we interviewed were single, and had moved to Japan without knowing anyone, they quickly sought out others for support and friendship. Through organizations like FEW, they met people in similar jobs or with similar interests. Several women mentioned that the friendships they had developed in Japan were closer than those "at home," because of the support that other foreign women could provide during periods of difficulties. One woman talked of her friends' becoming her "family" during holidays away from home. Another woman had not anticipated the extent to which she would become involved socially in Japan, particularly with other women. According to her estimate, she was one of the some 70 African-American expatriates working in Japan and quickly joined their network. The result was not only close female friendships, but also opportunities to participate in social activities she would otherwise never have encountered in the United States (e.g., invitations to the Jamaican embassy, to reggae concerts).

Thus, the women in the study recommended that others take advantage of the foreign professional women's networks and use friendships with women as key support systems for learning to adjust and become successful in Japan. Indeed, the women were pleased and surprised at the degree to which they were able to seek out and become part of close female networks and friendships among other foreign professional women. For many of them, their experience with meeting and socializing with Japanese women (or men) was less successful, however.

The Void in Socializing with the Japanese Women

For many of the foreign women professionals, their social worlds outside work revolved around activities with other foreigners. In a few cases, the pattern varied. Kiri, married to a Japanese man, had many Japanese friends through his connections and through her college networks. Linda, who had been engaged to a Japanese who later died, was also involved in extensive networks of Japanese friends. The two Japanese-American women also had links to many Japanese, because of their unique family situations. In both cases, they were able to move into Japanese society to some degree. In one case, the woman shared an apartment with a Japanese friend and had several cousins located around Tokyo. Through the friend and the cousins, the woman was able to become part of their social network and meet other young Japanese. The other woman had some contacts through her family but was never fully at ease socializing in those groups.

Most of the other foreign women commented on the difficulty of meeting and developing friendships with Japanese women. For the most part, the Japanese women were typically in jobs at very different (usually lower level) positions from the foreign women professionals. As a result, given the Japanese adherence to hierarchy and position, there was less commonality of interests between foreign and Japanese women at work or off the job.

Relationships with Men

The women we interviewed openly discussed their social lives off the job. While the focus was on relationships (or lack of them) with foreign men, they had recommendations regarding Japanese men as well.

Where are all the single foreign men? Uniformly, the single foreign women professionals cited lack of a social life with foreign men as their number one dissatisfaction with living in Japan. Repeatedly, when asked what they disliked about living and working in Japan, they commented on the shortage of available, congenial foreign men. One woman perceived that many foreign men moved to Japan in part to find a "Japanese girlfriend or wife who would take care of them." The men's fascination with and pursuit of the Japanese women prevented them from being interested in getting to know foreign women. The women advised others to be aware of the limitations of social life with foreign men in Japan and not to expect too much!

The mixed messages for Japanese men. Several of the women we interviewed warned against expecting to develop relationships with Japanese men. One woman commented that, as in the United States, she avoided any kind of serious social relationship with men from work. Her ability to keep a professional distance allowed her more flexibility on and off the job: she was able to give candy or send valentines without repercussion or assumption that such actions would lead to anything beyond congenial work relationships.

Others commented on what they perceived to be the expectations of Japanese men, noting that "sex is like a game" to them. Furthermore, some women commented that they experienced sexual harassment off the job as well, in social settings with Japanese men. Even so, as with the work related harassment, the women usually were able to halt the actions by tactfully telling the men they were uninterested. Thus, the women recommended not expecting too much from or seeking too aggressively relationships with Japanese men.

The support of husbands. Married women frequently mentioned their husbands as a major source of support and outlet for their frustrations at work. Amanda, the lawyer whose husband was a software engineer, commented that he helped her maintain self-esteem and equilibrium, in the face of snubs and obstacles at work. Indeed, her husband became more integrated into Japanese society and the culture than did she, making Japanese friends and learning the language.

Unfortunately, not all women were as pleased with their husbands' support. One woman, who arrived as a trailer, sought similar help from her husband. Lacking a job, she fell into depression, doubting herself and her skills. Her husband, on the other hand, had a new job, new culture, new colleagues and new challenges to deal with. As a result, he was unable to provide as much backing for her as she needed. Such mismatching between the transferees and the trailers is not uncommon but women trailers need to be aware of it. Anticipating the stresses that any job overseas may place on a relationship, women and their husbands or partners need to realize their reactions during early stages of an experience abroad may place extraordinary strains on them. The women in the study mentioned such tactics as taking time to assess the stresses, talking about how to manage them, and having a support system (i.e., friends) outside the relationship to help ease the strain.

RETURNING: PREPARE, PREPARE, PREPARE

Just as the women had suggestions about how to prepare before and during their initial period in Japan, they had numerous recommendations about how to prepare before returning to their home countries. The areas they focused on dealt mainly with (1) planning to return long before the actual move, (2) being realistic about possible opportunities when you return, and (3) anticipating culture shock and how to deal with it.

Planning the Return

By their very nature, the foreign women professionals we studied are aggressive and goal oriented, about their jobs and their careers. Nearly all admitted to having plans for their "post-Japan" careers. Several of the independent job seekers intended to remain in Japan 2–3 years and return for graduate study in the United States. Others, who already had graduate degrees, expected to be able to transfer to an office in the home countries (of the firms they worked for in Japan). Still others planned to capitalize on their Japan experience by starting their own consulting firms, whether in technical writing, compensation, or human resource management.

The expatriate women had different perspectives but also offered suggestions for long term planning. The woman with the international service organization lamented not having planned and obtained a guarantee for a job in her home office upon completion of her Japan assignment. Instead, because the assignment was so disastrous, she found no interest in any of the home offices in hiring her, leading her to decide to leave the organization and work altogether. Other expatriates, with more positive experiences, also recommended that women discuss long term career plans before they leave for Japan. One woman expected to return to the United States after a 2 year assignment, but only if offered a higher level, more responsible job. If she did not receive it, she planned to remain in Japan for another year.

As with other areas of advice, the women stressed the importance of taking the initiative in their careers and future moves. Several mentioned that they hoped to remain with the firms they had joined in Japan but acknowledged that to do so, they would have to initiate discussions and "find" or "create" a job for themselves elsewhere in the firm.

Being Realistic About Opportunities and Perceptions at Home

The women seemed to exhibit two divergent types of attitudes regarding how their Japan experiences would be viewed. They tended to split as a function of age: the younger, typically independent job seekers anticipated that their experiences in Japan would be welcomed and highly valued by potential employers in their home country. Linda, at the international public relations firm (based in New York), felt that her knowledge of the Japanese business environment would be viewed favorably. Expecting to return to the United States for graduate school within 1–2 years, she felt that the degree and her Japan background would give her a clear advantage over other people seeking jobs in the United States. Kiri, who anticipated returning to the United States in 8–10 years, believed that she would be able to capitalize on her knowledge of human resource management issues in Japan in establishing her own consulting firm.

The older women, transferees and independent job seekers alike, had more tempered attitudes about the value of their work experience in Japan. They each acknowledged the personal growth that the experience gave them but questioned how much their firms would appreciate and be able to use their knowledge of Japanese business and industry. The lawyer had talked to a majority of the corporate law partners in her firm, based in New York City, about her prospects and career, should she return to the head office. The conclusion she reached was that she would be required to work a year in the office before being considered for partner, several years behind her cohort group from law school. Furthermore, she had the impression that her years in Japan were viewed as blank pages, of little direct benefit to her career or to the firm. Interestingly, she was unperturbed about the news; her comment was that if it took a year longer to gain partnership, that was all right. On the other hand, she was not altogether convinced that she wanted to stay at the firm, in which case the news was even less troubling to her.

The women also recommended that anyone returning from Japan be realistic about the nature of the domestic job *and* the compensation package. The traditional transferees frequently commented on their surprise and delight at the generous packages they received in Japan. Several acknowledged that it would be difficult to return to domestic pay packages; indeed, one woman cited three colleagues who had left their firms to find other lucrative positions in Japan, rather than return to domestic positions and lower pay.

Beyond the compensation benefits, the women commented on the degree of autonomy they had in Japan and worried about having to adjust to jobs with much less freedom. Preparing for a drop in autonomy, for a less attractive compensation package, for a different type of stimulation in the job were all issues that many were aware of and dealing with.

Anticipating and Managing Culture Shock

A final area of recommendations dealt with the need for returning women to be prepared for the adjustment to a "new" culture and way of life. Research on returning expatriates (e.g., Napier and Peterson, 1989) consistently notes the dissatisfaction and frustration they face upon returning to their home countries. Some of the women commented that Tokyo was "now home," and to return to their "home" countries was likely to be quite difficult. Aside from simply being aware of the likely shock, they had several other suggestions.

The women frequently mentioned they had learned more about doing business from the Japanese than they expected. As we discussed, several talked about learning humility, graciousness and toughness from their Japanese counterparts. One woman's experiences negotiating with the Japanese also taught her to know her product better than she ever had. Several women talked of their developing a "gentle" side to their business dealings and learning the importance of entertaining as it contributes to negotiation and general business dealings. As one woman said, "It's difficult to be hostile to someone you've partied with."

Repeatedly, the women suggested that being open to new ways of doing business, being non-judgmental, and being entrepreneurial in discovering their own "best" style that worked in Japan were crucial to success. They went on to suggest that they planned to take those lessons when they returned to their home countries, anticipating that they could be better business people as a result.

Even more than the lessons they gained for their professional lives, the women suggested being open to growing personally. Several talked of developing an "inner self," of gaining personal confidence, of taking risks (or being forced to) and of "becoming a more interesting person." One woman commented that she had blocked her life in "20 year segments." Her Japan experience was the beginning of the "third 20 years," and had helped her focus on what she wanted to change about herself for the next era.

SUMMARY AND CONCLUSIONS

Clearly, the foreign women professionals we studied were finding ways to have fulfilling, albeit challenging, lives in Japan. Many had learned from current colleagues and friends how to handle work and outside work situations. Most, however, independently developed their own styles and approaches to living in Japan.

The fundamental recommendations for women appeared repeatedly to focus on being aware of the types of frustrations, challenges and situations foreign women professionals are likely to encounter in Japan. Interestingly, many women seemed to suggest even if there were no "good" solutions to certain situations (e.g., lack of foreign men for social relationships), it was nonetheless helpful that they be aware of or anticipate such challenges. Most unpleasant were the unexpected surprises, such as overt sexual harassment. Had the women known such incidents were common in Japan, many may have been less unnerved by them. Thus, understanding the Japanese and Japan's culture, learning how to adapt behavior to fit cultural norms in Japan, dealing with bias and harassment, drawing support from friendships with other women and, where possible, with men—these themes run through the recommendations that women gave, for both work and for non-work settings.

Despite all we learned during the research, many questions and issues arose that we were unable to investigate at all or as fully as we would have liked. In the next, and final, chapter, we review some of those issues and make suggestions about future directions for research and practice on foreign women professionals working outside their home countries.

Chapter 9

What Next for Foreign Women Professionals?

Nancy wrote much of Chapter 1 in Hanoi, Vietnam. I (Sully) sit in a small cafe in San Miguel de Allende, Mexico, writing the opening paragraphs of this concluding chapter. Just as Vietnam is developing rapidly, so too has Mexico become modern and international, transformed by Salinas, the North American Free Trade Agreement, and the arrival of Price Club, Burger King and ATT. My Mexican niece mail orders from Victoria's Secret; her fiancé is an international investment expert, competing with counterparts in New York and Hong Kong. Having spent my adolescence in San Miguel, 30 years ago, with crank telephones instead of fax machines, when Hershey's chocolate bars were prized imports, I am struck—hard—by the effects of globalization in Mexico!

The notion of globalization was the root of our desire to write *Western Women Working in Japan*. As we discussed in the early chapters, the effect of business becoming global is that women, particularly Western women professionals, will assume management and professional positions abroad. Their increasing presence demands attention, particularly since they appear to have experiences often quite different from foreign men's. We chose to study the experiences of foreign women professionals in Japan first because of its reputation for being one of the toughest environments for foreigners and for women. In addition, we wanted to build upon existing knowledge about expatriates in Japan (e.g., Black, 1988) and women in Asia (e.g., Adler, 1984b; 1994) to see whether that knowledge applied specifically to foreign women professionals in Japan.

Conducting the study, analyzing its results, and writing the book have produced both conclusions *and* questions. We were pleased to confirm much of the prior research on expatriates in general and on women expatriates in particular. Furthermore, the present study allowed us to amplify that knowledge with additional information and insights. Some of the information about women who find jobs independently, about how women find and structure their jobs in Japan, about how they deal with sexual harassment and their lives off the job—such knowledge should add to general research about women who work outside their home countries. As we gathered data, however, new avenues of inquiry emerged. Given the study's methodology and survey design, we were unable to pursue many of these new areas. Thus, we are left with many questions. In this final chapter, we will review some of the key findings and suggest future areas for investigation.

GENERAL FINDINGS

As stated, this study provided much support for previous work on expatriates. Several factors affect the adjustment of women expatriates, just as they do those of male expatriates. Women are positively influenced by the degree of job discretion they have, as well as how clearly their job tasks are defined. In addition, we found that the clarity of the subsidiary or branch unit's responsibilities within a multinational firm may influence women's adjustment. As Amanda the lawyer illustrated, the perceptions about expectations for her branch office from the headquarters office greatly influenced her job and its specific tasks.

Further, women's role clarity was related (albeit weakly) to their adjustment, similar to men's. Nevertheless, this concept may in fact have several dimensions (e.g., professional slights, sexual harassment) that differ for women expatriates from what men experience. Finally, the amount of time women spent in Japan also correlated to their work adjustment, confirming Black's (1988) findings for men.

Adler's (1984b) research on the advantages that expatriate women have over expatriate men in work relationships (e.g., visibility, access, open communication) were largely verified by our survey respondents and interviewees. In addition, as we expected, language ability appears to be important for adjustment and performance. What we did not anticipate as clearly was how much the impact seems to be modified by the positions women hold, and by the nature of their specific jobs. In particular, the extent and type of interaction that women have with Japanese tie closely to the degree to which they need and use Japanese. Thus any assumption that all foreign women professionals working in Japan need extensive language training needs to be tempered. This fits with Tung's (1988) work on the need to match expatriate *tasks* with appropriate cross-cultural and language training.

We also found that professional acceptance is more complex than we expected at first and that it depends greatly upon whom women interact with. Women in the study perceived, for example, that they were almost as well accepted professionally by clients in Japan as they would be in their home countries, although this acceptance took time to achieve. With other groups, professional acceptance appears more murky. Acceptance by Japanese bosses and subordinates seems to vary and depends on several factors, including women's ages and positions.

Finally, as past research on male expatriates has found, spouses or partners play a large role in women's adjustment to living in Japan. Related to this, and ignored in earlier literature, is the apparent negative effect that the lack of available foreign men has on the social life of single foreign professional women. While it makes good sense, it has never emerged as an issue for expatriates, probably because the research has focused on (usually married) men!

AREAS FOR EXPLORATION

As we researched foreign women professionals working in Japan, several ideas and avenues for future exploration emerged. First, the women repeatedly commented on how professional acceptance depended primarily on having clear, high demand expertise. An issue also unexplored for foreign men professionals, it raises interesting questions. For example, is it as important for men to have such clear expertise to be successful in Japan? Also, how can women establish or make known their expertise in a country like Japan, which values modesty? The tension between "showing what you know" and fitting cultural expectations of not bragging is a balance that several women noted.

Another area that emerged and that could be interesting for further research is the relationship between age and professional acceptance. In essence, the Japanese had difficulty accepting younger women in part because they refused to believe such young people could have the experience and wisdom to do a task successfully. Do young foreign professional men in Japan face similar questioning by the Japanese about their professional competence? Are there other countries where age would be such a factor? Moreover, given the Age Discrimination Act in the United States, age cannot be a factor in selection. Consequently, how can U.S. firms help younger foreign women professionals overcome such a "disadvantage" in establishing professional stature?

An intriguing avenue, first raised in Adler's (1984b) early research, relates to the advantages that foreign women professionals seem to have in overseas posts. In addition to visibility, some of the interviewees we met suggested that women are better at nurturing relationships than men. In countries where building and maintaining relationships are so critical, such talents could stand women in good stead. Also, do women manage better in indirect cultures, such as Japan, if they tend to be less aggressive than men tend to be? Do "female leadership" styles transfer better to certain cultures?

A final, and probably most central, question is whether women are indeed as successful as they report themselves to be. Without separate measures of their success and performance from a variety of perspectives, it is difficult to accept their ratings completely. Future investigation might explore the women's performance from the perspectives of their bosses, peers, or subordinates.

All of these ideas, and the issues raised within the chapters themselves, could demand more study in Japan. In addition, the same questions need attention in other countries and settings where foreign women professionals work. The experiences and challenges of women working in Japan doubtless vary markedly from those of women working in Spain, Thailand, Mexico, Vietnam, or Kuwait.

We hope the ideas and findings from the study and their implications will be of value for foreign women professionals and the organizations that hire them. The most important recommendation we offer, however, is that no firm should hesitate to look to women as potential candidates for posts in Japan; likewise, women should not reject out of hand the challenge of working in Japan. As the women we met have said in so many ways, to do so would be foolhardy. Clearly, women have "pierced" the bamboo wall in Japan. We look forward to finding other places where they can do the same.

Appendix A

Research Methodology

In Appendix A, we describe the basic research approach used during the project, including the sampling method and the data collection instruments.

SAMPLING

The sample for this study was drawn from two organizations in Tokyo, Japan. One is an organization for foreign professional and executive women working in and around Tokyo. The Foreign Executive Women (FEW) group, with about 200 members, was founded in the early 1980s as a voluntary professional organization. It holds monthly meetings for members to meet one another and hear presentations on topics relevant to conducting business as a foreign woman in Japan.

We used the membership of FEW as the basic sample group. Iris Harvey, a member of FEW and self-employed consultant in Japan, distributed a written survey (Appendix B) in November 1992 to each member of the organization; she sent follow up reminder postcards in early December 1992. Using the FEW membership list and her own extensive contacts in the foreign women professionals' community in Japan, she then selected 11 women for in-depth interviews. During a 1 week trip in Japan in December 1992, we interviewed these women, as well as nine others referred to us by those initial interviewees. The interviewees, as we discuss in Chapter 2, included women who had been transferred by their firms (i.e., expatriates), as well as those who went to Japan as "independent" job seekers or "trailers," accompanying spouses or partners and then seeking employment once in Japan. In addition to the women we interviewed, we also spoke with one male expatriate during the week.

In May 1993, we sent surveys to women who belonged to the American Chamber of Commerce in Japan (ACCJ) but who were not members of FEW. The 93 foreign women professionals who were ACCJ members received surveys and follow up postcards. Three surveys were returned as "undeliverable."

We received a total of 31 completed surveys. Combining surveys from the two groups yielded a total of 91 responses. The response rate was 39 percent from the ACCJ and 28 percent from FEW. The response rate for the total sample was 32 percent.

Of the respondents, 44 percent were married, 52 percent were 25–34 years old and 26 percent were 35–44 years old. In addition, 9 percent of the women held top management positions, 16 percent held middle management posts, and the rest held specialized positions such as account executive or legal counsel.

INSTRUMENTS

We used two primary instruments to collect information about foreign women professionals working in Japan, a written survey and interviews. We discuss each next.

Survey

The written survey covered areas that prior research had identified as important in expatriate adjustment as well as issues relevant to this particular sample (Appendix B). The survey used the general adjustment scales developed by Black (1988), which he later refined (Black, 1990). The measure consisted of 18 items that centered on the three components of adjustment: work adjustment, living conditions, and interaction with local nationals (in this case, Japanese).

A principal components factor analysis with varimax rotation was performed. We used one factor to help reduce the data: adjustment to work conditions (i.e., job responsibilities, performance standards, and supervisory responsibilities). It had excellent reliability (.92).

We used the other items individually to permit greater exploration of the women's situations. Those items included "adjustment to living conditions" (e.g., shopping, transportation, cost of living) and interaction with the Japanese (e.g., socializing with Japanese, interacting with Japanese in general and outside work, and speaking to Japanese in Japanese).

The items on *role ambiguity* and *role conflict* were based on Black's (1988) study of U.S. male expatriates in Japan. It consisted of five and four items, respectively. We also used Black's (1991) eight item measure of *role discretion*. All three scales had a reliability (Cronbach's alpha) of .85 or over.

Drawing upon Adler's (1984a,c) findings, we consulted our on-site colleague from FEW to develop a series of questions to assess whether women felt their gender affected their business relationships in Japan. In addition, in the survey to ACCJ respondents, we asked the women to compare their business relationships to what foreign men professionals in comparable jobs in Japan would experience. We used these items individually.

Other parts of the survey questioned respondents concerning their job satisfaction and job performance, as well as their commitment to the firms for which they work. Another series of questions probed how the respondents' business relationships compared to those they had prior to coming to Japan.

We measured prior overseas experience by the number of years previously spent abroad. Because we studied both women sent by firms and those who went independently to Japan, we expected that asking about *general* overseas experience might be more appropriate than *work* experience overseas. ACCJ respondents also gave information about how long they had been in their present positions.

The amount of time the women spent with Japanese *off the job* and the amount of work time they spent with Japanese *on the job* were measured as percentages of total time in each of those realms. The mean amount of time spent with Japanese off the job was 31 percent; the mean amount of time spent on the job was 61 percent.

Questions dealing with training and preparation asked what the women had experienced before taking their positions in Japan and queried whether their firms had provided training. Because so few women indicated they had received any information or training, we could not examine the influence of this variable on work or general adjustment.

Finally, the survey included several demographic questions: the women's functional area, their educational background, whether the women had children, their Japanese language ability, and whose decision it was to go to Japan. Other questions on the survey were not used for the study reported here.

Interviews

We developed a semi-structured interview protocol (Appendix C), which focused on five main issues: (1) the ways in which the women were chosen for and prepared for their jobs in Japan; (2) the relationship of ambiguity, conflict, and discretion in their roles and jobs on their work adjustment; (3) other factors that facilitated or inhibited women's work adjustment; (4) advantages and disadvantages that women had working in Japan; and (5) the impact their Japan experiences were expected to have on their future career opportunities and directions.

We interviewed 20 women, ranging in age from mid-20s to late-40s. The interviews took place mainly at the women's workplaces; we went to one woman's apartment and met two others in restaurants convenient to their places of business. The interviews lasted from an hour to nearly 3 hours. In all cases, the women were extremely cooperative and helpful, particularly in relaying concrete examples of the points we raised in our questions.

Appendix B

Survey Questionnaire

Please answer all of the items in this survey. Your answers will be completely confidential. Be as honest and candid as you can. If there is an item that just does not apply to your situation, please use N/A to indicate this. Thank you for your cooperation in completing this survey.

ABOUT YOUR BACKGROUND

The following background information will give us insight into what type of job you currently hold and how you got your job.

1. What is your current title?
    ___Chairman   ___Controller, Treasurer, Secretary   ___Division Manager
    ___President   ___Owner, Partner   ___Department Manager
    ___Vice President   ___General Manager
    ___Other (please specify) _____

2. What best describes your job's key function?
    ___Corporate management   ___Accounting/auditing
    ___Finance   ___Legal
    ___Marketing/sales   ___Computer services/engineering/systems
    ___Production   ___Human resources
    ___Other (please specify)_____

3. Age (years)
    ___Less than 25   ___45-49   ___61-65
    ___25-34   ___50-55   ___65+
    ___35-44   ___56-60

4. Education
    ___Some college   ___College degree (specify) _____
    ___Some post-graduate work   ___Graduate degree (specify) _____

5. Sex   ___Male   ___Female

6. Nationality _____

7. Marital Status
    ___Single   ___Married   ___Divorced

8. Children
    ___No   ___Yes /____how many children?

9. Do you have overseas experience prior to your current position?
    ___No   ___Yes / _____number of years in prior overseas position

9a.* How long have you been working in Japan in your present company? _____months

9b.   What is the national origin of the firm you work for now?
      U.S. _____   Japanese _____   Other (please specify) _____

10. Current Salary (base - million)
   ___ a. ¥3-4.5   ___ d. ¥7.5-9.0   ___ g. ¥12.0-13.5   ___ j. > ¥17.5
   ___ b. ¥4.5-6.0   ___ e. ¥9.0-10.5   ___ h. ¥13.5-15.0
   ___ c. ¥6.0-7.5   ___ f. ¥10.5-12.0   ___ i. ¥15.0-17.5

11. Which of the following do you receive?
   ___ Overseas allowance   ___ Home leave travel allowance
   ___ Housing allowance   ___ Education allowance
   ___ Cost of living adjustment

12. What would you estimate to be the total cost of your annual compensation package? (in yen)_____

ABOUT YOUR COMPANY

13. Which best describes your company?
   ___ Manufacturing and processing   ___ Wholesale/retail trade
   ___ Transportation/communications/public utility   ___ Service
   ___ Construction/engineering/mining/gas/oil   ___ Government
   ___ Finance/insurance/real estate/accounting   ___ Other (specify) _____

14. How many employees are in your parent company worldwide?
   ___ Under 100   ___ 500-999
   ___ 100-499   ___ 1000+

15. What are estimated worldwide sales for your parent company?
   ___ Less than $10 mil   ___ $200-249mil   ___ $400-449mil
   ___ $10-49mil   ___ $250-299mil   ___ $450-499mil
   ___ $100-149mil   ___ $300-349mil   ___ > $500mil
   ___ $150-199mil   ___ $350-399mil

YOUR ADJUSTMENT

16.   It is normal for an individual to have difficulty adjusting to living or working in a foreign country. Indicate the degree to which you, your partner/spouse, and children (if applicable) have adjusted to the following items by writing in the appropriate number beside each item, using the scale below.

Not at all Adjusted 1	Slightly Adjusted 2	Moderately Adjusted 3	Well Adjusted 4	Completely Adjusted 5

		Self	Partner/ Spouse	Children
____ A.	The culture in general	____	____	____
____ B.	Living conditions in general	____	____	____
____ C.	Social norms	____	____	____
____ D.	Food	____	____	____
____ E.	Shopping	____	____	____
____ F.	Cost of living	____	____	____
____ G.	Transportation	____	____	____
____ H.	Weather	____	____	____
____ I.	Entertainment/recreation facilities and opportunities	____	____	____
____ J.	Health care facilities	____	____	____
____ K.	Socializing with Japanese	____	____	____
____ L.	Interacting with Japanese in general	____	____	____
____ M.	Interacting with Japanese at work	____	____	____
____ N.	Speaking with Japanese	____	____	____
____ O.	Speaking with Japanese in their native language	____	____	____
____ P.	Your specific job responsibilities ____		____	____
____ Q.	Your performance standards and expectations	____	____	____
____ R.	Your supervisory responsibilities ____		____	____

CULTURAL TRAINING

Please indicate whether you agree with each of the following statements.

17.   The company allowed me, and where applicable, my family to visit Japan prior to making a final decision to accept the transfer.
___Yes ___No ___Not applicable to me

18.   The company utilized a trained professional (human resource psychologist, cross-cultural specialist) to interview me, and, where applicable, my family regarding the move to Japan.
___Yes ___No ___Not applicable to me

19.   The company gave me/us specific information regarding what to expect in Japan (costs, living conditions, job responsibility, social norms, business socializing).
___Yes ___No ___Not applicable to me

20.   The company put me/us in touch with others who had recently lived in Japan.
       ___Yes   ___No   ___Not applicable to me

21.   The company provided a specific person or organization who was responsible for assisting us once we arrived in Japan.
       ___Yes   ___No   ___Not applicable to me

22.   The company maintains an ongoing support program to help me adjust to life in Japan.
       ___Yes   ___No   ___Not applicable to me

23.   The company provided me with job specific training for my new position.
       ___Yes   ___No   ___Not applicable to me

24.   How satisfied were you with the overall support in moving to Japan provided by your company?
       ___Very satisfied   ___Somewhat satisfied   ___Not satisfied at all

COMPARISON OF YOUR POSITIONS

Using the scale below, please rate how your current position compares to the position you held just prior to your move to Japan. (Check one for each statement.)

	LESS THAN	ABOUT THE SAME	BETTER THAN
25. I have access to information which is needed to get my job done.	____	____	____
26. I have a trusting and professional relationship with my colleagues.	____	____	____
27. I have a trusting and professional relationship with my subordinates.	____	____	____
28. I have a trusting and professional relationship with my customers.	____	____	____
29. I have a trusting and professional relationship with my suppliers.	____	____	____
30. I have good visibility and access to senior management.	____	____	____
31. I get positive feedback for my individual contributions.	____	____	____

32. The next section deals with aspects of your current position. Indicate your agreement or disagreement with the following statements by writing in the appropriate number.

Strongly Disagree	Disagree	Somewhat Disagree	Neutral	Somewhat Agree	Agree	Strongly Agree
1	2	3	4	5	6	7

____A. Clear, planned goals exist for my job.

____B. A job description exists for my job.

____C. It is clear what my responsibilities are.

____D. I know exactly what is expected of me.

____E. I have to work under vague directives.

____F. I have to do things that should be done differently.

____G. I work under incompatible policies.

____H. I work with two groups that operate differently.

____I. I receive incompatible requests from two groups or people.

____J. I have discretion as to what work gets done.

____K. I have discretion as to how work gets done.

____L. I have authority to decide what tasks to delegate.

____M. I have discretion as to what tasks subordinates do.

____N. I have freedom to choose what to become an expert in.

____O. I have freedom to decide how much of a generalist or expert to become.

____P. I have authority to decide what work gets shared.

____Q. I have discretion as to what I am responsible for.

33. **Indicate your level of satisfaction with your job by using the following scale.**

Very Dissatisfied	Dissatisfied	Somewhat Dissatisfied	Neutral	Somewhat Satisfied	Satisfied	Very Satisfied
1	2	3	4	5	6	7

_____ A. Salary

_____ B. Bonus

_____ C. Benefits

_____ D. Job Autonomy

_____ E. Job Authority

_____ F. Job Responsibilities

_____ G. The way your supervisor manages you

_____ H. Performance recognition you are given

_____ I. Current co-workers (from your country)

_____ J. Current Japanese co-workers

_____ K. Long-term Career Implications

_____ L. Overall job situation

34. **Please rate your job performance in your job, using the following scale.** Be as honest and candid as you can. Circle the appropriate number.

1 = Unsatisfactory — Job performance is consistently below expectations in most areas of responsibilities

2 = Needs Improvement — Job performance has not fully met expectations in some areas of responsibility

3 = Fully Satisfactory — Results have consistently met expectations in all major areas of responsibility

4 = Exceeds Expectations — Job performance has consistently exceeded expectations in all major areas of responsibility

5 = Clearly Outstanding — Job performance has consistently far exceeded expectations in all major areas of responsibility

35. **If you have your own way, will you be working for this company three years from now?** Circle one.

Not Likely	Likely	Somewhat Unlikely	Neutral	Somewhat Likely	Likely	Extremely Likely
1	2	3	4	5	6	7

36. **How long do you plan to remain at this company?** (Please circle one box.)

<1 Year	1-2 Years	3-4 Years	5-6 Years	7-8 Years	9-10 Years	>10 Years
1	2	3	4	5	6	7

37. Based on your typical weekly activities, your job responsibilities and the type of people with whom you interact, how would you allocate your work week hours, represented by percentages, across the following groups. Please try to estimate a percentage for all applicable groups. Indicate "0" if not relevant.

a. Non-Japanese (includes supervisor, subordinates, clients, suppliers, etc.). _____ %

b. Individual work not needing collaboration with others. _____ %

c. Interaction with Japanese supervisor. _____ %

d. Interaction with Japanese subordinates. _____ %

e. Interaction with Japanese colleagues. _____ %

f. Interaction with Japanese clients, suppliers, others. _____ %

g. Other (please specify) _____ _____ %

    TOTAL _____100 %

38. In an average week, what percentage of your time is spent interacting with the Japanese?
     On-the-job _____ %   Off-the-job _____ %

39. Do you have a domestic sponsor in the home country office (or someone who is responsible for keeping in touch with you)?
     ___No   ___Yes   ___N/A

40. How would you evaluate your Japanese language ability?

	a. SPOKEN	b. READING	c. WRITTEN
Fluent			
Intermediate			
Basic			
None			

41. Who made the decision for you to take your present position in Japan?
     ___Primarily the suggestion of my company in the U.S.
     ___Primarily due to my instigation
     ___Family move
     ___Other (please explain) _____

42. Did the position that you now have exist before you took it?
     ___Yes ___No

43. Was there a woman in the position you now have before you took it?
     ___Yes ___No

44. What is your boss' nationality? _____

45. What is the nationality of the majority of your subordinates?
     _____

46. How many subordinates do you have? _____

47. Please fill in the information concerning the employees of the Japanese affiliate/firm where you now work. Approximations of the percentages/numbers are fine.

     a. How many people work in your affiliate/firm? _____

     b. What percentage of the workforce of the affiliate/firm is non-Japanese?
         _____

48. Please indicate on a scale of 1 to 5 (1 = strongly disagree; 5 = strongly agree) how much you agree with the following statements. If a question is not applicable, please write "N/A." When reading these statements, please think of Japanese with whom you come into contact in your work, such as colleagues, clients, subordinates, suppliers, boss, etc.

___a. The Japanese people that I work with give me sufficient information and support to adequately perform my job.

___b. I have a productive, trusting relationship with most of the Japanese I work with.

___c. I find that the Japanese I work with are curious about me.

___d. I find that the Japanese I work with remember me easily.

___e. It is rather easy for me to get new business in Japan.

___f. It is not difficult for me to get access to Japanese clients.

___g. My communication with the Japanese I work with is open.

___h. The Japanese people I work with seem comfortable working with me.

___i. It does not seem hard for me to attract Japanese clients.

___j. Generally speaking, the Japanese I work with seem to believe what I tell them.

___k. I have found that the Japanese I work with accept me as a professional in my field.

___l. It appears that I have good credibility with the Japanese with whom I work.

49.* Finally, we would like to know whether being a woman doing business in Japan affects your business relationships. For each statement below, please indicate whether you believe that you are worse off, better off, or the same compared to how it would be for a foreign man holding your job?

	Worse Off	Same	Better off
a. The Japanese people that I work with give me sufficient information and support to adequately perform my job.	_____	_____	_____
b. I have a productive, trusting relationship with most of the Japanese I work with.	_____	_____	_____
c. I find that the Japanese I work with are curious about me.	_____	_____	_____
d. I find that the Japanese I work with remember me easily.	_____	_____	_____
e. It is rather easy for me to get new business in Japan.	_____	_____	_____
f. It is not difficult for me to get access to Japanese clients.	_____	_____	_____
g. My communication with the Japanese I work with is open.	_____	_____	_____

		Worse Off	Same	Better Off
h.	The Japanese people I work with seem comfortable working with me.	_____	_____	_____
i.	It does not seem hard for me to attract Japanese clients.	_____	_____	_____
j.	Generally speaking, the Japanese I work with seem to believe what I tell them.	_____	_____	_____
k.	I have found that the Japanese I work with accept me as a professional in my field.	_____	_____	_____
l.	It appears that I have good credibility with the Japanese with whom I work.	_____	_____	_____

Thank you for taking the time to fill out this survey. Your participation is very important. If you would like a copy of this project's results, please write your name and address below, and we will send it to you when they are ready.

_____

_____

_____

_____

* Asked of Chamber of Commerce respondents only.

Appendix C

Interview Protocol

INTERVIEW QUESTIONS

FOREIGN EXECUTIVE WOMEN WORKING IN JAPAN

Preliminary:

Did you get a copy of the survey? Did you fill it out? If not, would you do so?

A.   Recruitment/Selection

1.   How did you find <u>this</u> position in Japan?

_____transfer

_____came as a trailing spouse

_____came independently and found a job

_____switched jobs

2.   Please describe the process that was used in selecting you for your present job/company? Were there any particular qualifications you needed to get the job, such as speaking Japanese? Is the process the same for all expatriates hired for this type of job?

3.   Were you asked whether you were a trailing spouse? Had children?

4.   What, if any, dual-career issues came up?

5.   What improvements would you make in recruitment/selection?

6.   Were you offered the same benefits as male expatriates (if hired within Japan)?

7.   To what extent was being a female an issue in being selected? If so, how? Were there any other issues? (e.g. age)

        7.5   How feasible is it for a woman to be transferred to Japan by a foreign firm?

8.   How did your firm show support or resistance for your taking this position? Please give

examples.

B.   Preparation:

(If didn't fill out a questionnaire.)

1. What kind of preparation did you have before you came:

    e.g. meeting person who previously held this position, training, language training?

    1.5   Do you speak Japanese?

    1.6   (To all.) Were <u>you</u> responsible for the preparation or did your firm provide it?

2.   Were expectations about your behavior, role, and status in this position discussed at that time?

    If so, how, and by whom?

3.   Was there any training for your family? If so, what kind?

4.   Did you anticipate any particularly challenge from being a woman?

C.   On-site

1.   Once you got on the job, how clear was it? If you understand the expectations of you in this

    job, how did you gain this understanding? If not, why do you think you don't have a clear

    understanding?

2.   Do you think the expectations would be as clear if you were doing this job in the U.S.?

3.   Does your <u>company</u> see your being female as an advantage or disadvantage? How? How does

    your company take advantage (in a positive way) of your being female or/and how does it help

    you overcome any disadvantages of your situation?

4.   Do you see being a woman as giving you any advantages in working with Japanese?

    Disadvantages? (Have this section of the questionnaire ready to provide some inspiration to the

    person.) Can you give us examples?

Now we'd like to ask a broader question dealing with your job:

5.   To what extent are company policies consistent across work groups? Are you ever frustrated

        that other work groups operate differently within your company?

6.   Do you ever feel conflict because/ Do you ever feel pulled in two directions because of

        different policies between HQ and here? Different ways of working between different groups?

        Please give us an example. How has this affected your ability to do your job?

7.   If you had to compare the freedom and authority you have here with a comparable job in the

        U.S., it would be:

        far, far less   far, far more

        1--------2--------3--------4--------5--------6--------7--------8--------9--------10

8.   What makes this job easier/more difficult to perform from a comparable job in the U.S.?

9.1. What is the most important factor in <u>your</u> success in Japan?

_____family adjustment/support

_____company support

_____qualifications for the job

_____personal characteristics

_____acceptance by the Japanese

_____(other)_____

9.2   Are you typical in this answer? How so?

9.3   What recommendations do you have on how to increase the success of women in Japan?

10.   How has being part of a dual-career couple affected your performance on the job?

11.   What recommendations do you have on how to increase the success of women in Japan?

D.   Return

1.   What are your plans for returning to your country?

2.   What are your company's plans for your return?

3.   What are the company's policies on repatriation?

> e.g.   ____job assured
>
> ____promotion/lateral move
>
> ____have to find your own job within the company

4.   Will this time in Japan have a positive or negative effect on your career? How does your company show that it has been a positive experience?

5.   Under what conditions will you return to your native country (for those not transferred here)? Do you think this will have been a positive experience for your career? Do you think employers will have thought so?

6.   What kind of dual-career issues do you think will surface when you return to your native country?

7.   How can the transition home be improved?

Bibliography

Abe, H. and Wiseman, R. L. (1983). A Cross-Cultural Confirmation of Intercultural Effectiveness. *International Journal of Intercultural Relations, 7*, 53–68.

Adler, Nancy J. (1984a). Expecting International Success: Female Managers Overseas. *Columbia Journal of World Business, 19*, (3), 79–85.

Adler, Nancy J. (1984b). Women Do Not Want International Careers and Other Myths About International Management. *Organizational Dynamics, 13*, (2), 66–79.

Adler, Nancy J. (1984c). Women in International Management: Where Are They? *California Management Review, 26*, (4), 78–89.

Adler, Nancy J. (1991). *International Dimensions of Organizational Behavior*. Boston: PWS–Kent.

Adler, Nancy J. (1993a). Women Managers in a Global Economy. *HR Magazine*, September, 52–55.

Adler, Nancy J. (1993b). Women Managers in a Global Economy. *Training and Development*, April, 31–36.

Adler, Nancy J. (1994). Women Managing Across Borders. In Adler, Nancy J. and Izraeli, Dafna N. (Editors). *Competitive Frontiers: Women Managers in a Global Economy*. Cambridge, Mass.: Blackwell Publishers, 22–42.

Adler, Nancy J. and Izraeli, Dafna N. (Editors). (1994). *Competitive Frontiers: Women Managers in a Global Economy*. Cambridge, Mass.: Blackwell Publishers.

Bartlett, C. and Ghoshal, S. (1988). Organizing for Worldwide Effectiveness: The Transnational Solution. *California Management Review, 31*, (1), 54–74.

Bartlett, C. and Ghoshal, S. (1989). *Managing Across Borders: The Transnational Solution*. Cambridge, Mass.: Harvard University Press.

Bartlett, C. and Ghoshal, S. (1992). What is a Global Manager? *Harvard Business Review*, 70, (5), 124–132.

Black, J. Stewart. (1988). Work Role Transitions: A Study of American Expatriate Managers in Japan. *Journal of International Business Studies*, 44, 497–515.

Black, J. Stewart. (1991). *A Tale of Three Countries*. Paper presented at the annual meeting of the Academy of Management, Miami, Florida, August.

Black, J. Stewart. (1992). Coming Home: The Relationship of Expatriate Expectations with Repatriation Adjustment and Job Performance. *Human Relations*, 45, 177–192.

Black, J. Stewart and Gregersen, H. B. (1991). When Yankee Comes Home: Factors Related to Expatriate and Spouse Repatriation Adjustment. *Journal of International Business Studies*, 122, (4), 671–694.

Black, J. Stewart and Gregersen, H. B. (1992). *O Kairinasai: Factors Related to Japanese Repatriation Adjustment*. Paper presented to the annual meeting of the Academy of Management, Las Vegas.

Black, J. Stewart, Gregersen, Hal, and Mendenhall, Mark. (1992). *Global Assignments*. San Francisco: Jossey-Bass Publishers.

Black, J. Stewart and Mendenhall, Mark. (1990). Cross-Cultural Training Effectiveness: A Review and Theoretical Framework for Future Research. *Academy of Management Review*, 15, 113–136.

Black, J. Stewart and Mendenhall, Mark. (1991). A Practical but Theory-Based Framework for Selecting Cross-Cultural Training Methods. In Mendenhall, M. and Oddou, G. (Editors). *Readings and Cases in International Human Resource Management*. Boston: PWS–Kent.

Black, J. Stewart, Stephens, Gregory K., and Rosener, Judy B. (1992). Women in Management Around the World: Some Glimpses. In Sekaran, U. and Leong, F. (Editors). *Womanpower*. Newbury Park, Calif.: Sage.

Black, J. Stewart and Stephens, J. G. (1989). Expatriate Adjustment and Intent to Stay in Pacific Rim Overseas Assignments. *Journal of Management*, 15, 529–544.

Brannen, Christalyn and Wilen, Tracey. (1993). *Doing Business with Japanese Men*. Berkeley, Calif.: Stone Bridge Press.

Carney, L. S. and O'Kelly, C. G. (1987). Barriers and Constraints to the Recruitment and Mobility of Female Managers in the Japanese Labor Force. *Human Resource Management*, 26, 193–216.

Church, A. T. (1982). Sojourner Adjustment. *Psychological Bulletin*, 9, 540–572.

The Discrete Charm of the Multicultural Multinational. (1994). *The Economist*, July 30, 57–58.

Dore, Ronald. (1987). *Taking Japan Seriously*. Stanford, Calif.: Stanford University Press.

Dowling, Peter, Schuler, Randall, and Welch, Denise. (1994). *International Dimensions of Human Resource Management*. Second Edition. Belmont, Calif.: Wadsworth Publishing.

Drucker, Peter F. (1986). The Changed World Economy. *Foreign Affairs*, Spring, 768–791.

Ettorre, Barbara. (1993). A Brave New World: Managing International Careers. *Management Review*, April, 10–15.

The Global 500: The World's Largest Industrial Corporations. (1992). *Fortune, 126,* (2), July 27, 176–232.

Hawes, F. and Kealey, D. J. (1981). An Empirical Study of Canadian Technical Assistance. *International Journal of Intercultural Relations, 5,* 239–258.

Hill, Charles W. L. (1994). *International Business: Competing in the Global Marketplace.* Burr Ridge, Ill.: Irwin.

Hixon, A. L. (1986). Why Corporations Make Haphazard Overseas Staffing Decisions. *Personnel Administrator, 31,* (3), 91–94.

Huddleston Jr., Jackson N. (1990). *Gaijin Kaisha: Running a Foreign Business in Japan.* Armonk, N.Y.: Sharpe.

Industries and Employment in the Year 2000: Summary of the Technological Innovation and Employment Report. (1986). *Look Japan,* Oct. 10.

Iyer, Pico. (1991). *The Lady and the Monk: Four Seasons in Kyoto.* New York: Knopf.

Japan Economic Report 33A. (1991). *Women in Japan's Work World See Slow Change from Labor Shortage, Equal Employment Law.* Washington, D.C.: Japan Economic Institute, August, 30.

Japan Economic Report 41A. (1994). *Education Mama Versus Working Mother: The Ideal, the Reality and a Possible Outcome.* Washington, D.C.: Japan Economic Institute, October 28.

Japan Economic Report 44A. (1993). *Recession and Respect: Is the Employment Scene Changing for Japanese Women?* Washington, D.C.: Japan Economic Institute, December 3.

Japan Survey. (1994). *The Economist,* July 9, 54.

Jelinek, Mariann and Adler, Nancy J. (1988). Women: World-Class Managers for Global Competition. *The Academy of Management Executive, 2,* (1), 11–19.

JIWMP News: Current Information on Women and Minor Workers in Japan. (1986). Tokyo: Japan Institute of Women's and Minor's Problems, July.

Job Seeking Women in Japan See Discrimination. (1994). *New York Times,* May 22, A4.

Kahalas, Harvey and Suchon, Kathleen. (1992). Interview with Harold A. Poling, Chairman, CEO, Ford Motor Company. *The Academy of Management Executive, 6,* (2), 71–82.

Kahn, R. L., Wolfe, D. M., Quinn, R. P., and Snock, J. D. (1964). *Organizational Stress.* New York: Wiley.

Karasek, R. (1979). Job Demands, Job Decision Latitude, and Mental Strain: Implications for Job Redesign. *Administrative Science Quarterly, 2,* 215–308.

Lam, Alice. (1992). *Women and Japanese Management.* London and New York: Routledge.

Lanier, A. R. (1979). Selecting and Preparing Personnel for Overseas Transfers, *Personnel Journal,* March, 160–163.

Lebra, Takie Sugiyama. (1992). Gender and Culture in the Japanese Political Economy: Self-Portrayals of Prominent Businesswomen. In Kumon, S. and Rosovsky, H. (Editors). *The Political Economy of Japan.* Volume 3. *Cultural and Social Dynamics.* Stanford, Calif.: Stanford University Press.

Martinez, Michelle Neely. (1991). The High Potential Woman. *HR Magazine,* June, 46–51.

Mendenhall, M., Dunbar, E., and Oddou, G. (1987). Expatriate Selection, Training and Career-Pathing: A Review and a Critique. *Human Resource Planning*, 26, (3), 331–345.

Mendenhall, M. and Oddou, G. (1985). The Dimensions of Expatriate Acculturation: A Review. *Academy of Management Review*, 10, 39–47.

Miller, E. L. (1973). The International Selection Decision: A Study of Some Dimensions of Managerial Behavior in the Selection Process. *Academy of Management Journal*, 16, (2), 239–252.

Napier, Nancy K. and Peterson, Richard B. (1989). Expatriate Re-Entry: What do Repatriates Have to Say? *Human Resource Planning*, 14, (1), 19–28.

Napier, Nancy K., Tibau, Jacques, Janssens, Maddy, and Pilenzo, Ron. (in press). The Role of the International Human Resource Manager: Managing from the Outside and the Inside. In Gerald R. Ferris, Sherman, D. Rosen, and Darold T. Barnum. (Editors). *Handbook of Human Resources Management*. Oxford, U.K.: Basil Blackwell.

Oddou, Gary R. (1991). Managing Your Expatriates: What the Successful Firms Do. *Human Resources Planning*, 14, (4), 301–308.

Ohmae, Kenichi. (1985). *Triad Power*. New York: The Free Press.

Parker, Barbara. (1991). Employment Globalization: Can Voluntary Expatriates Meet U.S. Hiring Needs Abroad? *Journal of Global Business*, Fall, 39–46.

Peterson, Richard B., Sargent, John, Napier, Nancy K., and Shim, Won-Shul. (1993). *The World's Largest Multinational Companies: Practices for Expatriates*. Paper presented at the Academy of International Business meetings, October 1993.

Phatak, A. V. (1989). *International Dimensions of Management*. Second Edition. Boston: PWS–Kent.

Piturro, Marlene C. (1992). Super Manager! *World Trade*, April, 80, 82.

PSST, Need a Body-Press? (1994). *The Economist*, August 6, 52.

Pyle, Kenneth B. (1991). How Japan Sees Itself. *The American Enterprise*, November/December, 28–39.

Reed, Steven R. (1993). *Making Common Sense of Japan*. Pittsburgh: University of Pittsburgh Press.

Reich, Robert B. (1991). Who Is Them? *Harvard Business Review*, March–April, 77–88.

Reischauer, Edwin O. (1974). *Japan: The Story of a Nation*. Tokyo: Charles E. Tuttle Company.

Rohlen, Thomas P. (1979). Permanent Employment Policies in Times of Recession. *Journal of Japanese Studies*, 5 (2), 235–272.

Schwartz, Felice N. (1992). *Breaking with Tradition: Women and Work, the New Facts of Life*. New York: Warner Books.

Solomon, Carlene Marmer. (1994). Staff Selection Impacts Global Success. *Personnel Journal*, January, 88–101.

Steinhoff, Patricia and Tanaka, Kazuko. (1994) Women Managers in Japan. In Adler, Nancy J. and Izraeli, Dafna N. (Editors). *Competitive Frontiers: Women Managers in a Global Economy*. Cambridge, Mass.: Blackwell Publishers.

Stone, Raymond J. (1991). Expatriate Selection and Failure. *Human Resource Planning Journal*, 14, (1), 9–18.

Taylor, Sully and Eder, Robert W. (1994). U.S. Expatriates and the Civil Rights

Act of 1991: Dissolving Boundaries. In S.B. Prasad (ed.) *Advances in International Comparative Management.* Greenwich, Conn.: JAI Press, 171–192.

Taylor, William. (1991). The Logic of Global Business: An Interview with ABB's Percy Barnevik. *Harvard Business Review, 69,* (2), 90–105.

Torbion, I. (1982). *Living Abroad: Personal Adjustment and Personnel Policy in the Overseas Setting.* New York: Wiley.

Trompenaars, Fons. (1993). *Riding the Waves of Culture.* New York: Irwin.

Tung, Rosalie. (1981). Selection and Training of Personnel for Overseas Assignments. *Columbia Journal of World Business, 16,* (1), 68–78.

Tung, Rosalie. (1988). *The New Expatriates: Managing Human Resources Abroad.* New York: Ballinger.

Tung, Rosalie. (1990). Language Training and Beyond: The Case of Japanese Multinationals, *Annals, 511,* 97–108.

World Development Report. (1992). Washington, D.C.: World Bank.

Index

About the Authors

NANCY K. NAPIER, Associate Dean for Academic and Student Affairs at Boise State University, worked for several years at Battelle Memorial Institute in contract research for Nissan, Hitachi, Mitsubishi, and Nippon Steel. She has taught and done research in the areas of strategic and human resource management, international management, and mergers and acquisition implementation. Her most recent reseaarch has been done in Europe, Japan, Southeast Asia, and Vietnam.

SULLY TAYLOR is an Assistant Professor of International Management at the School of Business Administration, Portland State University, and has taught in Spain and Japan. She has conducted cross-cultural training for NEC, Fujitsu, DEC, Aldus, and others. Her specialty is international human resource management and Japanese management.